LEADERSHIP
FROM AN
ISLAMIC AND WESTERN
PERSPECTIVE

Dr. Asan Vernyuy Wirba

This publication contains the opinions and ideas of its author. It is intended to provide helpful and informative material on the subjects addressed in the publication. The author and publisher specifically disclaim all responsibility for any liability, loss or risk, personal or otherwise, which is incurred as a consequence, directly or indirectly, of the use and application of any of the contents of this book.

WORKBOOK PRESS LLC
187 E Warm Springs Rd,
Suite B285 Las Vegas NV 89119 USA

Website: https://workbookpress.com/
Hotline: 1-888-818-4856
Email: admin@workbookpress.com

Ordering Information:
Quantity sales. Special discounts are available on quantity purchases by corporations, associations, and others. For details, contact the publisher at the address above.

Library of Congress Control Number: 2020904925

ISBN-13: 978-1-963718-31-7   Paperback Version
         978-1-963718-32-4   Digital Version

REV. DATE: 04/08/2024

LEADERSHIP

— FROM AN —

ISLAMIC AND WESTERN

PERSPECTIVE

Dr. ASAN VERNYUY WIRBA

Associate Professor
Department of Business Administration,
Jubail Industrial College (JIC)
Royal Commission for Jubail & Yanbu

Content

Preface

This book provides a comprehensive analysis of leadership, exploring both Islamic and Western viewpoints. The initial examination focuses on leadership from a Western perspective, drawing insights from esteemed scholars, practitioners, as well as leaders and followers. The subsequent examination delves into the Islamic perspective of leadership, which is rooted in the teachings of the Holy Quran and the exemplary lives of previous prophets, beginning with Prophet Adam (PBUH) to the seal of Prophet of Allah(God), Prophet Muhammad (PBUH), the four Rightly Guided Caliphs (Khulafa Al-Rashidun), and other virtuous leaders throughout the Islamic history.

This book provides an elucidation of leadership from both perspectives, as perceived by the author, with the intention of sharing it with you who are my local and global audience. We all live in a global village and it is good to share this book with you wherever you may be. Thus, the target audience includes the Muslim Ummah, Muslim Communities, One Nation Islam, and individuals from both Muslim and non-Muslim backgrounds, irrespective of their geographical location. The primary objective of this second edition of this book is to disseminate the author's personal viewpoint on leadership from both perspectives, as the author believes that knowledge is most valuable when shared. Furthermore, the author aim for this book is to serve as an inspiration for those individuals who are aspiring to become leaders or those who are already holding leadership positions within their respective communities, regardless of their geographical location or religious affiliation.

The decision to publish this second edition of the book is driven by the author's motivation, which arises from the current state of leadership in both the Muslim-Ummah and non-Muslim communities. In both western and Islamic societies, there is a noticeable dearth of effective leadership that encompasses compassion towards humanity, akin to the exemplary conduct demonstrated by Prophet Muhammad (PBUH), who was divinely sent by Allah (God) as a source of mercy for all of mankind. The leadership qualities exhibited by Prophet Muhammad (PBUH) were also evident in the actions of previous prophets, such as Isa (Jesus) and Musa (Moses), who firmly believed in the absolute oneness of Allah(God) and selflessly served their people and communities solely for the pleasure of Allah(God), without any personal or national interests. As leaders and followers of these prophets, we can derive valuable lessons from their exemplary lives and become effective leaders within our own communities, even though we may not possess the prophetic status. The inclusion of these prophets' examples in this book serves as a reminder to all leaders and followers, irrespective of their religious or non-religious affiliations, to learn from the wisdom of these great prophets and strive to become effective leaders and followers within our respective nations or communities, regardless of our diverse backgrounds. Unfortunately, today's leaders and followers often prioritize their own interests over the greater good of humanity, creating divisions and roles that serve only themselves, their people, their tribes, or their nations.

The current state of global affairs necessitates the presence of capable leaders who can steer the world towards a more cohesive and collaborative path. Presently, there is an increasing level of discord and fragmentation worldwide, which can be attributed to differing ideologies and political alliances. This is particularly evident in matters of global significance, such as the Palestinian Issues, the Russia-Ukraine conflict, and the escalating refugee crisis on a global scale. The leadership in the western world appears to possess a limited perspective, disregarding the existing realities across the globe. Consequently, this narrow outlook from western leaders, who were previously more cautious and democratic in their approach, further exacerbates the growing divisions at both national and international levels, fostering a sense of despair, particularly concerning international institutions like the United Nations (UN).

Effective leadership requires leaders to possess courage and fairness in their dealings with worldly affairs. It is crucial for leaders to refrain from taking sides and instead strive to be just and fair in the eyes of others and the international community. It is important to recognize that every individual and every people are equal in the eyes of Allah(God), and therefore, fairness and justice must be upheld. Failure to do so can lead to feelings of despair and hatred among people worldwide. The recent crisis in Gaza shows that Muslim youths all over the Islamic Ummah/ Muslims communities are united and the division is within the leaders of the Muslims Ummah/Muslims communities and that is a concern. They are all in the position of power in their various Muslims communities but are not united for the sake of the Ummah/one nation Islam/Muslims Ummah, which a concern. There is a need for unity amongst Muslims leaders and even non-Muslims leaders and followers alike. See Surah 49 Al-Hujurat (49:13) as translated into English by Khan and Al Hilali (1996, p.651), 49, O mankind! We have created you from a male and a female, and made you into nations and tribes, that you may know one another. Verily, the most honourable of you with Allah is that (believer) who has Taqwa [he is one of the Mutaqun (the pious— See V.2:2). Verily, Allah is All-Knowing, All-Aware.

The issues of human rights violations and abuse of power necessitate the presence of effective leadership from both perspectives. Those leaders who could translate into practice the call of Allah/God in the above Surah for unity in faith. However, some individuals within theMuslim-Ummah and non-Muslim Ummah view leadership as a means to accumulate wealth and gain political advantage, exploiting the citizens' concerns about their nation's economic state to further divide them. However, these individuals fail to acknowledge that leadership comes with the burden of responsibility and accountability, which will be thoroughly examined on the Day of Judgement.

The current global dearth of understanding pertaining to the notion of leadership has emerged as a significant matter of urgency and apprehension. These insufficiencies have led to the widespread proliferation of apprehension and unease among specific individuals across the globe, including both leaders and followers who have developed an intolerance towards individuals who differ from the native population, particularly newcomers. Numerous group leaders and politicians have capitalized on these circumstances to advance their political objectives centred on fostering division and animosity toward other as a mean of gaining power or maintaining power.

The rise of far-right movements in both Western countries and some certain Muslim nations has effectively exploited the fears and anxieties of its citizens, resulting in the creation of divisions and animosity towards individuals who do not share their ideology, religious beliefs or are immigrants to their various nations. These issues have consequently fostered intolerance between newly arrived citizens and their native counterparts in their host nation. The presence of such phenomena, characterized by hatred and division, is deeply concerning and requires urgent attention. Henceforth, without individuals of good will and good character who remain impartial and speak truth to the powers that be or to those in power, we risk losing what binds us all as human being which can undermining the credibility of the international community, and the united nation and it various institutions. The League of Nations suffered the same consequence and it is necessary to reform or strengthen the UN or it will remain powerless and less effective.

The present challenges faced by Western democracy and its leaders have led to a decline in their credibility among a considerable number of individuals. Should this pattern continue, it is plausible that our world may become divided into two conflicting factions, where the concept of democracy loses its significance and international organizations hold no influence. It is crucial for Western nations to actively promote peace and foster an environment where diverse opinions and ideologies can coexist harmoniously. Simultaneously, it is essential to uphold respect for international laws from all parties involved, without turning a blind eye to violations committed by allies or friendly nations. There must not be a blank check for those who disregard international laws, incite hatred among people, or promote fear and division among individuals worldwide, regardless of their religious affiliation and commit crime against humanity. Therefore, the author of this book defines leadership as selfless servitude purely for the pleasure of Allah(God).

Leadership is an immensely significant aspect that demands utmost seriousness. Failure to do so may result in leaders perpetrating genocides and crimes against humanity. Consequently, leadership is founded on trust and should be characterized by selflessness, solely driven by the desire to please Allah/God. Leaders and followers who serve others with the sole intention of pleasing Allah(God) will refrain from employing hate, fear, anxiety, and division for political gains. Instead, they will bear in mind that leadership is built on trust, and the actions of those in leadership positions will be scrutinized during the Day of Judgment. At that juncture, there will be no opportunity to return to Earth and engage in virtuous deeds. See Surah 23 Al Mu'minun (23:99-100), as translated into English by Khan and Al Hilali (1996, p.440), 99, Until, when death comes to one of them (those who joint partners with Allah), he says: "My Lord! Send me back. 100, "So that I may do good in that which I have left behind!" No! It is about a word that he Speaks; and behind them is Barzak (a barrier) until the Day when they will be resurrected. It is therefore important for leaders and follower to do good deeds here on earth than to be waiting for the Day of resurrection where there is no return to do good deeds. It is imperative for both leaders and followers to refrain from fostering animosity and discord in pursuit of authority. In order to avoid being deemed unsuccessful on the Day of Judgement, it is crucial to adhere to the principles outlined in religious texts that advocate for the practice of Islam, which emphasizes the belief in Allah(God) only.

The emergence of populism in Western societies and the rise of autocratic leaders within Muslim communities have resulted in the proliferation of misguided individuals and factions within Muslim communities. These entities employ inappropriate methods in their efforts to combat the arrogance and inflexibility exhibited by both systems, which are characterized by a disregard for the well-being of others and an inclination to assume the role of global enforcers. It is important to note that such behaviours do not find their origins in the teachings of the Bible, the Ten Commandments, the Quran, or the Sunnah of the Prophets, beginning with Prophet Adam (PBUH) and extending to the final Prophet of Allah/God and the Rightly Guided Caliphs. As leaders and followers, we should all draw inspiration from the leadership of Prophet Muhammad (PBUH) in Madinah, where he established a city-state and implemented the Madinah Constitution, which embraced the principles of truth and justice.

In the contemporary era, as I embark upon the endeavour of writing this book, it becomes apparent that even though the Muslim Ummah is divided among various nation-states, there is hope in it youths as demonstrated with the crisis in Gaza. The Muslim Ummah demonstrates solidarity with the people of Palestine, particularly those residing in Gaza, who are currently facing a dire situation that has garnered global attention. The international community, particularly Western leaders, appears to be lacking in their efforts to find a resolution to the two-state agenda and have given the state of Israel the green light to carpet bomb Gaza in the name of self-defence and forget the international humanitarian laws even in self-defence. Additionally, certain Muslim leaders are also absent, which is a tragic circumstance for both the people of Palestine and the Ummah as a whole. It is crucial for Muslim leaders to exercise caution when addressing the significant matter of Masjid Aqsa, as it holds immense importance for the Ummah, Islamic state, and Muslim communities. It is imperative that we do not disregard the essence of brotherhood that was exemplified during the time of Prophet Muhammad (PBUH) in the city-state of Madinah, irrespective of our respective nation-states. A unified voice is indispensable in addressing the predicament surrounding the third holy Masjid of the Ummah. Coexistence, or the two state is the solution to this crisis and there can be no winner unless the unthinkable is done, thus the absence to this problem is a concern and this requires effective leadership from both and support from others and the international community.

We Muslims can learn from brotherhood that exemplifies itself in Madinah, where there was a strong bond of brotherhood between the Helpers (Ansar) and the Migrants (Muhajirun) and other tribes that had been in existence there with no problems. The Ummah as it is now is in dire need of effective leaders and followers who emulate the ideals of Prophet Muhammad (PBUH) by adhering to the teachings of the Quran and the Sunnah, in order to prevent the division within the Ummah/ Muslims Communities that are divided into nations states and factions that engage in conflict and perceive one another as adversaries rather than brothers and sisters in Islam.

Leadersandfollowerswithinthe Muslim Ummah/Muslimscommunities/ Muslims societies should bear in mind and understand that leadership position is trust (Amanah), responsibility and accountable and they will accounted for by Allah/God for their actions when entrusted with the responsibility of leading their people. Those leaders who exploit their authority to oppress their citizens, instilling an atmosphere of fear, terror, and anxiety, whether it be directed from the West or within the Muslim Ummah, will be held responsible for their crimes against humanity. Consequently, the emergence of far-right politics and the influence of financial interests in Western politics and leadership is a cause for concern, as it may undermine the principles of democracy and render it a mere facade. Similarly, the rise of intolerant leaders and followers within the Muslim Ummah is also disconcerting.

The purpose of this book is to serve as a reminder to leaders and followers, regardless of their location in the West or within Muslim communities, about the significance of upholding the principles of justice, unity, and compassion. It is crucial for both leaders and followers to work towards promoting a sense of brotherhood and cooperation, guided by the teachings of Prophet Muhammad (peace be upon him), in order to overcome the challenges faced by the Muslim Ummah and the global community at large.

In recent times, there has been a noticeable increase in military coups in certain Muslim communities in Africa, particularly in the Francophone countries that were formerly colonized by France. This rise in coups can be attributed to the perception that France, as a nation, has exploited the resources of these countries for an extended period. Furthermore, there are allegations that France has imposed puppet governments in these nations to further its own interests, rather than prioritizing the interests of the respective countries and their citizens. Although the author does not endorse or support coups in general, it is important to acknowledge that the people in these countries are backing their military leaders due to the historical context of France's patronizing treatment of its colonies, which has contributed to the current situation.

It is noteworthy that if leaders in France and other Western nations had adhered to the principles outlined in the Bible and The Ten Commandments, their approach towards these nations may have been different. Therefore, it is imperative for leaders in the western world to uphold the Judaeo-Christian principles and the teachings of the Bible, while maintaining a reverential fear of God in all their endeavours. Similarly, Muslim leaders and their followers are expected to adhere to the teachings of the Quran and the Sunnah of the prophet Muhammad (PBUH) in their pursuit of leadership. These sources of guidance, particularly the Sunnah of the prophet Muhammad (PBUH) and the four Rightly Caliphs, can help prevent situations where individuals are mistreated or imprisoned for their beliefs and ideas. The issues mentioned above have contributed to voter apathy in the West and election coups in some Muslim countries, which is a cause for concern. Furthermore, some colonial powers continue to exhibit behaviour reminiscent of the past, creating problems in Africa, including anti-French and anti-Western sentiments. Given the current global landscape, it is imperative to move away from Western dominance and towards collaboration and mutual interests, resulting in a mutually beneficial outcome. However, the increasing prevalence of strong leaders and weak institutions in various regions worldwide is a worrying trend.

Effective leadership is crucial in Africa, particularly due to the absence of democratic processes that have resulted in military takeovers in former French colonies. This can be attributed to France's treatment of its colonies through agreements that are incompatible with the principles of a civilized society. Addressing this concern and not ignoring it is of utmost importance. The era of imperial powers has come to an end, and a new generation of African leaders is emerging. These leaders are demanding an end to colonial domination and cultural assimilation by France, while advocating for their rights and striving for the unity of the African continent. These issues, whether viewed from an Islamic or Western perspective, have inspired the author to write this book.

This book serves as a second edition and a continuation of the shared concept of leadership within both the Western and Islamic perspective. Furthermore, the author emphasizes the importance of recognizing Allah/God as the ultimate source of leadership, with the Quran and the Sunnah serving as the guiding principles for effective leadership. This recognition plays a critical role in addressing the current challenges in leadership and the misguided actions of fellow Muslims, which contribute to the lack of competent leadership within the Ummah. It is essential for both the Islamic Ummah and the non-Muslim Ummah (the Western world) to acknowledge that Allah/God is the creator of all things. Allah is all-powerful, surpassing human understanding, and possesses the ability to manifest His will.

This recognition is foundational for leaders and citizens alike, transcending religious boundaries and encompassing the global community. This notion is affirm in Surah Al Baqarah (2:117). See the English translation of the Quran by Khan and Al Hilali (1996, p.30), quote" The Originator of the heavens and the earth. When He decrees a matter, He only says to it: "Be! - and it is.". If we all know that the originator of leadership is Allah(God) and that we are only his servants on earth, we will not be arrogant to one another but lead our citizen for his pleasure and leadership become selfless because the reward of leading your own people come from Him Allah(God). See also Surah Ya-Sin (36:82) "Verily, His command, when He intends a thing, is only that He says to it, "Be! - and it is." Surah An-Nahl (16:40) which is translation in English by Khan and Al Hilali (1996, p.338) "Verily, Our Word unto a thing when We intend it, is only that We say unto it: "Be! - and it is." And in Surah Al-Qammar (54-50) translated English by Khan and Al Hilali (1996, p.674) "And Our commandment is but one as the twinkling of an eye".

The powers of Allah are there for us to see as Allah (God) says if you want to know Him look around you and that should give us as leaders the view that leadership is given to us by Allah(God) to serve our people to serve humanity and not to be their masters but only their servants. Allah(God) has created us as leaders and followers for a purpose which is to worship him and nothing else and also to be his vicegerent on earth, which means his representatives on earth. See Surah 2 Al-Baqarah (2:30). Therefore, from the above evidence, the author is convinced that if we Muslims and non-Muslims follow Allah (God) and His Messenger sand use the Quran and Sunnah of Prophet Muhammad (PBUH) and the four Rightly Guided Caliphs (Khalafah Al-Rashidun) we will flourish as was the case in the city state of Madinah under the leadership of Prophet Mohammad (PBU) and the Guided caliphs. During that time of Prophet Muhammad (PBUH) and the four Rightly Guided Khalifs, leadership was selfless and purely for the pleasure of Allah(God).

The author of this book hope that this book serve as a source of inspiration for individuals who hold leadership positions within their respective communities or those who aspire to serve their communities as ordinary citizens. The author emphasizes the importance of adhering to the teachings of the Quran and the Sunnah of the Prophet Mohammad (PBUH), as well as the teachings of all the Prophets before him, beginning with Prophet Adam (PBUH). As leaders and followers, it is our responsibility to guide people towards the path of Allah(God) while simultaneously leading our communities. The author encourages individuals to embody the qualities of faith and to strive towards becoming men and women of unwavering conviction. See Yusuf Ali's (1989, p.1221) comments 4432, which states that "The man of Faith who backs his Faith by righteous conduct is like the man of clear vision, who see things in their true perspective and walks with firm steps in the Way of Allah(God) and His Prophet(PBUH).

The man who does evil is like a blind man: The Light of Allah is all around him, but the man has made himself blind and can see nothing. He has rejected Faith and cannot even learn by other people's admonition." Again let us be leaders or followers who lead by example and are Allah (God) fearing and see leadership position as a trust from Allah(God) to humankind and that we will be accountable before Allah(God) in the days of judgment. We should be those whom in the day of judgement proclaim that we did our job or what is required of us as required by Allah/God as Prophet Mohammad (PBUH) proclaim in his last sermon to the Muslim-Ummah in mouth Arafat as he address the Muslim Ummah.

The current state of leadership in many parts of the world is concerning, as some leaders prioritize personal gain and division over the well-being of their citizens. This issue of leadership self-interest is particularly prevalent in the Western world, and in some Muslims countries where leaders often use fear, sham election and intolerance to gain political power. However, these problems are not limited to any one region or religion, which is a concern. It is important to remember that leaders will be held accountable on the Day of Judgment for their actions and decisions. The Quran and Sunnah provide guidance on what constitutes good leadership or effective ethical leadership, and Muslims should look to the example of Prophet Mohammad (PBUH) and the four Rightly Guided Caliphs for inspiration.

Thus effective leaders or rulers from an Islamic perspective is very important and Allah/God describe them in the Quran, as Muhsinun: those good doors who perform good deeds totally for Allah(God) pleasure only without any show-off or to gain praise or fame and do them in accordance with the Sunnah (legal ways) of Allah(God) the Messenger Muhammad (PBUH). The Quran identify effective leaders in Surah in surah 22 Al-Hajj (22:41) as translated into English by Khan and Al Hilali (1996, p.426-7). 41, Those (Muslim rulers) who, if given them power in the land, (they) enjoin Iqamat-Salat [i.e. to perform the five compulsory congregational Salat (prayers) (the male in mosques), to pay Zakat and they enjoin Al-Maruf (i.e. Islamic Monotheism and all that Islam order one to do), and forbid Al-Munkar (i.e. disbelief, polytheism and all that Islam has forbidden) [i.e. they make the Quran as the law of their country in all the spheres of life] And with Allah rests the end of (all) matters of (creatures). Performing Salat here means every Muslim, male or female, is obliged to offer his Salat (prayer) regularly five times a day at the specific times; the male in the mosque in congregation and the female at home. As the prophet (PBUH) has said: order your children to perform Salat (prayer) at the age of seven and beat them (about) it at the age of ten. The chief (of a family, town, and tribe) and the Muslim rulers of a country are held responsible before Allah/God in case of non-fulfilment of this obligation by the Muslims under their authority.

Who is this book for?

This book caters to a wide audience, irrespective of their diverse backgrounds or professions, encompassing both Muslims and non-Muslims alike. Furthermore, it serves as a comprehensive manual for individuals aspiring to assume leadership roles or follow such leaders, solely driven by the desire to please Allah/God on earth. These leaders and followers are regarded as representatives of Allah/God (vicegerents) as mentioned in Surah Al Baqarah (2:30). The author contends that the position of leadership is and should be regarded as a form of worship, drawing parallels to the leadership of Prophet Muhammad (PBUH) and the era of the Rightly four Guided Khalifs/Caliphs/vicegerents/successors, as well as certain virtuous leaders in the annals of Islamic and Western history.

Profile of the Author

Dr. Asan Vernyuy Wirba is a highly accomplished leader and manager who has had a distinguished career spanning over 17 years. Currently, he holds the position of Associate Professor of leadership and management at the Department of Business Administration in Jubail Industrial College (JIC), which is under the Royal Commission for Jubail and Yanbu. Located in Jubail Industrial City, Saudi Arabia, JIC is fortunate to have Dr. Wirba as a member of its faculty.

Dr. Wirba's expertise is vast and encompasses various domains such as teaching, training, research, business, and consulting. However, his additional passion after leadership and Management lies in the field of solar energy and academic management. With a Ph.D. from The University of Manchester in the United Kingdom, he has dedicated his research efforts to the study of leadership and management, with a great interest on Renewable Energy in the energy mixed.

The impact of Dr. Wirba's work is evident in his contributions to the academic community. He has authored several books and presented numerous research papers at prestigious international conferences and journals. Through these publications, he has shared his knowledge and insights, furthering the understanding of leadership, management, and the potential of Renewable Energy.

Dr. Wirba's dedication to his field and his commitment to advancing knowledge make him a valuable asset to the academic community. His expertise and contributions continue to shape the future of leadership and management, with a keen interest on Renewable Energy.

Acknowledgements

From its inception, many people contributed to leadership development from a Western and Islamic perspective. First, the author would like to express his appreciation for the support in editing the first edition of this book at the initial stage by Anastayzia Versachi, Seidou Hamidou, Mustapha Ahmed, Dr. Elvis Amowakwa, and Mohammed Francis Smith at the last step. He critically shaped the direction of this book. The author would also like to thank Dr. Shakoor Ahmed Ward, who read the book and gave his feedback earlier. Dr. Mohammad Hoq, Dr. Abdulwahab Shmailan, Yeva Guiea, Dr. Abdullahi Masud, Allan Latoga, Sulaiman Awal, Sherif Hassan, Abdou Zaki Asan, Dr. Amenu Foven Wirba, and JIC Library staff, Tawfiq A. Al-Zoori, Khaled Thaib Al Kharbi, Waleed

A. Al Masari, Ahsan Jamal, Sheraz Khurshid. A special thanks also goes to Mohammad Awwal Saidu for his input in the second edition of this book. All my thanks go to all of them.

The author also wants to thank his wife, Aisha Musa, son, Mohammad Asan Wirba, and Abdullah Asan Wirba, for being patient while writing this book's second edition. Finally, thanks to my parents and Brother Al Haji Sulaiman Inua and Mother Alima Vejai, who has always encouraged the author throughout his life. Not to mention my late father, Mallam Inua Wirba, who worked tirelessly for Islam in Cameroon's and more importantly in Kumbo-Nso Bui Division, North West Province of Cameroon where he was the founder and established the first Anglo-

Arabic Schools in Cameroon, specifically in the North West Province (NWP). May Allah (God)forgive his sins and grant him paradise (Janahtul Ferdaus). We all as his children and grandchildren are all indebted to his mission and vision for his community, particularly the Muslim communities he fought for until his last hours on earth with regards to Islam and Islamic education in Cameroon. May Allah be pleased with his soul.

Chapter 1

Introduction

This book commences by undertaking a comparative analysis of Western and Islamic perspectives on leadership. In the exploration of the Western perspective on leadership, a comprehensive overview is presented, encompassing the viewpoints of various Western scholars, practitioners, and professionals in the field of leadership. It is important to note that the moral and ethical dimensions of leadership are duly acknowledged and incorporated within the examination of both perspectives. The author of this book advocates for a transformative shift in the comprehension of leadership and that Allah(God) is and should be the tenant of leadership from both perspective, positing that leadership is an altruistic form of servitude, solely dedicated to the gratification of Allah(God). Furthermore, the author asserts that leaders and followers are divinely appointed representatives of Allah(God) on Earth, as elucidated in Surah Al-Baqarah (2:30). Ultimately, the book contends that leadership theories are designed to enlighten and guide the implementation of optimal leadership practices.

The Islamic perspective of leadership is rooted in the teachings of the Quran and the Sunnah of the Prophets of Allah(God), spanning from prophet Adam (PBUH) to the revered Prophet Muhammad (PBUH), as well as the four Guided Caliphs and other virtuous leaders throughout history. This book delves into the fundamental principles and values that underpin leadership in Islam. The Islamic perspective of leadership draws inspiration from the exemplary leadership of Prophet Muhammad (PBUH), particularly his role in establishing an Islamic city-state in Madinah with a great constitution embracing all aspects of human life. Thus, when seeking a paradigm of effective leadership, one need not look far, but rather examine the model of leadership demonstrated by Prophet Muhammad(PBUH) in Madinah, as well as the commendable examples of effective leadership set by the Four Rightly Guided Caliphs(al-Khulafā' al-Rashidun)and the preceding Prophets, commencing with prophet Adam (PBUH).

Leadership has been and will always be one of the most discussed and written-about concepts in the history of Mankind and Civilization. We are not the first and will not be the last in trying to understand what is meant by a good leader or an effective leadership. Leadership will always continue to captivate all our minds, hearts, and imaginations, irrespective of our background, either Muslims or non-Muslims. Generations after generations are still searching for an elusive answer as to what makes a good and effective leader.

This book seeks to answer this elusive question of what makes a good or an effective leadership from both Islamic and Western perspective. Hence, the exploration of the concept of leadership is an ongoing and captivating endeavor by many scholars, practitioners and professionals. It is hope that this book serves as a reminder to both Western and Islamic leaders and their followers of the importance of an effective leadership. It is also important to note that leadership is a trust and that those who assume the responsibility of leadership in their various nation's states or Muslims communities are first accountable to Allah(God). They are Allah(God) representative on Earth. In other words, leaders and followers in the west and Muslims communities must comprehend that their roles within nations, communities, and societies carry significant obligations that will be evaluated during the Day of Judgement. These responsibilities of leadership necessitate careful consideration and humility in delivering it, since it is a trust (Amanah).

Hence throughout the course of human existence, the progression of the human race has been profoundly influenced by the existence of exceptional individuals who assume the roles of leaders and followers. Notably, across various generations, Prophets have been dispatched by Allah(God) to guide humanity with the purpose of reminding and guiding them towards the unity of Allah(God) and the importance of adhering to His guidance in our roles as leaders and followers, despite the disobedience exhibited by certain individuals and leaders. Furthermore, when Allah/God appoints a prophet to a specific community, that prophet possesses fluency in the language of the people in order to effectively communicate Allah(God) Message and teachings. As a result, it becomes our responsibility as human beings to choose leaders who can embody our collective aspirations and ambitions.

Henceforth, the concept of leadership continues to captivate individuals across generations, irrespective of their faith or beliefs. Numerous scholars and practitioners have made efforts to address the issue of leadership, with some focusing on writing books that primarily emphasize the development of proficiency and success in leadership, often overlooking the significance of moral and ethical considerations in leadership practice and others like this book try to inject the ethical and moral perspective of leadership as the way of contributing to the understanding of leadership from both perspectives.

This book is being written with a focus on the increasing apprehension prevailing among individuals and groups in contemporary society regarding the moral and ethical behavior exhibited by leaders within their respective communities and nation-states. Addressing such inquiries can be a formidable undertaking given the inherent characteristics of leadership roles, which predominantly centre on personal authority and power rather than prioritizing accountability to Allah/God only. Unfortunately, it is evident in the writing of this book that the reverence for Allah/God no longer holds a significant place in the hearts and minds of some of those people who hold leadership positions in both Western and Islamic/Muslim communities. Instead, many leaders today seek power for personal gain, prioritizing their own interests over the well- being of their constituents. They engage in embezzlement of public funds for personal use and that of their families, leaving their citizens to fend for themselves, which is a tragic abuse of power. It is disheartening to witness individuals investing their own resources to secure leadership positions, losing sight of their true purpose and forgetting that they will ultimately be held accountable for their actions on the Day of Judgment.

Some leaders perceive leadership as a means to achieve esteem and prestige, while others are driven by patriotism and personal advancement in life, as well as the desire to exert control over others. For certain individuals, it serves as a shortcut to wealth and fame, whereas others see it as an opportunity to exercise power and engage in selfless service. Irrespective of the motives propelling these leaders towards positions of leadership, this book serves as a reminder that true leadership is characterized by selfless servitude solely for the purpose of pleasing Allah/God. Any other objective pursued in the pursuit of leadership is destined to fail in the eyes of Allah(God). The aspiration to lead should originate from a desire to please Allah/God, with the understanding that by doing so, one will effectively serve their communities and societies, thereby fostering dignity and prosperity for all.

The concept of leadership in this book is characterized as selfless servitude, solely for the pleasure of Allah/God, as exemplified by the previous Prophets, beginning with prophet Adam (PBUH) and culminating with the final Prophet Mohammad (PBUH), as well as the four Guided Caliphs, pious leaders, and followers who were motivated not by self-interest or self-aggrandizement, but rather by the desire to carry out Allah's work on earth as Khalifah on earth (vicegerent). See Surah Al Baqarah (2:30) as translated into English by Khan and Al Hilali (1996, p.16), 30, "And (remember) when your Lord said to the angels: "Verily, I am going to place (mankind) generations after generations on earth." Which means that man is a Khaliah or vicegerent of Allah/God on earth who know that the originator of leadership is Allah/God and that he is only a servant or a care taker on earth. As representatives of Allah/God, it is imperative for us to bear in mind the underlying purpose behind the creation of mankind. In order to fulfil our role as vicegerents, we must adhere to the divine laws set forth by Allah(God), not only in relation to ourselves but also towards our fellow human beings and even the animal kingdom. It is incumbent upon humanity to exercise restraint and limit their desires in accordance with their genuine needs, as bestowed upon us by Allah(God), utilizing our intellect and the guidance provided by religion.

Consequently, it becomes essential to prevent any form of transgression, whether one assumes a position of leadership or follows the lead of others. Those who choose to transgress, regardless of their role, will inevitably face the full consequences of their actions on the Day of Judgement. The primary objective of this book is to serve as a reminder to both leaders and followers that true leadership entails selfless servitude, solely aimed at pleasing Allah/God, as exemplified by the noble conduct of previous Prophets, guided Caliphs, and devout leaders and followers. Their actions were not driven by personal gain or self-aggrandizement, but rather by an unwavering commitment to carry out Allah/God work on earth as Khalifah (vicegerent), as stated in Surah Al Baqarah (2:30).

Many institutions have emerged to examine leadership in Western and Islamic societies, emphasizing its importance and relevance. Nevertheless, the problem of effective leadership persists despite the establishment of these institutions. This is primarily because they neglect to incorporate an Islamic viewpoint on leadership, which is based on the teachings of the Quran and the Sunnah of the Prophets, starting with Adam (PBUH) and concluding with the last Prophet of Allah/God, Mohammad (PBUH), as well as the four Guided Caliphs.

To address this issue, it is imperative that we examine the leadership model of Prophet Mohammad (PBUH) and his principles in building the city states of Madinah, as well as the leadership styles of the four Guided Caliphs in leading their respective communities. Despite the endeavours of scholars, practitioners, and experts to comprehend the intricacies of leadership by devising diverse theories to elucidate the leadership process, they have not succeeded in doing so by utilizing the appropriate premise, which is that the originator of leadership is Allah/God. As representatives of Allah/God on earth, both leaders and followers are obligated to adhere to the established laws in order to serve as models of righteousness.

This responsibility mirrors that of the prophets and Messengers who were sent by Allah/God, with their central focus being the worship of Allah/God and the adherence to His laws. Unfortunately, the current state of leadership is marred by scandals, indicating a significant departure from the leadership styles and skills demonstrated during the time of the prophets, particularly Prophet Muhammad (PBUH) and the four guided Caliphs who served as exemplary models of good leadership. In contemporary times, numerous leaders exploit the fears and anxieties of their citizens, intentionally fostering divisions within communities for personal or political gain, whether in Western societies or Muslim communities. It is crucial to recognize that these leaders and their supporters will be held accountable for their crimes against humanity, as their actions perpetuate division and hatred towards others.

Upon reviewing the literature on leadership, it becomes apparent that the concept of leadership is complex. The multifaceted nature of leadership is inherent, and the Western perspective on its definition encompasses a comprehensive understanding of this concept. Leadership, in this context, can be defined as the ability of an individual to guide, inspire, and influence others towards the achievement of common goals. It involves the possession of certain qualities and skills that enable one to effectively navigate complex situations, make informed decisions, and foster positive change within an organization or community. Furthermore, leadership in the Western context emphasizes the importance of ethical conduct, integrity, and accountability, as leaders are expected to act as role models and uphold high standards of behaviour. This viewpoint henceforth acknowledges the ever-changing aspect of leadership, acknowledging that it can be cultivated and improved through practical experience, educational pursuits, and introspection. Ultimately, leadership from a Western perspective is distinguished by its focus on cooperation, inclusiveness, and the advancement of shared achievements.

Northouse (2010, p. 1) argues that the results from all fields of study about leadership show that leadership is a much more sophisticated and complex phenomenon. Northouse (2013) further argues that the "Collectively of the research findings on leadership provide a picture of a process that is far more sophisticated and complex than the often-simplistic view presented in some of the popular books on leadership". Northouse (2013) further argue that "Leadership research is increasing dramatically, and findings underscore that there is a wide variety of different theoretical approaches to explain the complexities of the leadership process."

Winston and Patterson (2009), on the other hand, argue that even the 90+ dimensions of leadership are insufficient to comprehend leadership. In contrast, Sharma et al.'s (2019) study on leadership demonstrates that the research field on leadership is wide open for novel researchers to explore in the future. To others leadership is fascinating topic and at the same time is an interesting topic in which many scholars and practitioners have spent a great deal of time studying, researching, lecturing, and writing. Many practitioners and researchers have put a great deal of emphasis on understanding an effective leadership or good leadership.

Today as the author is writing this book a simple search on the internet will demonstrate that a large array of ideas, opinions, thought, research, and theory of leadership exist and overwhelming. Some scholar are of the view that leadership is a complex idea. Others argue that leadership can be boiled down into a couple of simple principles. For some researchers who studied the history of leadership have the opinion that leadership ideas are varied over the centuries and then try to understand why. Some contemporary leadership scholars have various contradicting ideas on leadership and also the definition of leadership. Some scholar studying leadership from a neuroscience perspective utilizing magnetic resonance imaging (MRI) as a means of understanding leadership. Whatever is the view of different scholars about leadership it is important to know that leadership is very important and remain vital for all irrespective of their believes and values.

The success or failure of any societal or organizational change is largely attributed to leadership, making it the primary factor. Effective leadership entails a leader's sincere introspection, enabling them to consistently question their own mind-set, beliefs, opinions, and outlook on life, self-esteem, and personal growth. This self-reflection empowers leaders, as well as followers, to consistently contribute positively to society, companies, or business organizations, and those in their vicinity. Achieving this requires professional development, fostering a constructive corporate culture, and demonstrating leadership qualities, particularly during challenging circumstances and crises.

To fully explore the topic of leadership from both Islamic and Western perspectives, it is necessary to begin by examining leadership through a Western lens. This involves analysing scholarly definitions of leadership and conducting a thorough review of leadership literature. This approach emphasizes the importance of moral and ethical leadership, recognizing it as the most critical aspect of effective leadership. Despite the sensitive nature of this topic, as it relates to the central theme of Allah(God) as the originator of leadership and leaders as representatives on earth, it is crucial to address it in order to promote a paradigm shift towards a more ethical and morally grounded approach to leadership.

Leadership is viewed as a selfless act, solely for the pleasure of Allah(God), and guided by Allah(God) laws rather than human-made laws that contradict the creator. Therefore, the content of leadership is and should be derived from the Quran and the Sunnah of the Prophets of Allah/God, beginning with Prophet Adam (PBHU) and culminating with the final Prophet Mohammad (PBUH) and the four Guided Caliphs.

Chapter two is dedicated to the examination of Leadership from a western perspective, it is important to acknowledge the viewpoints of scholars such as Rost (1991, p. 127) who reject the moral definition of leadership. Rost emphasizes that leadership ethics should be incorporated into the description of leadership, as they pertain to the leadership process rather than the content of leadership. Similarly, Kellerman (2004, p. 45) argues that it is crucial for scholars to remind us that leadership is not inherently a moral concept. According to Kellerman, leaders possess a range of qualities and characteristics, both positive and negative, similar to the general population. To assume that all leaders are virtuous individuals is to deliberately ignore the realities of the human condition, thereby severely limiting our potential to become more effective leaders. On the other hand, Northouse (2010, p. 12) argues that even though there is a lot written about leadership, it has been a big challenge for practitioners and researchers who want to understand what leadership is. He argues that leadership is a highly valued phenomenon that is very complex. On the other hand, Rost (1991, p. 98) casts doubt on whether earlier leadership studies were about leadership or what is understood as good management. Some leadership scholars argue that leadership is a twentieth-century concept, while others believe it dates back to ancient Greece and Rome. When Plato and Machiavelli lived, the first research or studies on leadership were mostly about power and influence. However, leadership studies have move on and many theories have been developed to enhance our understanding of leadership.

Many scholars have written some theories to explain leadership for example, the Great Man Theory was the most prevalent of earlier leadership theories. Great Man Theory concludes that great leaders were born, not made, with innate qualities that enabled them to lead and those scholars who adhere to this theory try to find a universal characteristic of leadership and there was not such characteristic that were universal of leadership. Writers like Northouse (2010, p. 20–21), sum up some of these characteristics as including intelligence, determination, self-assurance, honesty, and sociability. Northouse (2010, p. 1) also argue that a review of the scholarly literature on leadership reveals a vast array of theoretical approaches to explaining the complexities of the leadership process. Some researcher and scholars conceptualizes leadership as a trait or behavior.

However, there is yet a universally accepted definition of leadership. Stogdill (1974, p. 7) in his book acknowledges that there are nearly as many definitions of leadership as there are people who have attempted to define it. Thus leadership as a concept is dynamic and changes in perception across time and space. To really capture the spirit and the understanding of leadership we need to start the understanding of it from the right premise. The right premise according to this book is that Allah/God is the originator of leadership and that we as vicegerent/Khalifa/Caliphs of Allah/God on earth and that if we follow the reason for creation and follow Allah/God laws as did the Prophets of Allah starting from Adam (PBUH) to the finality of the Prophets, prophet Mohammad (PBUH) and the four Guided Khalifas ways we as leaders in our various communities will render our duties to our people or citizen in the right way and that is leadership. The subsequent section will centres its attention on the principles and elucidation of leadership as perceived through the lens of Western ideology. Consequently, what precisely constitutes leadership from a Western standpoint?

The next chapter focuses on the concept and definition of leadership from a Western Perspective.

Chapter 2

The Concept and Definition of Leadership from a Western Perspective

There are many definitions of leadership as there are many scholars who tried to define it and therefore there is no universal definition of leadership. The Western perspective on the definition of leadership encompasses a comprehensive understanding of leadership. Some scholars of Leadership, defined leadership as the ability of an individual to guide, inspire, and influence others towards the achievement of common goals. Which involves the possession of certain qualities and skills that enable one to effectively navigate complex situations, make informed decisions, and foster positive change within an organization or community.

In addition, the Western viewpoint places significant emphasis on ethical behaviour, integrity, and accountability in leadership, with leaders being held to the standard of serving as exemplars and maintaining elevated levels of conduct. This standpoint acknowledges the fluidity of leadership, acknowledging that it can be cultivated and improved through practical involvement, educational pursuits, and introspection. Ultimately, leadership from a Western perspective is distinguished by its focus on fostering collaboration, inclusiveness, and the advancement of collective achievements. Hence, Rost (1991, p. 102) defines leadership as a relationship of influence between leaders and followers who intend genuine change that reflects mutual goals. In this process, the leader interacts with the follower based on a shared goals. In this book shared goals, mutual interest should be based on ethical considerations and beliefs and the Quran and the Sunnah of the Prophets should be the guiding principles.

According to Newstrom (2011, p. 171), leadership influences and encourages others to work enthusiastically toward achieving goals. On the other hand, Robbins and Judge (2012) argue that leadership is the ability to get a group to work toward a vision or set of goals. Furthermore, they argue that an organization requires strong leadership and management for optimal effectiveness. In essence, leadership is a relationship of influence between a leader and follower, as it cannot exist without a leader and a follower. Dubrin (2007), on the other hand, argues that leadership is "the ability to give people the confidence and support they need to help the organization reach its goals." Similarly, Yukl (2006, p. 8) defines leadership as "the process of influencing others to understand and agree on what needs to be done and how to do it, and the process of facilitating individual and collective efforts to achieve shared objectives."

Burns (1978, p. 19) in the study of leadership differentiates transactional and transformational leadership and suggests that transactional leadership occurs when one person initiates contact with others for an exchange of something of value; that is, a leader approaches followers with the intent to exchange. Transactional leadership focuses on short-term, day-to-day leadership.

Avolio et al. (2003, p. 287) assert that leadership entails persuading individuals to forego their interests temporarily in favor of the collective good. Furthermore, Burns (1978, p. 19) defines leadership as leaders influencing followers to act for specific goals that reflect the values and motivations, wants and needs, aspirations, and expectations of both leaders and followers. The genius of leadership lies in how leaders understand and act on their followers' values and goals. According to Yukl (2006), leadership is the process of influencing others to understand and agree on what is to be done and how it is to be done, as well as facilitating individual and collective efforts to achieve shared objectives. On the other hand, Hagen et al. (1998) argue that leadership is how leaders change other people's thoughts, actions, and values. Bass (1990, pp. 19–20), argue that leadership is the interaction between two or more group members that frequently involves restructuring the situation and the members' perceptions and expectations. Leaders are change agents or individuals whose actions have a more significant impact on others than on themselves. A group member demonstrates leadership when they modify the motivation or skills of other group members.

Northouse (2010, p. 3) defines leadership as the process by which an individual influences a group of individuals to accomplish a common objective. De Pree (1990) defines leadership as stewardship, emphasizing the significance of building relationships, initiating ideas, and establishing enduring organizational values. Rather than focusing on the how of corporate life, he explains the whys and demonstrates that the first duty of a leader is to define reality, and the last is to express gratitude. The skilful leader must stimulate efficiency by enabling others to realize their individual and organizational potential. In addition to developing, communicating, and defending civility and values, they must foster new leaders and strengthen the corporate culture. According to Wirba (2020), leadership is selfless purely for the pleasure of Allah/ God and this book still hold firm on this definition of leadership.

West and Ainscow (1991, p. 29) define leadership as influencing group behaviour toward a common goal. Kotter (1990) argues that leadership is the ability to develop a vision, set a new direction for an organization, and persuade others to move in that direction. Leadership is defined by Mullins (1987, p. 225) as a relationship through which one person influences the behaviour of others. Covey (1990) argue in his book entitle "The 7 Habits of Highly Effective People" that leaders listen to others with genuine empathy and try to understand them before they try to be understood. Which way ones looks at leadership it is understandable that there is great necessity for effective leadership.

Rost (1991, p. 101) in his book on leadership critically argues that while the industrialized leadership model has served the American people well since the late 1800s, it is increasingly failing to meet their needs as the twenty-first-century approaches. He proposed a post-industrial leadership paradigm with core values such as collaboration, common good, global concern, diversity, pluralism in structure, and participation, client orientation, civic virtues, and freedom of expression, critical dialogue, qualitative language and methodologies, substantive justice, consensus-oriented policy processes. These are values; he argues that they must be incorporated into the new definition of leadership.

Rost (1991) observation is caching up with America today where many political leaders are striving to create division amongst its citizens, a tribal way of looking at leadership which is really failing the American people and democracy in general. For those of all who grow up believing in democracy and the role of law it seems that some political leadership are failing the American people and democracy on least some mindful people step up to rescuer democracy from decay. Once again leadership is vital for democracy and the role of law. Leadership position is very essential and should not be hijack by those who want to divide citizens by tapping into their fears and worries rather on citizens share values and objectivity.

Bass (1997) define leadership as influencing a group to achieve its objectives and directing the organization to become more cohesive and coherent. Winston and Patterson (2006) provide an integrative definition of leadership and conclude, "A leader is one or more people who select, equip, train, and influence one or more follower(s) with diverse gifts, abilities, and skills and focus the follower(s) on the organizational mission and objectives, causing the follower(s) to willingly and enthusiastically expend spiritual, emotional, and physical energy in a concerted, coordinated effort to achieve the organizational mission and objectives." Despite the differences in leadership functions, Northouse (2010) noted that leaders are also involved in planning and organizing tasks to complete the job (i.e., management function). Similarly, managers frequently assist groups in achieving their objectives (i.e., leadership function). Leadership is distinct from management, despite the fact that the two share similarities. For example, they are both concerned with influence, working with others, and achieving their objectives. Northouse, (2010).

According to other authors on leadership, leadership entails making sound and, at times, difficult decisions, developing and articulating a clear vision, establishing attainable goals, and equipping followers with the knowledge and resources necessary to achieve those goals. Others believethatleadershipisthecapacityofanindividualorgrouptoinfluence and direct followers or other members of an organization to assist them in achieving their objectives. Harvard Business Review (2004) cites Prentice (1961) as defining leadership as "the accomplishment of a goal through the direction of human assistants" and a successful leader as one who can understand people's motivations and enlist employee participation in a manner that aligns individual needs and interests with the group's purpose. He advocated for democratic leadership that fosters the learning and growth of employees without encouraging anarchy. The observations of Prentice regarding how leaders can motivate employees to support the organization's goals are timeless and reflective of the leader's role in an organization.

According to Prentice, leadership entails much more than "understanding people," "treating others kindly," and "not pushing others around." Sometimes it is believed that there is no division of authority in a democracy or that everyone is their boss. This is absurd, especially in the business world. But business leadership can be democratic if it gives every employee the best chance to move up in the company without causing chaos. According to him, a leader's role is to identify roles and responsibilities within the group that allows each member to satisfy a primary motivation or interest. In contrast, Greenleaf's (1970) theory of servant leadership asserts that the servant-leader is, first and foremost, a servant. It starts with the innate desire to serve and to serve first. Then, the conscious decision makes one a leader who inspires others. This person is strikingly distinct from those who are leaders first, possibly due to the need to satisfy an unusual power drive or to acquire material possessions. Two extreme types are the leader-first and the servant-first individuals. Some shadings and blending's are a component of the infinite diversity of human nature.

The differences manifest in the care taken by servant-first individuals to ensure that the highest priority needs of others are met. The servant-leader prioritizes the development and prosperity of the people and communities to which they belong. In contrast to traditional leadership, in which the person at the top of the pyramid usually gets and uses the most power, the servant-leader shares power, puts the needs of others first, and encourages others to grow and do their best. In addition, servant leadership is not about seeking personal power, prestige, or material rewards. Thus, proper motivation is service to others, not control or the exercise of power. The proponents of servant leadership recognize that servant leadership is the basis of effective leadership.

Eicher-Catt (2005, p. 17) criticizes Servant Leadership, claiming that the values attributed to it are gender biased and accuses the theory of perpetuating a theology of leadership that upholds androcentric patriarchal norms and insidiously perpetuates a long-standing masculine-feminine, master-slave political economy. There are leadership authors who are critical of spiritual leadership or moral leadership as prescribed in the Quran and Bible, but the author of this book makes a strong case for returning to the roots of leadership, which cannot be separated from the spiritual being of a leader and followers. Finally, when analysing the definitions of leadership from a Western standpoint, it is crucial to acknowledge the significant contributions made by Western leadership scholars and practitioners. However, these definitions lack the recognition of Allah(God) as the ultimate source of leadership and humanity as Allah(God) representatives on earth. In other words, the Bible, The Ten Commandments, and the teachings of Jesus should be central in the definition and content of leadership from a Western perspective which can lead guiding principles for leadership practices.

Additionally, a review of numerous definitions of leadership from a Western viewpoint reveals a lesser emphasis on the moral and ethical aspects of leadership, which is a cause for concern. These aspects should serve as the guiding principles and practices of leadership to prevent instances of scandal in various domains or issues such as politics, religion, and other affairs. It is important to note that Allah(God) has created all individuals with the purpose of worshiping Him alone.

Therefore, the primary duty of both leaders and followers should be to worship Allah/God, abide by His laws, and act as His representatives on earth. It is evidence here in this book that, the purpose of life is very simple, Allah/God created mankind to worship Him. See Surah 51 Adh-Dhariyat (51:56-58) as translated into English by Khan and Al Hilali (1996, p.660-1). 56, "And I (Allah) not created the Jinn and mankind except that they worship Me (Alone). 57, I seek not any provision from them (i.e. provision for themselves or for My creatures) nor do I ask that they should feed Me(i.e. feed themselves or My creatures). 58, Verily, Allah is the All-Provider, Owner of Power, The Strongest. Therefore, the author of this book define leadership from an Islamic perspective which is sees leadership or leadership position as serve less servitude purely for the pleasure of Allah(God).

We as leaders and followers are vicegerent of Allah (God) on earth. Therefore, the principles of leadership content must be from the Quran and the Sunnah of the prophets starting from Adam (PBUH) to the final prophet of Allah/God Mohammad (PBUH) and the four Guided Khalips. And also from the western perspective the content of leadership should be from the Bible, The Ten Commandments or the teaching of Jesus, Moses and other prophets of Allah(God).

The erosion of the political environment in the traditional West is becomingincreasinglyapparent, particularlywithregardstointernational affairs. The blind support of regimes that do not respect international laws by Western leaders is a cause for concern, as it has left the world cynical of their motives. For example, the strong support of Israel by the United States, Britain, France, Germany, and other European states has had a negative impact on their image in the Islamic world and beyond, even in their own nations, as evidenced by the demonstrations in the streets of the Arab, Muslim worlds, and around the world during the recent crisis in Gaza. Despite preaching democracy, the West supports autocracy or regimes that do not fully comply with international laws and this is concerning.

Western leaders privately pander to aggressive domestic pressure groups, while advocating peace and tranquility in public. The erosion of democratic principles and truth, particularly in the Western world, is a growing concern, particularly with regards to the actions of some of their leaders. To prevent a complete failure of democracy and the role of law, it is suggested that individuals and leaders follow the guidance of Allah(God) as taught in the Quran, the Bible, the Ten Commandments, and the teachings of past prophets such as Jesus and Moses, which are based on Divine Laws. While man-made laws have their limitations, Divine laws are essential in ensuring that mankind remains accountable.

There is a pressing requirement for a fundamental change in the way leadership is perceived, particularly from a western standpoint. The focus and substance of leadership ought to be directed towards moral and ethical principles, firmly rooted in the teachings of the Quran, Sunnah of the prophets, four Rightly Guided Khalifas, Sharia from the Muslim perspective, and the Bible, the Ten Commandments and the teaching of Jesus and other Allah/God prophets from a western perspective. Additionally, when relevant, it should also draw from the Divine Laws and the teachings of Moses and Jesus. Therefore, the guiding principles of leadership should be derived from the Quran, Bible, or any scripture of Allah/God to guide mankind on earth. For instance, the Ten Commandments provide a simple yet powerful example of ethical conduct, such as refraining from stealing, keeping the Sabbath holy, and fearing Allah/God alone. Great leaders and followers draw inspiration from the teachings of the Quran or the Bible. This book serves as a reminder of the leadership principles that can be drawn from the Ten Commandments, the teachings of Moses, and the previous prophets, including Prophet Muhammad (PBUH), the final prophet of Allah/God on earth, and the four Rightly Guided Khalifas/Caliphs/Vicegerents/ Successors. All the above observations about leadership from a western perspective which requires a paradigm shift.

A Paradigm Shift

The concept of a paradigm shift involves examining leadership through the lens of morality, ethics, and scripture, i.e. the Quran, the Sunnah and the Bible, Ten Commandments and other religious principles. The role of morality and ethics in leadership is of utmost importance. A Western perspective of leadership that emphasizes moral and ethical aspects of leadership is crucial. By adopting an ethical and moral perspective on leadership might help in addressing and mitigating numerous scandals that have plagued human history and mankind in the west and non-western societies and more importantly in the realms of politics, finance, and other human institutions. There is a pressing demand for leadership from a Western perspective to adhere to the Bible, Ten Commandments, and other religious guidelines that dictate the behaviours of both leaders and followers.

Paradigm shift, as advocated in the present book, involves replacing the prevailing mind-set of "win at all costs" with a more collaborative and mutually beneficial approach which is rooted in the belief that Allah (God)is and should be at the centre of all human decisions and endeavours, emphasizes the supremacy of divine laws over man-made laws.

The prevalence of ethical scandals in the corporate and business world serves as a constant reminder of the importance of addressing the ethical and moral decay in leadership, which necessitates spiritual guidance and attention. Prominent examples of such scandals include the Enron crisis, WorldCom, Parmalat, National Irish Bank (NIB), Allied Irish Bank (AIB), the Sanlu Company Melamine Incident, and the Volkswagen diesel emissions scandal. These instances underscore the urgent need for leaders who prioritize ethics, morality, and, most importantly, the spiritual aspect of humanity. The global emergence of prominent scandals and the participation of leaders in unethical behaviours have garnered heightened awareness regarding the significance of ethical and moral leadership, a matter of concern for all individuals. This book is written as a reminder to both leaders and followers to uphold moral and ethical principles and at the same time put Allah(God) at the centre of their decision process. The undeniable deterioration in ethical and moral principles among leaders and followers necessitates that as an authors and practitioners of leadership, we must not adopt a passive stance, hoping that these scandals will naturally dissipate. We should keep on reminding ourselves and others whether leaders or follower of the necessity of ethic, morale and the fear of Allah/God in all our endeavors. Allah(God) created us for a purpose and we must therefore seek guidance from Allah(God) and all these guidance are found in the Quran and the Bible or the Ten Commandments and other religious principles.

Green and Odom (2003) highlight in their writings on leadership the detrimental effects of Enron's lack of ethical leadership, which resulted in harm to thousands of employees and necessitated greater government regulation. The author of this book posits the notion that a shift is imperative, wherein our dependence on governmental regulations alone should be surpassed. Instead, the author advocates for a rekindling of our leaders' cognizance regarding the significance of spirituality and the pursuit of divine guidance from Allah/God in their decision-making endeavours. The proposition put forth suggests that leaders ought to perceive their responsibilities as a manifestation of worship, wherein their ultimate recompense emanates from Allah/God, rather than being contingent upon the approval of the populace, acquaintances, or kin.

Knight and O'Leary (2018) posit that the root cause of ethical leadership failures can be traced back to the self-centred focus that has been perpetuated by Enlightenment ideals and humanistic thinking on autonomy. They argue that contemporary concerns with material and symbolic success have further reinforced this preoccupation with the self, leading to corporate scandals and ethical failures. To address this issue, the authors suggest adopting Aristotelian virtue ethics, which prioritize community values and solidarity over individualistic heroism. This approach offers a potential solution to challenging self-centeredness and promoting ethical leadership.

Furthermore, Plinio et al. (2010) conducted an extensive qualitative investigation, shedding additional light on the significance of embracing a virtue-centred methodology towards leadership. Their study revealed that organizations currently confront substantial challenges in terms of deficient ethical conduct and a dearth of ethical leadership. This observation is not ground breaking, and unless there is a shift in our perspective and a comprehensive comprehension of the fundamental origins of these predicaments, it is anticipated that similar scandals will persist in the future.

Ethical Leadership

The definition of ethics in the Western world began with Plato and Aristotle. To this effect, Northouse (2010) argues that from the perspective of the Western tradition, the development of ethical theory dates back to Plato (427-347BC) and Aristotle (384-322BC) and that ethics comes from ethos, a Greek word meaning character, conduct, and custom. Northouse (2010) argue that the ethical theory provides a system of rules or principles that guide us in deciding what is right or wrong and good or bad in a particular situation. Hence in this book the author goes beyond this notion of ethical rules or principles argue by Aristotle or Plato and argue that the principles of leadership either from the Islamic and western perspective should be from the Quran, and the Sunnah of the Prophets especially the final prophet of Allah/ God Mohammad (PBUH) and the four Rightly Guided Khalifas from the Islamic perspectives and from the Western perspective of leadership from the Bible, Ten Commandments, from the prophets and from any scripture of Allah/God and not forgetting Divine laws that guides all mankind irrespective of their faith.

Some Western scholars like Yukl (2012), on the other hand, argues that ethics is central to leadership because of the nature of the relationship between leaders and followers. Leaders influence followers and, therefore, will affect them negatively or positively through their character or behaviours. They can also influence followers in the quest for a common goal and, at the same time, treat their followers as individuals with respect and dignity.

This argument from Yukl is good but we need Allah/God principle as regards to leaders and followers and how they should behave with one another based on the scripture, for example the Quran and the Bible. If we can follow divine principles or decree we will be in better position to lead as Allah/God want us to treat one another. For example the values of justice, equality, and liberty to assist followers in understanding the importance of ethics are very important and should be practiced by leaders and followers based on the scripture. The values that the leaders uphold are instrumental in influencing followers and therefore should have roots in the scripture. Our leaders should be models for others to follow and not using their followers for their own personal interest by creating division, fears and worries for their personal gains. Zero some mentality by leaders today is a concern.

The far right political ideology is gaining whole in many countries today especially in the west. These right wing groups in the west that are gaining ground are mostly anti-immigration and Islamophobia violence because their leaders blame others for their problems and some of their leaders are use sing the concept of we and them to gain popularity and create division among people. Therefore ethical and moral leadership is essential in our societies today ever than before and we must all stand for ethical and moral leadership.

The writing of this book is a reminder of what we should be doing and be warning and reminding our leaders and follower of the importance of ethical and moral leadership in our societies. Western scholar like Ciulla (1995) had started reminding us of the important of ethical leadership by arguing that most scholars and practitioners who write about leadership rest on the altar and not practice by those who supposed to do so. Kanungo and Mendonca (1998) also argue about the importance of ethical leadership in an organization by stating that a leader's ethical conduct guided by moral principles gives credibility to the organization. Thus, what is ethical leadership?

Definition of Ethical Leadership.

There are many definitions of ethical leadership, and the author will examine some of them in this book. The concept of ethical leadership refers to a set of principles and values that guide the behavior of leaders in an ethical manner. It involves the ability to make decisions that are morally sound and just, while also considering the interests of all stakeholders involved. Ethical leadership is characterized by honesty, integrity, transparency, and accountability, and it is essential for promoting trust, respect, and credibility within organizations. Effective ethical leadership requires a deep understanding of ethical principles, as well as the ability to apply them in real-world situations. It is a critical component of organizational success, as it fosters a culture of ethical behavior and promotes the well-being of all individuals involved. Trevino et al. (2005, p.120) define ethical leadership as the demonstration of normatively appropriate conduct through personal actions and interpersonal relationships and the promotion of such conduct to followers through two-way communication, reinforcement, and decision-making. They contended that a moral and ethical leadership's traits and characteristics are honesty, trustworthiness, integrity, and the moral nature of that leader's conduct.

Leaders are role models and guides to their followers; if they do not act or function morally, it may affect followers. Therefore, they should be credible and consistent with what they say or do. They should walk the talk and talk the walk. The University of Villanovan (2021) define ethical leadership as a form of leadership in which individuals demonstrate conduct for the common good that is acceptable and appropriate in every area of their life. To them, ethical leadership has three significant traits: Being the Example, championing the importance of ethics, and communicating. For them, leading by example is very important because actions speak louder than words. To champion the importance of ethics it is the role of an ethical leader who focuses on the overall importance of ethics, including ethical standards and other ethical issues, and how these factors can influence society and primarily teach peers about ethics, especially in cases where workers are faced with an ethical issue in the workplace or organisation.

Ethical leaders communicate because it is their job to communicate with each team member and allow for open conversation. On the other hand, Bhasin (2021) defines ethical leadership as a type of leadership incorporated by leaders who demonstrate appropriate and ethical behavioral conduct inside and outside the organization. Leaders with ethical leadership styles exhibit good values via their words and actions, plus they do what is right, show integrity, and do not overlook wrongdoing. For him, ethical leadership is; leading by example, being willing to evolve, respecting everyone equally, communicating openly, managing stress effectively, and mediating fairly.

According to Kennedy (2022), ethical leadership is basing all management decisions, values, and morals on specific principles such as fairness, equality, honesty, respect, and accountability. These values form the basis of any ethical leadership. He gave the example of ethical leadership as a case of managers who manage several employees in an organization and respect all the members, listen to their views and opinions, supports their interests and beliefs, and encourage the subordinates to always act in fairness, practice honesty, and be considerate of each other. On the other hand, Greenleaf (1977, p.20), who theorized servant leadership, states, "Service to followers is the primary responsibility of leaders and the essence of ethical leadership." Brown et al. (2005, p.120) define ethical leadership as "the demonstration of normatively appropriate conduct through personal actions and interpersonal relationships, and the promotion of such conduct to followers through two-way communication, reinforcement, and decision-making." Ng and Feldman's (2015) study on ethical leadership finds support for ethical leadership's effect on followers' job attitudes, job performance, and other employee outcomes.

De Hoogh and Den Hartog (2009) defined ethical leadership as the process in which a leader influences group activities to attain organizational goals in a socially responsible way. For them, this definition should consider that a leader is ethical, moral, and caring and that their actions should benefit all stakeholders, including followers, the organization, and society. In support of this notion of ethical leadership, Kanungo (2001) argued that the ethical leader must engage in righteous acts and avoid harmful acts toward others, and their actions must be based on altruistic motives rather than self-centred. Surely ethical leadership behaviour should be stable behaviours across the spectrum. In other words, leaders cannot be ethical publicly and act unethical privately because Allah/God sees our acts as public or private. Again we are reminded in this book that we are all Khaliah's or vicegerent, and Allah is all seers and knowers of all things, both public and private. See Surah Al- Sajdah (32:6) as cited the English translation of Quran by Khan and Al Hilali (1996, p.522) that is He: The All-Knower of the unseen and the seen, the All-Mighty, the Most Merciful.

Thus, ethical leadership should enable people always to do the right thing irrespective of time and location, private or public. Allah/God sees us all the time and knows our movement and, more importantly, our intentions. We cannot forget Freedman and Steward (2006) who argue that ethical leadership is about "raising the bar," helping people to realize their hope and dreams, creating value for stakeholders, and doing these tasks with the intensity and importance that "ethics" connotes. Furthermore, they attest that there must be room for mistakes, humor, and humanity, which is sometimes missing in our current leader's behavior.

Yukl (2006) examined ethical leadership and concluded that "the ethical leader promotes honesty and mirrors his or her actions with values and beliefs." Kanungo (2001) attests to the fact that ethical leaders engage in deeds and behaviors that benefit others, and at the same time, they abstain from behaviors that can cause any hurt to others. Heifetz (2006), on the other hand, proposes that the primary responsibility of ethical leaders is to deal with conflict among followers and instruct them in the right way.

Furthermore, Heifetz (1994) attests to the fact that the overriding responsibility of leaders is to create a work atmosphere characterized by empathy, trust, and nurturing and to help followers to change and grow when faced with a difficult situation. In essence, ethical leadership influences followers to do the right things. Hickman (1998, p.361) subsequently quotes Aristotle's advice regarding ethics. Subsequently, Burns (1978, p.134) captured the essence or the spirit of ethical leadership when he argues that transforming leadership ultimately becomes moral in that it raises the level of human conduct and ethical aspiration of both leaders and leaders, and thus it has a transforming effect on both. Greenleaf (1977) attests to the fact that leaders need to serve followers and devote themselves to the ethical development of followers. At the same time, those who advocate Authentic Leadership believe that being ethical is true to oneself. However, Posakoff et al. (1990) argue that Transformational Leadership is a leadership style that is often said to be closely related to Ethical Leadership. Hence, Yukl (1994) also attests to the fact that Transformational Leadership is a process in which leaders and followers assist each other to reach a greater level of morality and motivation.

Yukl(2010) acknowledges that influential Transformational leaders see themselves as change agents, are risk takers, belief in people and care about the needs of others, are open to learning, believe in disciplined thinking and analysis, and become visionaries. Dubrin (2007), on the other hand, suggests that ethical leaders should have; 1) honesty, trustworthiness, and integrity; 2 treating all parties that will be affected by the leader's decision moderately; 3) helping people to achieve a common goal; 4holding respect for the individual; and; 5) working in silence and behind the scenes to make ethical achievements. All the above are guarded against the abuse of power by leaders and, at the same time, provide guidelines for determining when exercising influence is considered proper. Good leadership is all about having a trusting relationship with followers by treating them with respect, honesty and care with compassion. Ethics are behaviours that are stimulated by right and wrong, while the moral is inspired by religion.

Furthermore, Werphehowski (2007) examines Ethical Leadership from a spiritual perspective and argues that an ethical leader is one who reconciles humanity back to God and restores followers from the bondage of sin. Followers of the ethical leader will see divine immanence in such as life… unfolding of God's agency in liberating pardon, sovereign judgement, creaturely blessing, and faithful love over against the damage brought by sin, suffering, death, and hopelessness. Haven discus ethical leadership it is important to examine moral leadership. Thus, what is moral leadership?

Moral Leadership

The call for moral leadership is based on the same framework as ethical leadership as noted above. Moral leadership is a concept that has garnered significant attention in the academic realm. It refers to the ability of a leader to guide and influence others towards ethical and moral behaviour. This type of leadership is characterized by a strong sense of integrity, honesty, and accountability. It is grounded in the belief that leaders have a responsibility to act in the best interest of their followers and society as a whole.

Moral leadership is often contrasted with transactional leadership, which is focused on achieving specific goals and objectives through the use of rewards and punishments. While transactional leadership can be effective in certain contexts, it is often criticized for its lack of concern for ethical considerations. In contrast, moral leadership emphasizes the importance of ethical decision-making and the development of a strong moral compass. This type of leadership is particularly important in today's complex and rapidly changing world, where leaders are faced with a multitude of ethical dilemmas and challenges. Effective moral leadership requires a deep understanding of ethical principles and values, as well as the ability to apply them in real-world situations. It also requires a willingness to take responsibility for one's actions and to hold others accountable for theirs. Overall, moral leadership is a critical component of effective leadership in any context. It is essential for promoting ethical behaviour, building trust and credibility, and creating a positive and productive organizational culture.

Nair (1994) argued that leaders, especially those in business and politics, have lost their moral purpose and sense of idealism. Subsequently, Guadiani (1997) also argued that many citizens no longer have faith in their leaders, and the media have discovered unethical leaders in unlikely places, such as the clergy and college and university presidents. Bennis (1984) also asked, where have the leaders gone? He ascertains that leaders like Gandhi, Kennedy, and Martin Luther King, all lie slain. Kanungo and Mendonca (1998) argued that organizations are structures without a soul and ethical leadership and that organizational leaders must be more sensitive to their moral obligations to the broader society. Cheng et al. (2004, p.91) define moral leadership as "a leader's behaviour that demonstrates superior virtues, self-discipline, and unselfishness." According to Dov Seidman (2021), moral leadership is a leader's conduct that exemplifies solid moral values, selflessness, and integrity. For him, decision-making in moral leadership is guided by an inherent ethical system and moral purpose. Self-disciplined, compassionate, and responsible moral leaders prefer to lead and inspire others by setting an example and establishing moral goals. He asserts that moral leadership in professional ethics emphasizes honesty, trustworthiness, and reliability. Such a leader does not abuse power; they are impartial and prepared to put organizational needs before their own. Unfortunately, we live in a world where many leaders and followers have no moral or ethical behaviours, which is not very comforting.

Many people today worship money and are ready to do anything for it. Therefore, there is a need for moral leadership because moral leaders can hold all their employees to the same ethical values and standards, are against ethical violations, and promote a culture of unity and inclusion at work and wherever they may be. Moral leaders are truthful to themselves and others and recognize the need to be human. Hence according to Leychsalmy (2021), moral leadership is a framework and set of principles informing leaders in how they approach everything they do: how leaders interact with others, Moral leadership is rooted in, and guided by, a moral framework and set of principles that inform how leaders approach everything they do. He argues that moral leaders are accountable, pursue excellence and think about consequences before they act. Thus, moral leaders should avoid favoritism, prejudice, and blame. Moral leadership provides values or meaning for people to live by, inspiration to act, and motivation to hold oneself accountable. Moral and ethical leadership are core to human values and how we relate to one another as individuals and groups within our diverse societies and communities. To be a Khalifah or vicegerent of Allah/God on earth requires moral and ethical leadership because a vicegerent is a divinely connected representative of Allah in the human form as a mercy to humankind who has to be good. Thus, "being the vicegerent of the Creator, that is, ruling the world in compliance with His laws."

As vicegerent, we are in charge of executing Allah (God) laws on earth wherever we may be or following them wherever we may be.

We as vicegerent should be aware that everything available in eatthis universe is not explicitly ours but belongs to the Creator of this universe, i.e., Allah(God). Therefore, as vicegerent and human beings, we cannot misuse all these natural resources given to us by Allah(God) beyond our needs, wants, and desires, for we will be accountable for it on the Day of Judgment. Haven briefly discusses the ethical and moral perspective in leadership and the need to put Allah/God in the centre of leadership from both perspective is vital for those leaders and followers. Furthermore, examining some leadership theories from a Western perspective is essential in this book and therefore the next chapter focuses on the theories of leadership.

Chapter 3

Theories of Leadership from a Western Perspective

There are many theories of leadership. Each theory endeavors to inform practice. In this book, the author examines each theory and allows readers to conclude how lessons can be learned to inform practice. In other words, various leadership theories were developed over time for us to learn and draw lessons from as leaders and followers of our different communities and societies. Some theories, especially the earlier theories of leadership, focus on the characteristics and behaviours of successful leaders, and later theories begin to consider the role of followers and the contextual nature of leadership. Some of these theories are the great man theory, trait theory of leadership, behavioural theories, contingency theories, and contemporary leadership theories such as charismatic leadership, transformational leadership, transactional leadership, and servant leadership theory.

Thus, leadership theories are a fundamental aspect of the academic discourse on leadership. These theories aim to provide a comprehensive understanding of the nature of leadership, its functions, and the factors that contribute to effective leadership. The study of leadership theories is essential for individuals seeking to develop their leadership skills and for organizations seeking to cultivate effective leadership practices. The various leadership theories that have been developed over time as noted above include trait theory, behavioural theory, contingency theory, transformational theory, and situational theory, among others. Each of these theories offers a unique perspective on leadership and provides insights into the different approaches that can be adopted to achieve effective leadership. The study of leadership theories is an ongoing process, as new theories continue to emerge and existing theories are refined and expanded upon. Ultimately, the goal of leadership theory is to provide a framework for understanding the complex nature of leadership and to guide the development of effective leadership practices. In this chapter we will start with the great man approach to leadership.

The Great Man Approach and the Trait Approach to Leadership

The Great Man approach to leadership is a theoretical framework that posits that effective leadership is primarily determined by the innate qualities and characteristics of the leader. This approach suggests that certain individuals possess inherent traits that make them more likely to succeed as leaders, such as intelligence, charisma, and confidence. Proponents of this approach argue that these traits are largely unteachable and that leadership is therefore a natural and innate ability.

The Great Man approach has been criticized for its lack of empirical evidence and its failure to account for the role of situational factors in leadership. Critics argue that effective leadership is not solely determined by individual traits, but rather by a complex interplay of individual characteristics, situational factors, and group dynamics. Additionally, this approach has been criticized for its potential to perpetuate gender and other biases, as it tends to focus on traditionally masculine traits and characteristics. Despite these criticisms, the Great Man approach remains a popular theoretical framework in leadership studies, particularly in the fields of psychology and sociology. Many scholars continue to explore the role of individual traits and characteristics in leadership, while also acknowledging the importance of situational factors and group dynamics. Ultimately, the Great Man approach represents one of many theoretical perspectives on leadership, and its limitations and strengths should be carefully considered in any analysis of leadership effectiveness.

Daft (2018) attests to the fact that the Great Man approach is a leadership perspective that seeks to identify the inherited traits leaders possess that distinguish them from people who are not leaders. The basic assumption of the great man approach to leadership is that great leaders are born, not made. Thus, the term 'Great Man' is used because leadership was conceptualized as a single 'Great Man' who put everything together and influenced others to follow along based on inherited traits, qualities, and abilities. Thus, the Trait Approach arose from the 'Great Man' theory to identify the key characteristics of successful leaders. It was believed that critical leadership traits could be isolated through this approach and that people with such traits could then be recruited, selected, and installed in leadership positions. This approach to leadership placed more emphasis on the personal qualities of leaders and thus implied that leaders were born with innate qualities. The Trait Approach examines an individual's characteristics and looks for the essential traits consistently identified with leaders or people viewed as leaders. In other words, the trait approach or theory attempts to identify the personality traits or characteristics most often associated with successful leaders. To this effect, Daft (2018) argues that the trait theory assumes that people inherit certain qualities and traits that make them better suited to leadership.

Traits are the distinguishing personal characteristics of a leader, such as intelligence, honesty, self-confidence, and appearance. The Trait Approach to leadership is concentrated on the personal characteristics of leaders, which distinguish them from non-leaders. Hughes et al. (1985, p. 287) observe that the Trait theorists assumed leadership in terms of the innate personal characteristics of particular individuals.

Accordingly, they sought to identify common personality traits which distinguish leaders from non-leaders, regardless of circumstances or organizational setting. On the other hand, Stogdill (1948, cited in Bass 1990) doubts the evidence for this theory. Having failed to find consistent evidence to suggest that personal factors play a part in who becomes a successful leader, he concludes that the personal factors associated with effective leadership are substantially affected by the requirements of the situation in which the leader emerges. In other words, a person does not become a leader by some combination of traits, but the pattern of personal characteristics of the leader must bear some relationship with the followers' characteristics, activities, and goals.

Stogdill, according to Hughes et al. (1985, p. 264), did not himself accept the importance of traits for leadership but did observe that Trait theorists seemed to agree that intelligence, dominance, self-confidence, achievement, drive, and interpersonal skills were the most important personal attributes. It is important to note that if leaders are viewed as being born and not made, the implication is that training and development for leadership are less important than the selection of leaders. Previously, the literature on the Trait Approach had primarily focused on physical factors, such as height, physique, appearance, and age. Nevertheless, typical expressions from those who support the Trait perspective of leadership, are, 'He is born to be a leader, or 'She is a natural leader,' are not especially helpful in explaining which of these qualities are essential or why.

The Trait Approach failed to produce a definitive list of leadership traits, and, as mentioned above, it also failed to take situations into account. Additionally, it should have addressed how leadership traits affect group members and their work. These are some of the criticism of the Traits Approach. Burham (1975, p.205) affirms that studies of leaders in different situations have failed to discover any particular syndrome of personality traits that regularly characterize such individuals and differentiate between leaders and non-leaders. For him, the Trait Approach is not helpful for training and development because individual personal attributes are relatively stable and fixed and therefore need to be amenable to change. Thus, the results of trait studies were inconclusive in that, although some leaders might have possessed certain traits, their absence did not necessarily mean that the person was not a leader; at best, it could be said that some traits, such as task motivation, technical skills, intelligence, social skills, emotional control, and charisma, did appear more frequently than others. In examining the strength, Northouse (2010, p.25–7) affirmed that it has several identifiable strengths.

First, the Trait Approach is intuitively appealing. It fits clearly with our notion that leaders are the individuals who are out front and leading the way in our society. The second strength of the Trait Approach is that it has a century of research to back it up. No other theory can boast of the breadth and depth of studies conducted on the Trait Approach. Thirdly, the Trait Approach highlights the leader component in the leadership process. Finally, the Trait Approach has given us some benchmarks for what we need to look for to be leaders. In examining the weakness of the Trait Approach, Northouse (Ibid) points out that this approach has several shortcomings: 1) the failure of this theory to delimit a definitive list of leadership traits is a problem. The list of emerging traits appears endless; they should have considered situations; 2) it has resulted in highly subjective determinations of the most critical leadership traits; 3) it is not a helpful approach to training and development for leadership because traits are identified, and they are not easy to change. Therefore, other approaches to leadership had to be found, leading to the behavioral approach.

The Behavioural / Style Approach

The study of behavioral aspects in leadership has garnered significant attention in academic research. Scholars have extensively explored the various behaviors exhibited by leaders and their impact on organizational outcomes. This field of study aims to understand the specific actions, traits, and characteristics that leaders display in their roles, and how these behaviors influence the performance and effectiveness of their teams or organizations. By examining the behavioral dimensions of leadership, researchers seek to provide valuable insights into the complex dynamics of leadership and contribute to the development of effective leadership practices. Thus the Behavioral Approach is different from the Trait Approach in that, whereas the latter focuses on the supposed personal characteristics of the leader, the former emphasizes the observable behavior of the leader. In other words, the Behavioral Approach focuses on what leaders do. Furthermore, a behavioral approach often focuses on two kinds of behavior, task-related and relationship related.

Task behaviors facilitate goal accomplishment, helping group members achieve their objectives, while relationship behaviors help subordinates feel comfortable with themselves, with each other, and the situation in which they find themselves. Hersey and Blanshard were early advocates of this approach and even developed instruments to measure leadership behavior. According to Northouse (1997), the Behavioral Approach reminds leaders that their actions towards others are interpreted on task and relationship levels. Therefore, this approach allows leaders to reflect on their behavior by looking at it in terms of the two general dimensions of task and relationship behaviors.

The leadership style approach is a theoretical framework that seeks to understand and analyze the various leadership styles that exist within organizations. This approach posits that leadership is not a one-size-fits-all concept, but rather a complex phenomenon that is influenced by a variety of factors, including the leader's personality, the organizational culture, and the nature of the task at hand.

The style approach to leadership is based on the premise that there are several distinct leadership styles, each of which is characterized by a unique set of behaviors and attitudes. These styles include autocratic, democratic, laissez-faire, transformational, and transactional leadership. Each of these styles has its own strengths and weaknesses, and the most effective leaders are those who are able to adapt their style to the specific needs of their followers and the situation at hand. One of the key contributions of the style approach to leadership is its emphasis on the importance of situational factors in determining the most effective leadership style. This approach recognizes that different situations require different leadership styles, and that effective leaders are those who are able to identify and adapt to these situational demands.

Overall, the style approach to leadership provides a valuable framework for understanding the complex nature of leadership and the various factors that influence it. By recognizing the importance of situational factors and the need for leaders to adapt their style to the specific needs of their followers and the situation at hand, this approach can help organizations to develop more effective leaders and achieve their goals more efficiently. Furthermore, Northouse (1997, p. 71) argues that this approach to leadership stresses that there is no one best leadership style. Instead, leaders need to be flexible and adapt their style to the requirements of the situation.

Northouse (2010, p.78) discussed the strengths of the Style Approach and concluded that this approach marked a significant shift in the general focus of leadership research. This approach also broadened the scope of leadership research to include the behaviors of the leaders and what they do in various situations. Secondly, a wide range of studies on leadership Style validates and gives credibility to the basic tenets of the approach. Thirdly, on the conceptual level, researchers of the Style Approach have ascertained that a leader's style consists primarily of two significant behaviors: task and relationship. Finally, this approach is heuristic. In the area of criticism, Northouse (2010, p.79) argues that the Style Approach has failed to find a universal style of leadership that could be effective in almost every situation. According to Den Hartog and Koopman (2001), the focus shifted from whom leaders are to what leaders do. In other words, people can learn to become leaders through teaching and observation. This theory or approach assumes that leaders can become successful and effective according to what they do, not the characteristics of the leader, as in the case of the trait approach to leadership. Many examples of research have been done about the behavioral approach to leadership, such as the studies done by the University of Iowa Studies, Ohio State University Studies, the University of Michigan Studies, and the University of Texas Study.

Situational Approach to Leadership

The Situational Approach to leadership is much more focused on how leaders should adapt their style to suit the demands of the followers or the organization (Northouse, 1997). The basic premise of this theory is that different situations demand different leadership styles. The Situational Approach to Leadership is a theoretical framework that posits that effective leadership is contingent upon the specific situation at hand. This approach emphasizes the importance of adapting one's leadership style to suit the needs of the situation and the individuals involved.

The Situational Approach to Leadership was first introduced by Paul Hersey and Ken Blanchard in the late 1960s and has since been widely studied and applied in various organizational contexts. According to the Situational Approach to Leadership, there is no one-size-fits-all leadership style that is universally effective. Instead, leaders must assess the situation and the needs of their followers in order to determine the most appropriate leadership style to employ. The Situational Approach to Leadership identifies four distinct leadership styles: directing, coaching, supporting, and delegating. Each of these styles is appropriate for different situations and requires different levels of involvement and direction from the leader. The Situational Approach to Leadership has been widely applied in organizational settings, particularly in the areas of management and human resources. It has been used to develop training programs for leaders and to inform organizational policies and practices.

The Situational Approach to Leadership has also been studied in relation to other leadership theories, such as transformational leadership and servant leadership, and has been found to complement and enhance these approaches. Overall, the Situational Approach to Leadership provides a valuable framework for understanding the complex and dynamic nature of leadership. By emphasizing the importance of situational factors and individual needs, this approach offers a nuanced and flexible approach to leadership that can be adapted to a wide range of organizational contexts. Therefore, an effective leader adapts his or her style to the demands of different situations. Effective leadership behavior in the Situational Approach depends on the task, the characteristics of the group, and the interpersonal relationships within the group.

The prominent scholar who has contributed to this theory is Fiedler, whose Contingency Theory postulates that there is no single best way for managers to lead. Situations will create different leadership style requirements for a manager. Thus, there are many best ways for school principals, leaders, or managers to lead. Fiedler defines the condition of a managerial task into three factors; 1) Leader-member relations. How well do the manager and the employees get along? A leader who is more trusted and has more influence on the group would be better than a leader who is not trusted. 2) Task structure. Is the job highly structured, relatively unstructured. For example, a task where the team and leader have little knowledge of achieving them is viewed as unfavorable. 3) A leader's position powers are the amount of power a leader has to direct the group and provide reward or punishment. The more power the leader has, the more favorable his situation. Fiedler identifies power as being either strong or weak. Based on the above, managers were rated whether they were relationship-oriented or task-oriented. For example, a manager who is task-oriented tends to do better in situations with good leader-member relationships. It is important to note here that there is no good or bad leadership style; each person or leader has his or her preferences for leadership.

Path-Goal Theory

The Path-Goal Theory is a leadership theory that focuses on how leaders can effectively motivate and guide their followers towards achieving their goals. This theory suggests that leaders should adopt different leadership styles based on the needs and characteristics of their followers, as well as the situational context. By providing clear goals, removing obstacles, and offering rewards and support, leaders can enhance the motivation and satisfaction of their followers, ultimately leading to improved performance and goal attainment.

The Path-Goal Theory emphasizes the importance of the leader's role in clarifying the path to success and providing the necessary support to facilitate followers' progress. Path-Goal Theory focuses on how leaders motivate subordinates to accomplish agreed goals. The rationale underlying this theory of leadership is to influence both employee performance and employee satisfaction by focusing on employee motivation (Northouse, 1997, p.88).

Northouse (1997) states that the Path-Goal Theory emphasizes the relationship between the leader's style and the characteristics of the subordinates and their work setting. Path-Goal Theory explains how leaders motivate subordinates to be productive and satisfied with their work. The basic principle of Path-Goal Theory is from Expectancy Theory, which suggests that employees will be motivated if they feel competent if they think their efforts will, and if they feel the payoff for their work is worthwhile. A leader can help subordinates by selecting a (directive, supportive, participative, or achievement-oriented) one that provides what is missing for subordinates in a particular work setting. The leader's responsibility is to help subordinates to reach their goals by directing, guiding, and coaching them along the way (Northouse, 2004, pp123-143). Write (1996, p.62) cites House (1971, p.324), who asserts that the central tenet of Path-Goal Theory is that the motivational functions of the leader consist of an increasing personal payoff to the subordinate for work-goal attainment and making the path to these payoffs easier to function by clarifying it, reducing roadblocks and pitfalls, increasing the opportunities for personal satisfaction. Leader behaviour is acceptable and satisfying to subordinates to the extent that the subordinates see such behaviour as either an immediate source of satisfaction or instrumental to future satisfaction.

Finally, Write (1996, p.63) argues that Path-Goal Theory asserts that (a) the leader's behaviour will exert a beneficial influence on subordinates' motivation to perform, on their job satisfaction, and their acceptance of the leader, to the extent that it smoothies the path to the achievement of their goal; and (b) the leadership behaviour which performs this function will vary depending on the characteristics of the subordinates and their working environment.

Furthermore, the most supported and influential contingency theory to date is probably House's Path-Goal Theory of Leadership, developed in 1971. The theory describes how a leader's behaviour influences subordinate' satisfaction and performance (Yukl, 1989). Path-Goal Theory assumes that the leader must clean the road for the employees and eliminate problems leading to defined goals so that the employees can function more efficiently Den Hartog & Koopman, (2001).

Servant Leadership Theory

The theory of servant leadership is a formal concept in the field of leadership studies. It posits that effective leadership is characterized by a focus on serving the needs of others, rather than the self-interest of the leader. This approach emphasizes the importance of empathy, humility, and a commitment to the growth and development of those being led. The servant leader is seen as a facilitator of the success of others, rather than a controller or authoritarian figure. This theory has gained significant attention in recent years, as organizations seek to create more collaborative and inclusive cultures that prioritize the well-being of all stakeholders. Robert Greenleaf (1970) first proposed Servant-Leadership in 1970. This theory of leadership is a theoretical framework that advocates a leader's primary motivation as service to others.

According to Greenleaf (1970), the great leader is seen as a servant first. This leadership theory is very close to the Islamic perspective of leadership. From the Islamic leadership perspective, the content or guide to the definition of leadership is the Quran and the Sunnah of the Prophet Muhammad (PBUH).

Servant Leadership emphasizes increased service to others; a holistic approach to work, promoting a sense of community; and the sharing of power in decision-making. Central to the Servant-Leadership framework are the followings; (1) service to others, (2) holistic approach to work, (3) promoting a sense of community (4) sharing of power in decision-making. Other attributes of Servant Leadership are listening, empathy, healing, awareness, persuasion, conceptualization, foresight, stewardship, commitment to the growth of people, and building community. There is a lot to be learned from this fascinating leadership theory. However, some have criticized this theory. For example, Stone, Russel, and Patterson (2003) call the theory systematically undefined and lacking in empirical support. On the other hand, Eicher-Catt (2005, p.17) argues that the values attributed to Servant-Leadership are gender biased and accuses the theory of perpetuating a theology of leadership that upholds androcentric patriarchal norms and that it insidiously perpetuates a long-standing masculine-feminine, master-slave political economy. The next set of leadership theories is the Transformational and Transactional Leadership Theory.

Ethical Theory

The study of ethical theory is a fundamental aspect of philosophical inquiry. It involves the examination and analysis of various ethical systems and principles, with the aim of understanding the nature of morality and ethical decision-making. Ethical theory seeks to provide a framework for evaluating and justifying moral judgments, and to identify the principles and values that underlie ethical behaviour. This field of study is essential for individuals who wish to engage in ethical reasoning and decision-making, and for those who seek to understand the ethical dimensions of various social, political, and economic issues. Ethics comes from ethos, which means character, conduct, and customs

Ethical Theory falls into two broad categories; theories relating to a leader's behaviour and others relating to a leader's character. Theories relating to conduct are of two types. The first are those related to conducting and consequences, and then some relate to rules that advocate leaders' conduct. Theories related to consequences are called teleological theories. These theories examine whether a leader's actions, behaviour, and conduct have a positive outcome. Those theories related to duty or rules are called deontological theories (meaning duty in Greek word). This theory focuses on the actions that lead to consequences and whether the actions are good or bad.

Finally, the theories related to the character as a virtue-based approach. However, if we look at ethical leadership from Islamic perspective is focused on the willingness of the leader and the follower to willingly submit to the will of Allah/God. Ethical leaders from Islamic perspective have to consult with his followers, be just and allow freedom of thought. That is why in Islam there is no compulsion in religion. See Surah Al Bakarah 2 (2:256) as translated in English by Khan and Al Hilaili (1996, p.65) There is no compulsion in religion. Verily the Right path has become distinct from the wrong path, whoever disbelieve in Taghut and believe in Allah, then he has grasped the most trustworthy handhold that will never break. And Allah is All-Hearer, All-Knower. Targhut here means anything worshiped other than the Real Allah/God, i.e. all the false deities. It may be Satan, devils, idols, stones, stars, angel and human beings.

In essence no compulsion in religion means do not force anyone to become Muslim, for Islam is plain and clear, and its proofs and evidence are plain and clear. Therefore, there is no need to force anyone to embrace Islam. Rather, whoever God directs to Islam, opens his heart for it and enlightens his mind, will embrace Islam with certainty. Whoever God blinds his heart and seals his hearing and sight, then he will not benefit from being forced to embrace Islam. It was reported that; the Ansar (helper) were the reason behind revealing this Ayah, although its indication is general in meaning. Thus compulsion in Islam have no place.

There are many verses of the Quran that relate to Surah Al Baqarah 2(2:256) meaning no compulsion in religion. For example Surah Yunus 10(10:99-100) as translated to English by Khan and Al Hilaili (1996, p.276), 99,And had your Lord willed, those on earth would have believed, all of them together. So will you (O Mohammad (PBUH) then compel mankind, until they become believers. 100, It is not for any person to believe, except by the leave of Allah, and He will put the wrath on those who are heedless. See Surah Hud 11(11:28) as translated into English by Khan and Al Hilaili (1996, p.282), 28, He said: "O my people! Tell me, if I have a clear proof from my Lord, and a Mercy (Prophedhood) has come to me from Hi, but that (Mercy) has been obscured from your sight. Shall we compel you to accept it (Islamic Monotheism) when you have a strong hatred for it?

See also Surah Al Kahf 18(18:29), as translated into English by Khan and Al Hilaili (1996, p.372) 29, And say: "The truth is from your Lord." Then whoever will let him believe; and whoever wills, let him disbelieve. Verily, We have prepared for the Zalimun(polytheists and wrongdoers), a Fire whose walls will be surrounding them (disbelievers) in the Oneness of Allah). And if they ask for help (relief, water), they will be granted water like boiling oil, that will scald their faces. Terrible is the drink, and an evil Murtafaq (dwelling, resting place)! Surah Al-Ghashiyah 88(88: 21) as translated by Khan and Al Hilaili (1996, p.770), 21, So remind them (O Muhammad (PBUH) you are only one who reminds.

Teleological Approach

There are three approaches to assessing whether outcomes are ethical. The first, Ethical Egoism, describes actions designed to obtain the greatest good for the leader. Second, Utilitarianism refers to the leader's actions to find the greatest good for the most significant number of people. Third, Altruism designates the actions of leaders that show concern for others' interests, even if the interest is against the leader's self-interest.

The teleological approach is a philosophical perspective that focuses on the purpose or end goal of a particular phenomenon or entity. It posits that the ultimate purpose or telos of something determines its nature, function, and value. This approach is often employed in various fields of study, including ethics, biology, and theology, to understand and analyze the underlying purpose or design of a given subject.

In ethics, the teleological approach seeks to determine the moral worth of an action by examining its consequences and whether they align with the desired end goal. This consequentialist perspective emphasizes the importance of achieving the greatest overall good or happiness for the greatest number of individuals. By considering the ultimate purpose or telos of human life, this approach aims to guide ethical decision-making and promote the well-being of individuals and society as a whole. In biology, the teleological approach is utilized to understand the purpose or function of various biological structures and processes. It acknowledges that organisms and their components are intricately designed to fulfil specific functions that contribute to their survival and reproduction.

In examining the adaptive nature of these structures and processes, scientists can gain insights into the underlying purpose and evolutionary significance of different biological phenomena. In theology, the teleological approach is employed to explore the purpose or end goal of human existence in relation to a divine being or higher power. It seeks to understand the ultimate purpose or telos of human life and the role of individuals in fulfilling this purpose. This approach often involves examining religious texts, doctrines, and philosophical arguments to gain a deeper understanding of the divine plan and the moral obligations that arise from it. Overall, the teleological approach provides a framework for analysing and interpreting various phenomena by considering their ultimate purpose or end goal. By examining the underlying design, function, and value of a subject, this approach allows for a comprehensive understanding of its nature and significance in different fields of study.

Deontological Approach

This approach comes from 'does', a Greek word meaning duty. This aspect looks at the outcome. For example, telling the truth, being fair, keeping promises, and respecting others are actions and behaviours that leaders should exhibit while dealing with others in their communities by doing what is right. The deontological approach is a philosophical framework that emphasizes the moral duty or obligation of an individual to act in accordance with certain ethical principles, regardless of the consequences of their actions. This approach is often contrasted with consequentialism, which evaluates the morality of an action based on its outcomes or consequences.

In the deontological approach, the ethical principles that guide an individual's actions are considered to be universal and absolute, and are not subject to negotiation or compromise. These principles may be derived from religious or secular sources, and may include concepts such as respect for human dignity, the sanctity of life, and the importance of honesty and integrity. One of the key features of the deontological approach is the emphasis on the intention behind an action, rather than its outcomes. This means that an action may be considered morally right or wrong based on the motives of the individual performing it, rather than the consequences that result. For example, lying may be considered morally wrong in the deontological approach, even if it leads to a positive outcome, because it violates the principle of honesty and integrity. Overall, the deontological approach provides a framework for individuals to make ethical decisions based on their moral duty and obligation, rather than the potential benefits or harms of their actions.

Virtue-based Approach

This theory is related to leaders and their character. The virtue can be learned and engaged in with practice and experience. Examples of ethical virtues that can be learned are generosity, courage, sociability, honesty, self-control, justice, modesty, perseverance, integrity, fidelity, humility, and trustfulness. The virtue-based approach is a philosophical framework that emphasizes the cultivation and practice of virtues as a means to achieve moral excellence and ethical behaviour. This approach posits that individuals should strive to develop and embody virtues such as honesty, compassion, courage, and justice in their actions and decisions. By focusing on the development of virtuous character traits, the virtue-based approach aims to guide individuals towards leading a morally upright and fulfilling life. This approach is rooted in ancient Greek philosophy, particularly the works of Aristotle, who argued that virtues are essential for human flourishing and the attainment of eudemonia, or a state of well-being and fulfilment. In contemporary ethical discourse, the virtue-based approach continues to be a prominent perspective, offering valuable insights into the nature of moral conduct and the cultivation of virtuous character.

Transformational Leadership

Transformational leadership is a leadership style that emphasizes the importance of inspiring and motivating followers to achieve their full potential. This approach is characterized by a leader who is able to articulate a clear vision for the organization, and who is able to inspire and empower followers to work towards achieving that vision. Transformational leaders are known for their ability to create a sense of purpose and meaning for their followers, and for their ability to foster a culture of innovation and creativity. This leadership style is often contrasted with transactional leadership, which is focused on the exchange of rewards and punishments for performance. While both styles have their strengths and weaknesses, transformational leadership is generally seen as more effective in promoting long-term organizational success and employee satisfaction.

Bass and Avolio (1996) define Transformational Leadership as a process by which leaders take action to try to increase the awareness in their associates of what is proper and necessary, to raise their associates' motivational maturity, and to move them to go beyond their self-interests for the good of the group, the organization, or society. According to Bass and Avolio (1996), such leaders provide their associates with a sense of purpose that goes beyond a simple exchange of rewards for the effort provided. On the other hand, Phillips (1999, pp.23-24) argues that Transformational leaders have a bias for action and a sense of urgency centred have shared goals. They act with respect for the values of the people they represent. They are visionary and decisive. They have an intuitive understanding of human nature that combines with the ability to care, establish trust, and build alliances, and they have the know-how to create and manage change successfully.

According to Northouse (2010, p171), Transformational Leadership is a process that changes and transforms people. It concerns emotion, values, ethical standards, and long-term goals. Transformational Leadership involves a distinctive form of influence that moves followers to accomplish more than is usually expected of them. It is a process that often incorporates charismatic and visionary Leadership. Thus, for him, Transformational Leadership is the process whereby a person engages with others and creates a connection that raises the level of motivation and morality in both the leader and the follower.

Hunt (2005) described the increasing popularity of theories, studies, and case studies about the transformational leader. More than other frameworks, Transformational Leadership focuses on the significant role that leaders can play in promoting both personal and organizational change and the role of leaders in assisting their employees in meeting and exceeding expectations about performance (Avolio, 2005). Northouse (2010, p.186) examines the strength of the Transformational Approach and believes that, firstly, Transformational Leadership has many different perspectives, including a series of qualitative studies of prominent leaders and CEOs in large, well-known organizations. Secondly, this theory has intuitive appeal. Thirdly, it is a process between followers and leaders. Fourth is more than other leadership models. Fifth, it strongly emphasizes followers' needs, values, and morals.

Finally, there is substantial evidence that Transformational Leadership is an effective form of Leadership. In contrast to the strength of Transformational Leadership by Northouse (2010, p187), there is also criticism. First, the criticism is that Transformational Leadership lacks conceptual clarity. The second criticism is on how it is measured. Thirdly, critics argue that it treats Leadership as a personality trait or personal predisposition rather than a behaviour that people can learn. The fourth criticism is that it is elitist and antidemocratic. Transformational Leadership involves changing people's values and moving them to a new vision. However, who will determine whether the new directions are good and more affirming? Who decides that a new vision is the best? These are some questions that show or question the strength of Transformational Leadership. Thus, this theory focuses on how leaders inspire followers to accomplish goals that surpass the follower's direct self-interest.

Accordingto Bass(1997), Transformationleadersmarshaltheirfollowers through idealized influence (charisma), inspirational motivation, rational inspiration, high-performance expectations, and compelling articulation of a vision. Thus, the transformational leadership theory focuses on how leaders motivate followers to follow goals that exceed their immediate self-interest. Transformational leaders evoke values of trust, teamwork, and self-development. Transformational Leadership views their followers as idealized influence.

Transactional Leadership

Bass and Avolio (1996) define Transactional Leadership as gaining compliance from associates through contracts with the leader. The contractual relations may be explicit or implicit. The leader clarifies expectations and may exchange promises of reward or disciplinary threats for the desired effort and performance levels. The constructive style is labelled Contingent Reward, and the corrective style is labelled Management-by-Exception, which can be either active or passive.

According to Burns (1989), transactional leadership refers to the bulk of leadership models, which focus on the exchanges between leaders and their followers. For example, politicians who win votes by promising no new taxes demonstrate Transactional Leadership. Similarly, managers who offer promotions to employees who surpass their goals are exhibiting Transactional Leadership. In the classroom, teachers are transactional whentheygivestudentsagradeforcompletedwork. Wecanobservethese transactional leadership aspects in our organizations today. Therefore, Transitional Leadership is alive and used in many aspects of our life by many leaders and followers. Furthermore, Transactional leadership is a prominent leadership style that focuses on the exchange of rewards and punishments between leaders and followers. This style is characterized by a transactional relationship, where leaders provide rewards, such as promotions or bonuses, in exchange for followers' compliance and performance. Conversely, leaders also administer punishments, such as demotions or reprimands, when followers fail to meet expectations or deviate from established norms. Transactional leadership is rooted in the principles of contingency theory, which posits that effective leadership is contingent upon the alignment of leader behaviours with follower needs and expectations. In this regard, transactional leaders employ a transactional approach to motivate and influence their followers. They establish clear expectations and goals, and provide specific instructions and guidelines to ensure that followers understand what is expected of them. Additionally, transactional leaders closely monitor performance and provide feedback to ensure that followers are meeting the established standards.

One of the key features of transactional leadership is the use of contingent rewards. Transactional leaders offer rewards to followers who meet or exceed performance expectations. These rewards can take various forms, such as salary increases, promotions, or recognition. By linking rewards to performance, transactional leaders create a sense of motivation and incentivize followers to strive for excellence. Another important aspect of transactional leadership is the use of management by exception. Transactional leaders actively monitor followers' performance and intervene when deviations from established norms occur. They employ two types of management by exception: active and passive. Active management by exception involves proactively identifying and addressing problems or deviations from standards, while passive management by exception occurs when leaders only intervene when problems become significant or performance falls below acceptable levels.

Transactional leadership has been widely studied and has shown both positive and negative outcomes. On the positive side, transactional leadership can lead to increased follower satisfaction, motivation, and performance. The clear expectations and rewards offered by transactional leaders can create a sense of fairness and transparency, which in turn fosters trust and commitment among followers. However, transactional leadership has also been criticized for its focus on extrinsic motivation and its limited ability to foster creativity and innovation among followers. In conclusion, transactional leadership is a leadership style that emphasizes the exchange of rewards and punishments between leaders and followers. It is based on the principles of contingency theory and employs a transactional approach to motivate and influence followers. While transactional leadership has its merits, it is important to recognize its limitations and consider alternative leadership styles that may better foster creativity and innovation.

Authentic Leadership

Authentic Leadership is one of the newest areas of leadership research, and it emerges after the Transformational and Transactional Leaderships popularity. Transformational Leadership's popularity is that the leader goes beyond his self-interest for the follower's good.

The main focus of Authentic Leadership is whether Leadership is genuine and honest. Thus, this theory is about the authenticity of leaders and their Leadership. However, according to many writers on Leadership, Authentic Leadership is still in its formative phase of development. Therefore, there is a need for continuous development in understanding authentic Leadership. The need for authenticity in Leadership emerges from failures in corporate and non-corporate settings—the Enron, WorldCom, and Bearing Bank scandal of Singapore.

The same sentiment is shared by Northouse (2010, p.205) when he argues that in recent times upheavals in society have energized a tremendous demand for Authentic Leadership. The corporate scandals at companies like WorldCom and Enron and massive failures in the banking industry have also created fear and uncertainty. People have become more apprehensive and insecure about what is happening around them, and, as a result, they long for bona fide Leadership they can trust and for honest and good leaders. Based on the above observation, it becomes apparent that people, writers, and practitioners of Leadership continuously search for answers from trustworthy and honest leaders, which can lead to the development of Authentic Leadership as a concept. These are some things that heighten the attention of researchers on the subject and, at the same time, lead to the study of Authentic Leadership, trustworthy, honest, and real Leadership.

Authentic leadership is a concept that has gained significant attention in the field of leadership studies. It refers to a leadership approach that emphasizes the genuine and true nature of leaders, as well as their ability to inspire and motivate others through their own personal values and beliefs. This leadership style is characterized by leaders who are self-aware, transparent, and consistent in their actions and decisions. They are able to build trust and credibility with their followers by being true to themselves and their principles.

Authentic leaders are not afraid to show vulnerability and admit their mistakes, as they understand that this can foster a culture of openness and learning within their organizations. They are also able to effectively communicate their vision and goals, and align them with the values and aspirations of their followers. By doing so, they are able to create a sense of purpose and meaning in the work that their followers do, which in turn leads to higher levels of engagement and commitment. Furthermore, authentic leaders are able to build strong and positive relationships with their followers. They genuinely care about the well-being and development of their employees, and actively support and empower them to reach their full potential. This creates a sense of loyalty and dedication among followers, as they feel valued and appreciated by their leader.

In conclusion, authentic leadership is a valuable and effective approach to leadership that focuses on the genuine and true nature of leaders. It emphasizes self-awareness, transparency, consistency, and the ability to inspire and motivate others through personal values and beliefs. By embodying these qualities, authentic leaders are able to build trust, create a sense of purpose, and foster strong relationships with their followers.

Northouse (2010, p.206) argues that Authentic Leadership appears easy to define on the surface, but in actuality, it is a complex process that is difficult to characterize and that there is no single accepted definition of Authentic Leadership. As such, he asserts that Authentic Leadership can benefit from three viewpoints; intrapersonal, developmental, and interpersonal, and that each definition is unique and helpful in clarifying the meaning of Authentic Leadership. The same interpretation by Klenke (2007), who points to the fact that the concept of Authentic Leadership has been treated extensively in various disciplines, including Humanistic Psychology (Maslow, 1971; Rogers, 1959), Developmental Psychology (Ericson, 1995), and existential philosophy (Heidegger, 1963/2002; Sarte,1994) and it also has in Religious Studies and History. To that end, he cites Terry (1993, p.139), who asserted that authenticity is ubiquitous, calling us to be true to ourselves and accurate to the world, authentic in ourselves and honest in the world; when authenticity is acknowledged, we admit our foibles, mistakes and protected secrets, the parts of ourselves and society that are fearful and hide in the shadows of existence. Klenke (2007) focused on the role of the self in Authentic Leadership through three identity lenses; (a) self–identity, (b) leader identity, and (c) spiritual identity. For Klenke (2007), the self-identity system encompasses the intrapersonal self-defined internal dispositions and abilities. The leader identity system reflects the interpersonal self as defined by the leader's relationship with others. Thus, what is Authentic Leadership?

Avolio et al. (2004) defined Authentic leaders as those individuals who are deeply aware of how they think and behave and others as being aware of their own and others' values/moral perspective, knowledge, and strength, aware of the context in which they operate and who are confident, hopeful, optimistic, resilient, and high on moral justice character.

Haven examines some theories of Leadership above. It is essential to add some leaders' quotations: The task of Leadership is not to put greatness into people but to elicit it, for the greatness is there already. (John Buchan) The best executive is the one who has enough sense to pick good men to do what he wants done and the self-restraint to keep from meddling with them while they do it.' (Theodore Roosevelt) To lead people, walk beside them as for the best leaders, the people do not notice their existence: the following best, the people honour and praise. The next, the people fear; and the next, the people, when the best leader's work, they say, we did it ourselves! (Lao-Tsu), Refrain from following where the path may lead. Go instead where there is no path and leave a trail. (Harold R. McAindon). The most crucial thing in examining leadership theories is to inform practice because the knowledge of leadership theories may help interact better with others. The next chapter is focuses on leadership from an Islamic perspective.

Chapter 4

Islamic Perspective of Leadership

The Islamic perspective on leadership is a topic of great significance in the academic discourse especially amongst some Muslims scholar and practitioners. It is a subject that has been studied extensively by scholars and researchers alike, with the aim of understanding the principles and values that underpin Islamic leadership. The Islamic perspective on leadership is rooted in the teachings of the Quran and the Sunnah of the prophets, starting from prophet Adam (PBUH) and more importantly the final prophet of Allah/God Prophet Muhammad (PBUH), and also the Rightly four Guided Khalifah/Caliphs, which provide guidance on the qualities and characteristics that a leader should possess. These teachings from the Quran and the Sunnah of the prophets (PBUH) and the four Rightly Guided Caliphs emphasize the importance of justice, compassion, humility, and wisdom in leadership. It stresses the need for leaders to act as role models for their followers. Furthermore, the Islamic perspective on leadership recognizes the importance of consultation and consensus-building in decision-making, and encourages leaders to seek the opinions and advice of those around them.

Overall, the Islamic perspective on leadership offers a unique and valuable perspective on the nature of leadership in general, and provides a framework for understanding the role of leaders and followers in the society. Thus, leadership from an Islamic perspective is highly sought-after and valued by Muslims today more than ever in the history of Islam, due to some short comings of leadership in the Muslim Ummah and the failure of Muslim communities and societies to show exemplary leadership qualities and statesmanship similar to those qualities of leadership exemplified by Prophet Mohammad (SAW) and during the leadership of the four Rightly Guided caliphs at their time. Islam is a way of life, and there is a need for leaders who can enhance this way of life by being good examples and a model for the Muslim Ummah.

Good Muslims leaders and followers would establish prayer and maintain charity as a way of life so that the needy within the Ummah feel being included and heard and listen to by their leaders. Hence, there is a need for effective leadership in the Muslim Ummah and the world in general. The Muslim Ummah needs exemplary leaders who lead by example and protect their citizens from any harm or distress and at the same time follow Quran and the Sunnah of the Prophet (PBUH).

Throughout the history of mankind Allah(God) always sent prophets to lead mankind through the right part. These prophets were the leaders of their various communities starting with prophet Adam (PBUH) especially the final prophet of Allah(God) prophet Mohammad (PBUH). Allah/God sending of prophets to mankind was to guidance mankind which is a great sign of Allah/God love for humanity. Initially, the Angel thought that they were the ones who deserve to be Allah(God) representative on earth, but Allah (God) is all Knower. See Surah 2 Al Baqarah (2:30). In other words, Allah(God) always has a great care for humankind throughout history and civilization. The care and trust that Allah (God) for humankind is affirmed in Surah Al Baqarah (2:30) in that Allah/God placed mankind as His vicegerent on earth and the Angel were surprise of the choice of mankind being Allah/ Vicegerent on earth. See Surah As- Sajdah (32:24) as translated in English by Khan and

Al-Hilali (1996, p.524) 24- "And we made from among them (Children of Israel), leaders, giving guidance under our command when they were patient and used to believe with certainty in Our Ayat (proofs, pieces of evidence, verses, lessons, signs, and revelation.

Thus, the Islamic perspective of leadership as envisaged in this book is the leadership that was demonstrate by previous prophets and more importantly by Prophet Mohammad (PBUH) and the four Rightly Guided khalifs/Caliphs. Under their leadership of these prophets and the four Guided Caliphs, all their followers were protected, served, guided to serve Allah/God only and also follow Allah/ God laws on earth Divine Laws (Sharia).

Sharia holds significant importance for both leaders and followers within the Islamic perspective. It is commonly referred to as Islamic law and encompasses a collection of principles and guidelines derived from the Quran and the Sunnah, which are the teachings and practices of the Prophet Muhammad (PBUH). Regarded as the divine law of Allah, Sharia is believed to offer a comprehensive framework governing the moral, social, and legal aspects of life for Muslims. Its scope encompasses a wide range of topics, including personal hygiene, prayer, fasting, charity, marriage, divorce, inheritance, criminal law, and international relations. By providing a just and equitable system, Sharia promotes social harmony and individual well-being. The foundation of leadership should be rooted in the Quran, the Sunnah of the Prophet, and the exemplary conduct of the rightly guided Khalifs, as well as other pious leaders from the past and present. Following the demise of Prophet Mohammad (PBUH) in 632 CE, the caliphs assumed leadership of the Muslim Ummah at the time. The passing of the Prophet Mohammad (PBUH) was a profound shock to the Muslim Ummah, with many struggling to come to terms with the notion of their prophet' (PBUH) eternal departure. Despite disbelief and sorrow among the followers of the prophet (PBUH), it was imperative to select a successor to lead the Islamic Ummah. During the process of preparing the deceased body of the esteemed Holy Prophet of Islam for burial, the Ansar of Madina convened at their designated gathering spot known as 'Saqeefa Bani Sa'dah' to deliberate upon the matter of succession to the revered Holy Prophet. Being the final prophet, there would be no prophet to succeed him. Additionally, as the leader of the Muslim community, it was imperative to establish a successor who would assume the role of guiding the Muslim community after the passing of Prophet Muhammad (PBUH).

During the meeting of the Ansars at Saqeefa Bani Sa'idah', Sa'd bin Ubadah, a prominent leader among them, passionately advocated for the selection of a successor to the Holy Prophet Muhammad (PBUH) from the Ansars to manage the temporal affairs of the Muslims Ummah. He contended that the Ansars, who had provided refuge to the Holy Prophet Muhammad (PBUH) and his companions when they were persecuted by their own people the Quraishi in Makkah and had played a pivotal role in the growth and spread of Islam, had a rightful claim to the leadership of the Muslims Ummah. As the capital of the Muslim state was located in their city in Madinah, it was only fitting that an Ansar should be appointed as the head of the State after the passing of the Holy Prophet (PBUH). Sa'd's speech was met with resounding applause from the Ansars, who were swayed by his compelling arguments and appeared to be on the verge of selecting him as their leader in succession to the Holy Prophet Muhammad (PBUH).

During the meeting at Saqeefa Bani Sa'idah, the emigrants were informed that the Ansars had gathered to select a successor to the Holy Prophet Muhammad (PBUH). This news created a critical situation as the decision of choosing a successor was crucial for the survival of the Muslim community. The emigrants were aware that any wrong decision could jeopardize the future of Islam. Although the burial of the Holy

Prophet Muhammad (PBUH) was a matter of priority, the question of succession was a matter of life and death. In order to prevent any hasty or incorrect decision, Abu Bakr, Umar, and Abu Ubaidah decided to negotiate with the Ansars at Saqeefa Bani Sa'idah before it was too late. When Abu Bakr, Umar, and Abu Ubaidah arrived at Saqeefa Bani Sa'idah, the Ansars were on the brink of selecting Sa'id bin Ubadah, their leader, as the successor to the Holy Prophet Muhammad (PBUH).

Abu Bakr, taking the opportunity, emphasized the seriousness of the situation to the gathered people. He highlighted that this matter was not limited to the citizens of Madina alone; it held significance for all the Arab Muslims. It was unlikely that all the Arab tribes would accept the leadership of the Ansars, especially considering the existing divisions among the two major Ansar tribes. Abu Bakr argued that, given the circumstances, the Quraish, who were the guardians of the Kaaba, were the most suitable to lead the Muslim community. Directing his appeal to the Ansar, he stated, "O Ansar, no one can deny the superiority of your religious position or the greatness of your eminence in Islam. Allah chose you as the supporters of His religion and His Messenger.

The Prophet (PBUH) was sent to you upon his migration from Makkah, and the majority of his companions and wives come from your ranks. Indeed, in terms of status, you are second only to the earliest companions. Therefore, it would be fair if we assume the role of Amirat while you accept the ministry. You should not be stubborn in your stance. We assure you that we will not make any decisions without consulting you." After Abu Bakr's address, Habab bin Mandhar, a leader of the Ansars, expressed his belief that the right to leadership, or Amirat, belonged to the Ansars and that they could not relinquish this right. He suggested that the Ansars could compromise by having two Amir's, one from the Ansars and one from the emigrants. In response, Umar argued that

Islam advocated for unity, with one God, one Prophet, and one Quran. Therefore, it was logical to have one Amir for the Muslim community. Umar warned that if the proposal of having two Amir was accepted, others would also demand the right to elect an Amir from their group, leading to the fragmentation of the Islamic polity. He stressed that, in the interest of maintaining the solidarity of Islam, it was crucial to have only one Amir, and that this Amir should be from the Quraish, the tribe of the Holy Prophet.

A heated exchange of words ensued between Habab and Umar. In an attempt to appeal to the Ansars, Abu Ubaida reminded them that they were the first to support Islam and urged them not to be the first to contribute to the disintegration of the religion. The Ansars appeared to hesitate in their demand after Abu Bakr's statement, indicating that it had some effect on them. Abu Bakr (RA) then reiterated that the proposal was solely based on the interest and solidarity of Islam, and to prove their sincerity, he declared that he did not covet the office and presented Umar and Abu Ubaida as potential successors.

This softened the attitude of the Ansars, and Zaid bin Thabit, an eminent Ansar leader, supported the proposal that the successor should be selected from among the Quraish, as the Holy Prophet was also from the Quraish. Another Ansar leader, Bashir bin Sa'd, reminded the Ansars that their position of superiority in holy jihad wars and religion was to please Allah and obey the Holy Prophet, and that they should not make it a ground for self-aggrandizement. He also emphasized that the Quraish had the strongest claim for the succession of the Holy Prophet, and they should not quarrel with them on this issue. The situation took a dramatic turn, resulting in a shift of preference among the Ansars towards selecting a leader from the Quraish. Capitalizing on this opportunity, Abu Bakr reiterated his proposal that either Umar or Abu Ubaida be chosen.

In response to Abu Bakr's suggestion, Umar promptly stood up and expressed his admiration for Abu Bakr, acknowledging him as the most outstanding among the Muslims. Umar highlighted Abu Bakr's significant contributions, such as being the "Second of the Two" in the Cave, being appointed as 'Amir-ul-Haj', and being entrusted with leading the prayers during the Holy Prophet's illness. Umar emphasized that Abu Bakr held a special place among the companions, being the closest and most beloved to the Holy Prophet Muhammad(PBUH). Consequently, Umar and Abu Ubaida recognized Abu Bakr's superiority and requested him to extend his hand so that they could pledge their allegiance to him. Umar then proceeded to make Abu Bakr stand, and with utmost reverence, he touched Abu Bakr's hand as a symbolic gesture of allegiance. Following Umar, Abu Ubaida also pledged his allegiance to Abu Bakr. Subsequently, all the Ansars present there followed suit, offering their allegiance to Abu Bakr one by one. Thus, after careful deliberation, Abu Bakr Siddiq was chosen as the next caliph/khalifa "successor" of the prophet as the leader of the Islamic Ummah. For some companions Abu Bakr was chosen as a caliph because of his character and judgement and also because during Prophet Muhammad (PBUH) time Abu Bakr (RA) some time was chosen to lead prayer as noted above. Umar ibn al-Khattab (RA), a notable associate and companion of the Prophet Muhammad (PBUH), proposed the nomination of Abu Bakr, a close friend, father in-law of the Prophet and ally of the Prophet Muhammad (PBUH). Following further endorsement from the companions, Abu Bakr was officially appointed as the inaugural caliph, the religious successor to Prophet Muhammad (PBUH), within the same year after a good deliberations between the Ansar and the Immigrant. However, it is important to note here that the holy Prophet Mohammad (PBUH) himself never left any instructions for the selection of a leader of the Muslim Ummah after him.

However, it was the choice of the companions after great deliberations amongst them to choose Abu Bakr (RA) as the next Khalifa, even though some Muslims at the time thought that Ali (RA) who was a close relative of the Prophet should have been chosen as the caliph after the passing away of the Prophet (PBUH). Furthermore, some companions were of the opinion that the designation of Prophet Muhammad (PBUH) successor at Ghadir Khumm was a subject of dispute among his companions. Some companions argued that Ali ibn Abi Talib, prophet Muhammad (PBUH) cousin and son-in-law, should have been chosen by prophet Muhammad (PBUH) himself even though the Prophet (PBUH) did not choose who to succeed him. Ali (RA) being the Prophet Muhammad (PBUH) closest living male relative and his son-in-law through his marriage to Fatimah, eventually ascended to the position of the fourth Caliph and not the first Caliph after the passing of the Prophet (PBUH) as some would have wanted.

The divergence in opinions concerning the rightful heir of Prophet Muhammad (PBUH) is believed by certain analysts to have led to a substantial schism within the Islamic faith, ultimately leading to the establishment of the Sunni and Shi'a sects, which endure to the present era, however, Allah/God Know best. Ali (RA) was a cousin and son-in-law of the Prophet and therefore some thought by right he should have been chosen as the Caliph, but Abu Bakr was chosen and became the first Caliph/Khalifah/ "successor" of the Prophet Mohammad (PBUH).
In this book the author will discuss the four Rightly Guided Caliphs (Khulafah Al-Rashidun) as the leaders of the Muslim Ummah so that lessons can be learn especially those who are inspired to be leaders of today and tomorrow. Furthermore, regarding the succession of prophet Mohammad (PBUH), especially during the Umayyad period (661-750), some Muslims believed that kinship to the Prophet (PBUH) should have been the criteria for the legitimacy of the leadership of the Muslim Ummah due to some faction within the Ummah at the time. Therefore, some Muslims during the time acknowledge the kinship factor as a

legitimate leadership position from the Qu)raish, the Prophet (PBUH) tribe, to which the four Rightly Guided Caliphs/khalifs' "successors" all belonged.

After the passing of the Prophet (BUH) there were four Rightly Guided Caliphs (Khulafah Al-Rashidun)/khalifs) namely: Abu Bakr (RA), Umar RA), Uthman (RA), and Ali (RA); their era w known to many Muslims as the golden age of Islam because these caliphs were "Rightly Guided Caliphs" (Khulafah Al Rashidun) also because of their close personal associations with Prophet Muhammad (PBUH). Moreover, these Rightly Guided Caliphs were responsible for establishing an administrative and judicial organization of their Muslim communities as required by Islam.

During the period of the four Guided Khilafahs, there were no clear distinction between spiritual and worldly affairs. In other words, there was no separation of religion and the state. Henceforth, there are some terminologies that need to be addressed in this book to enhance the understanding of leadership from the Islamic perspective. These terminologies are for example, Caliph/Khalifah/ "successor," which means successor or vicegerent and is in the Quran in Surah al Baqarah (2:30) and Surah Sad (38:26), which are discussed subsequently in this book. There are also other terminologies like Amir, which could mean a prince, commander, or leader. Prophet Muhammad (PBUH) has used the word Amir to emphasize that when a group of Muslims is on a mission or journey, they choose or elect an Amir to lead them. Imam is also used in the Islamic leadership perspective but, in most cases, signifies leading people to prayers, and it can also mean a leader as well.

Leadership from an Islamic perspective is a trust (Amanah). The first trust and obedience of leaders and followers is to Allah/God and His prophets (PBUH). Allah/God is the one who entrusted his prophets with the leadership to deliver Allah (God) message to their various people and especially our beloved prophet Mohammad (PBUH) to deliver Allah(God) message to the Islamic Ummah/Muslims Ummah/ Muslims communities all over the world and he was being accountable for his deeds. This trust that Allah(God) has entrusted to humankind to be his caretaker or representative on earth is affirmed in Surah Al Baqarah (2:30)n the English translation of the Quran by Khan and Al Hilali (1996, p.16) And (remember) when your Lord said to the angels: Verily I am going to place (mankind) generations after generations on earth".

See Surah 4: An-Nisa (4:58), as translated into English by Khan and Al Hilali (1996, p. 122); Verily Allah commands that you should render back the trust to those to whom they are due: and that when you judge between men, you judge with justice. Verily, how excellent is the teaching He (Allah) gives you! Indeed, Allah is Ever All-Hearer, All-Seer." Also, See Surah 3: Al -Imran (3:189), as translated in English by Khan and Al Hilali (1996, p.108), "And to Allah belongs the dominion of the heavens and the earth, and Allah has power over all things." Subsequently, in Surah 33 A-Ahzab (33.72), also translated into English by Khan and Al Hilali (1996, p. 538), 7. "Truly, we did offer Al-Amanah (the trust or moral responsibility or honesty and all the duties which Allah has ordained) to the heavens and the earth, and the mountains, but they declined to bear it and were afraid of it (i.e., afraid of Allah's Torment). But man bore it. Verily he was unjust (to himself) and ignorant (of its result)."

Thus, leadership from an Islamic perspective is trust (Amanah) and should be performed as a form of worship (Ibadah) which means obedience, submission, and devotion to God, by following His Divine Law as prescribed in the Quran.

The highest form of worship is the belief in the Oneness of Allah. (i.e., there is no God but Allah) Moreover, the lowest in the scale of worship is removing obstacles and dirt from the way." Henceforth, leaders, and followers should be able to remove obstacles from others ways. Seeking knowledge is one of the highest forms of worship. The Prophet (PBUH) in one of his Hadith said that, "Seeking knowledge is a (religious) duty on every Muslim." In another saying, he said: "Seeking knowledge for one hour is better than praying for seventy years." All these are related to leadership in all aspects. "Receiving your friend with a smile is a type of charity, and putting some water in your neighbour's bucket is a charity." Performing one's duties is considered an act of worship, and kindness to others is an act of worship; as a leader, we should be kind to others. Therefore, leaders and followers in the Muslim world should follow Divine Laws (Sharia).

Muslim leaders should be keepers to their followers and vice versa. They should be fair and just to their followers, judge them in truth, and not follow their desires and transgression. See Surah Sad (38:26) as translated in English by Khan and Al Hilali (1996, p.572) O Dawud (David)! Verily, We have placed you as a successor on the earth, so judge you between men in truth (and justice) and follow not your desire, for it will mislead you from the Path of Allah. Verily, those who wander astray from the Path of Allah (shall) have severe torment because they forget the day of Reckoning. Therefore, leaders serve with grace and follow the truth, not their desires, for the day of Reckoning is awaiting them. However, some leaders in Muslims Ummah today lack the leadership ability that Allah/God asked Dawud (David) to render to his people. See Surah Al-Anbiya (21:73) as translated in English by Khan and Al Hilali (1996, p.414) "And We made them leaders, guiding (mankind) by our command, and We revealed to them the doing of the good deed, performing Salat (Iqamat as Salat), and the giving of Zakat and of Us (Alone) they were the worshipers."

Clearly, from the above Surah, it is clear that leadership from an Islamic perspective is vicegerent and is individual as well as positional leadership, whether political, tribal or any form of leadership. We should follow Allah/God prescriptions in the Quran and the Sunnah, which is why the content of leadership is and should be from the Quran and Sunnah of the Prophet (PBUH).

Today in the Muslim Ummah/, Muslims communities we need effective leaders who exemplifies the leadership of the Prophet Muhammad (PBUH) and the four Guided Khalifas, and also followers who adhere to Islamic laws (Sharia) and principles. We need Leaders who are trusted and are accountable to the followers and to Allah/God. For example, during the Caliphate of Umar Ibn Al Khattab (RA) his governance was based on mutual consultation, justice, equality, and profound respect for freedoms - principles that resonate deeply in our present times. We need to have such a spirit of justice, accountability to Allah/God first and second to their followers. These leaders should be responsibility and have respect for human dignity.

Umar Ibn Al Khattab (RA) once said "I fear the day when the disbelievers are proud of their falsehood. And the Muslims are shy of their faith" Muslims leaders and followers should not shy away from their faith rather they should hold firm to their faith. The quote from Khalif Umar (RA) reflect a state of mind of some Muslims leaders and followers who shy away from their faith. And that "We were the most humiliated people on earth and Allah/God gave us honour through Islam. If we ever seek honour through anything else, Allah/God will humiliate us again".

As a leader of the Muslim Ummah as Khaliah, Umar (RA) was known to be humble, aware of the significance and seriousness of his responsibility. For example, at night, he was known for going around to inspect the conditions of Muslims communities to know and have a first-hand knowledge and information about his followers, not sitting in his office and getting the information from his officers. Those night tours weren't common before his reign, and weren't done at the same pace even after his death.

As a statesman, Umar Ibn Al Khataab (RA) during his reign established a political structure to hold the vast Islamic state together. And he divided the state into provinces and appointed governors, whom he did not allow to exceed two years in power, out of fear it would influence their roles. His sense of responsibility and kindness also extended to animals, whom he valued because they are God's creations. Omar is often quoted declaring that "if a mule stumbled in Iraq, he was responsible for not having the road paved."

The significant of all these quotes above from Umar Ibn Al Khataab (RA) are example of effective leadership that should be copied and exemplifier by our Muslims leaders and follower today. Our Muslims leaders and followers should not shy away from their responsibilities. Similarly the spirit of accountability and responsibilities was also expressed by Abu Bakr when he was made Khalifa/Caliph/Amir, the leader) of the Muslim Ummah after the death of the prophet Mohammad (PBUH), and he was chosen to be the first Caliph. In his acceptance speech he said: "I have been made your leader, and I am not better than anyone of you. Support me if I do well, and correct me if I do wrong (Al Salabi, 2001). Follow me as long as I follow the commands of Allah/ God and His Prophet(PBUH); if I do not follow their commands, then you do not have to follow me.

A similar statement was made by the second Khalifah/Calipha Umar during his inaugural speech, as cited in Al-Salabi, (2001)" If you find crookedness in my behaviour, you have to straighten me out." A person in the audience responded to him by saying if we find crookedness in your behaviour, we will straighten you out even if we have to use the sword. Omar expressed his happiness with this response because they were neither afraid of the leader nor were they shy about telling him the truth and reminding him of his duties as Khalifiah of the Muslim Ummah. All leaders from an Islamic perspective are accountable to Allah/God and the people they lead or as individuals. No one is above the law (sharia), and his/her behaviour should be a good example to their communities and beyond.

Accountability is key to leadership from an Islamic perspective and there are some emphasis in the Quran. See Surah Isra (17:13-15) as translated to English by Khan and Al Hilali (p.354-e355), 13-And We have fastened every man's deed to his neck, and on the Day of Resurrection, We shall bring out for him a book which he will find wide open. 14. (It will be said to him): "Read your book. You yourself are sufficient as a reckoner against you this Day. 15. Whoever goes right, then he goes right only for his benefit of his own self. And whoever goes astray, then he goes astray to his own loss. No one laden with burdens can bear another's burden. And We never punish until We have sent a Messenger (to give warning). Thus, the spirit of effective leadership is necessary, i.e., leaders who are aware of their position as a leader and accountable to Allah/God and to his followers, which creates a sense of brotherhood that was a cornerstone of Islam as existed in early Islam in Madinah were the Ansar (helpers) and the Muhajirun (immigrant) beame one. Ansar, also known as Helpers, and Muhajirun, commonly referred to as Immigrants. During this time in Madina, Muslims were the keeper of one another. They became brothers and sisters to each other, and the proper fundamentals of brotherhood were established and cemented through Islam and not only country-connected or tribal affiliation.

Today in the Muslim Ummah some of our leaders and followers care more about their own citizens rather than the Rope of Allah(God) which, Quran, whereby, Islam is at the Centre of this brotherhood. Allah/God affirmed brotherhood and unity of Muslims in Surah 3 Al-Imran (3:103) as translated in Khan and Al Hilali (1996, p.93) "And hold fast, all of you together, to the Rope of Allah (i.e., this Quran), and be not divided among yourself, and remember Allah's Favour on you, for you were enemies one to another, but He joined your hearts together, so that, by His Grace, you become brethren (in Islamic Faith), and you were on the brink of a pit of Fire, and He saved you from it. Thus, Allah makes His Ayat (proof, evidence, verse, lesson, sign, and revelation. Clear to you that you may be guided".

Muslim leaders of their Ummah/Muslims communities should hold firm to the Rope of Allah and stay together and not become divided because of nationalism and citizenship but because of Islam. We should not be disbelievers of the Ayat (proof, evidence, verse, lessons, signs, revelation, etc. of Allah/God. We should not have to disobey Allah/ God but seek His guidance to lead in the right way. See Surah Al-Imran (3:112). Again we should hold firm to the Rope of Allah and not be divided. We should guard against divisions because the disbelievers are ready to create division among us, for example, by creating a division between Sunni Muslims and Shia Muslims, Arab or African Muslims, or Asian or European or Turkish or Egyptian Muslims. See Surah Al- Anfal (8:62-64) as translated by Khan and Al Hilali (1996, p.236) "And if they intend to deceive you, then verily, Allah is All-Sufficient for you. He it is Who has supported you with His Help with the believers" 63- "And He has united their (i.e. believers') hearts. If you had spent all that is in the earth, you could not have united their hearts, but Allah has united them. Certainly He is All-Mighty, All-Wise". 64- "O Prophet Muhammad (PBUH)! Allah is Sufficient for you and for the believers who follow you".

We can see a good example of good leadership from Khalifah Umar Ibn Khataab (RA) when he valued individual freedoms and applied the principle of equality among Muslims and non-Muslims within the borders of the Islamic state. For example, when it came to him that the son of Amr bin As, a companion of the Prophet and the ruler has abused and beat up a Coptic Christian. Khalifah Omar Ibn Al Khataab (RA) ordered the son of Amr to be punished in public on the hands of the victim. He then was quoted telling both, the father and son: "Since when have you turned men into slaves, whereas they are born free of their mothers?"

Leaders of our Muslim Ummah should draw from the above verses of the Quran and the example of Khaliah Umar Ibn Al Khataab RA) when dealing with citizens of the Muslim Ummah and making sure to unity among Muslim base on Islam and not on citizenship or nationalism or the differences of the sect(Mazhab).

The author argue that there is an absent of effective leadership in the Muslim Ummah today the kind of leadership that was exemplify during Prophets Muhammad (PBUH) time and that of the four Rightly Guided Khalifs/Caliphs/Vicegerent/Successor. We in the Muslim Ummah need to go back to Islam and make sure that our leadership principles are guided by the Quran and the Sunnah of the prophets and more importantly Prophet Mohammad (PBUH) and the four Rightly Guided Khalifs.

Muslim communities and countries are divided based on nation states. These divisions have created a sense of nationalism, and power-grabbing by some leaders as a source of wealth accumulation and prestige not because of uniting the Ummah and establishing prayers, giving arms, and propagation of Islam, although there is no compulsion on faith. Some Muslim leaders and followers today are nationalistic and careless about other Muslims living in their nation states, which is a problem and a concern hence the writing of this book. Where is the brotherhood established during the prophet Muhammad(PBUH) time in Madinah?

We should all learn from the brotherhood that the prophet (PBUH) when immigrated to Madinah established a sincere brotherhood amongst Muslims brothers and sisters. We should learn from the story narrated by Dawud ibn Ali about Khalifah Omar Ibn Al Khataab (RA) as once saying: "If a lost sheep under my care were to die on the banks of the Euphrates, I would expect Allah the Exalted to question me about it on the Day of Resurrection." This is the kind of care and respect even for animals these Khalifs used have for those under their care as citizens of the Ummah. We as Ummah and as a people need to avoid divisions amongst Muslim countries based on race or religion, tribe or ethnicity, for example Arab Muslim, African Muslim, Kurdish, Shia, and Sunni Muslims, creating nationalistic sentiments which is not good for the Ummah.

We all know that the Ummah of today is divided by nation states but we can do better by allowing other Muslims who chose to reside within the other Muslim communities or nation state to feel welcome and protected. Thus, everywhere a Muslims is or chose to work and live there, he or she should be welcome and protected as any citizen without any discrimination. We as leaders and follower should not forget that we are all brothers and sisters and that our unity is based on Islam mainly for the pleasure of Allah/God and our beloved Prophet Muhammad (PBUH), the Rightly Guided Khalifs, pious predecessor's leaders of the Ummah who adhere to different schools of thought but remained united despite their disagreement. As Muslims or leaders or followers, we should let our differences, or of our geographical location, disunite us, for we are all Muslims. Location or geographical location or nation states should not impede our brotherhood in Islam.

It is obvious from the look of things today in the Muslims Ummah leaders and followers of Muslim Ummah seem to only help their own citizens only and not giving a helping hand or extending their favors to other brother Muslims leaving and residing in their various states or nations. Yes your own citizens are important to you first but that should not hinder leaders from caring and protecting their brethren who have chosen to reside in your nation state either for political reason or economic reason or whatever is the reason Again we have forgotten the brotherhood that was built in Madinah during the prophet time and during the guided Caliphs, whereby the likes of Bilal Ibn Rabah formerly enslaved person, was given the post of the one who called for prayer (Muazin) in the Prophet Muhammad (PBUH) Masjid. His example is for us Muslims leaders and follower should follow and remain brothers and sisters in Islam. Let us emulate such good example and not bent on futile nationalism rather than Islam our Deen. Unless we recognize each other as brothers in Islam and that we are all Muslim brotherhood irrespective of tribes and nations, we will keep on leading based on our desires or on the desire of disbelievers who want us not to be united. The concept of divides and rule is alive in the Muslim Ummah and we can all do better.

Some of these problems of lack of unity and brotherhood in the Muslims Ummah or community as prescribed in the Quran is a concern. See Surah Al Imran (3:103) which states that Muslims should hold firmly to the rope of Allah/God together and do not become divided. And remember the favor of Allah on to us. 103, And hold fast, all of you together, to the Rope of Allah (i.e. this Quran), and be not divided among yourselves, and remember Allah's Favour on you, for you were enemies one to another but He joined your hearts together, so that, by His Grace, you became brethren (in Islamic Faith), and you were on the brink of a pit of Fire, and He saved you from it. Thus, Allah(God) makes

His Ayat (proofs, evidences, verses, lessons, signs, revelations, etc.,) clear to you, that you may be guided.

Thus, leadership from an Islamic perspective is a trust (Amanah) and those in the position of leadership in the Muslim Ummah today and tomorrow will be asked of what they did with the position of leadership that Allah/God gave or permit them to lead the Ummah during the Day of Judgment. Therefore leaders in the Muslims Ummah should be aware of their responsibility and accountability to their citizens and to Allah/ God. I would like to share this quote from Khalifah Umar Ibn Al Khataab (RA) when he said "No amount of worrying can change the future. Go easy on yourself, for the outcome of all affairs is determined by God's decree. If something is meant to go elsewhere, it will never come your way, but if it is yours by destiny, from you it cannot flee."

Leaders should and followers of the Ummah should take note of this quote and do right and avoid doing wrong and leave the rest to Allah/ God. Once leaders and followers know that they have done right they should leave the rest to Allah/God, but this does not mean that we should fold our arms and said this is the destiny Allah(God) have chart for us as Muslims and even non-Muslim. Thus, Islam regards leadership as a responsibility entrusted to them to exercise to subordinates or followers or humankind in general. From an Islamic perspective, a good leader calls or invites his followers to do things Allah(God) has ordained or commanded them to do and forbids what Allah/God does not want them to do.

The fundamental role of a leader and follower is to be servant of Allah(God) on earth. Leaders and followers are all vicegerent of Allah/ God on earth. We are all Allah(God) representatives on earth. See Surah Fatir (35:39), Al Baqarah (2:30), Al-Anam (6:165), and Al-Ahzab

(33:72). Leaders and followers' role as Allah((God) vicegerent on earth are to acknowledge that Allah(God) is the originator of leadership and that humankind responsibility is to Allah/God, and that they should take care of all things that Allah/God had made for him/her to use in this world and also follow His Divine Laws (Sharia). See Surah Ibrahim (14:32-34) as translated in English by Khan and Al Hilali (1996, p.321) "Allah is He Who has created the heavens and the earth, and send down water (rain) from the sky, and thereby brought forth fruits as provision for you; and He has made the ships to be of service to you, that they may sail through the sea by His Command; and He has made rivers (also) to be of service to you. 33. And He has made the sun and the moon, both constantly pursuing their course, to be of service to you; and He made the night and the day, to be of service to you.34. And He gives you of all that you asked for, and if you count the blessing of Allah, never will you be able to count them. Verily, man is indeed an extreme wrongdoer, a disbeliever (an extreme ingrate who denies Allah's Blessing by disbelief, by worshiping others besides Allah, and by disobeying Allah and His Prophet Mohammad (PBUH).

Also See Surah Al Furqan (25:2), Al Qammar (54:49), Hud (11:6), and Al-Arar (7:10) as translated in English by Khan and Al Hilali (1996, p.200), And indeed, We gave you an authority on the earth and appointed for you therein provisions (for your life). Little thank-you give. Therefore, as vicegerent, we need to be grateful to Allah/God and do our duties as a form of worship. We as leaders and followers should follow the basic principles of Islam by worshiping Allah/God and follow the Sunnah of the Prophets of Allah/God starting from Adam to Prophet Mohammad (PBUH) at the same time being just and fair to others.

Leadership from an Islamic perspective is ideal and should be practised by all Muslims leaders and followers because Allah/God made humanity his Khalifa/vicegerent on earth. As such, we leaders and followers are responsible in the eye of Allah/God for our deeds. If they treat others wrong or discriminate against others as individuals as leaders or followers, we will be accountable for it during the Day of Judgment. That is why in Islam put responsibility and accountability as individual deed and no one will be responsible or accountable for others' deeds.

We need to be self-reflective and try to emulate the kind of brotherhood and sisterhood that was practiced in Madinah during our beloved prophet Muhammad (PBUH) time and during the period of the four Rightly Guided Khalifas. Justice was the cornerstone of the leaders, accountability was there and good brotherhood between the Ansar (the helpers) and Muhajirun (Immigrant). See Surah An-Nisa (4:58) as translated in English by Khan and Al Hilali (1996, p.122) "Verily, Allah command you that you should render back the trusts to those, to whom they are due, and that when you judge between men, you judge with justice. Verily, how excellent is the teaching which He (Allah) gives you! Truly, Allah is Ever All-Hearing, All-Seer. Thus, some Muslim leaders and some followers lack the courage to be just and fair, especially when judging men.

Some leaders and some followers in some Muslim countries are more concerned with what comes with leadership position such as wealth and power. Some of these leaders and some followers are concerned about amassing more wealth for themselves and their families and may have forgotten that they will be accountable to Allah/God on the last day for their deeds. Some leaders and followers take their own money to buy their leadership positions, knowing fully well that they will be accountable on the Day of Judgment for their deeds and for the position they occupy as leaders. Some leaders in Muslim countries have nationalistic inclination while forgetting the Islamic Ummah, one nation Islamic brothers and sisters. Some of these leaders in the Muslim world cannot grant nationalities to other Muslims born in their various countries. However, in some Western countries, when a child is born in their country this child automatically becomes a citizen, even if their parents are not citizens of that nation. This is a challenge for leaders and followers of the Muslim Ummah or Muslims communities or countries. This problem alone creates the notion of we and them sentiment, for example you do not belong here, go to your country where you come from which divides the Muslim Ummah into nation- state and nationalism instead of brotherhood of Islam as was exemplify in Madinah during the prophet Muhammad(PBUH) time between the Ansar (helpers) and the Muhajirun (Immigrants).

There is a need for continuous renewal within Muslim Ummah or countries, as practiced by some western countries, especially the United States and Great Britain. The adoption of continuous renewal means that there is always a new blood of citizens from around the world who bring with them a new vitality and drive. The likes of great entrepreneurs who have made it America is a good example and why can we not practice such polices in some Muslims countries?

There are many examples in the history of Islam that reflect continuous renewal. For example, Bilal was captive slave who became the person who call for prayer in the Prophet Mohammad (PBUH) Masjid. The president of the United State Barak Obama whose father was a student from Kenya and he became the President of the United States of America. The present prime Minister of United Kingdom who had Indian origins. This remind us Muslim that it can be possible if we welcome others to our land and give them the right to become citizens of the Ummah and can rise to the top and can contribute to the new country development and their children as well.

When there are crisis's in the Muslims Ummah or Muslims communities or countries some of our leaders do not try to rescue their brothers and sisters and give them refugee status but prefers to put money on the United Nations system to help those refugees, who are brothers and sisters in Islam. We leaders and followers in various Muslims communities need to create Baitul-Mall or some public funds that is always ready to help those in crisis, especially our brothers and sister in Islam. The Kingdom of Saudi Arabia is doing a great job with this regard, especially King Salman Humanitarian Aid &Relief Centre. This initiative by King Salman, the King of Saudi Arabia is great and I hope this could be duplicated in many Muslims countries and coordinated as similarly as that of the UN especially for the Muslims Ummah or for humanity at large. Thus, Muslim are brother and sisters and therefore need one another in time of crises. Hence a Muslim is a brother and sister to one another, he does not oppress his brother or sister, nor does he fail him, or her, nor does he lie to him, or her, nor does he hold him or her in contempt. Taqwa (piety) is right the only thing that makes a difference between Muslims. The Ummah is inviolable for another Muslim: his blood, his property, and honour. Prophet Mohammad (PBUH) in one of his Hadith said: None of you truly believes until he loves his brother what he loves for himself," Narrated by (Bukhari & Muslim). See Surah Hujjurat (49:10). "The believers are nothing but brothers. So make reconciliation between your brothers, and fear Allah, that you may receive mercy."

Muslim leaders should be attracting Muslim intellectuals from all over the Ummah to settle and contribute to the strength of the Ummah where ever they may be. Thus, the most significant challenges of the Ummah (Muslim communities) do not lie with the West or in the differences in ideologies between Shia and Sunni, or other aspects but with Muslims failing to practice the spirit of brotherhood that was the cornerstone of Islam in Madinah.

The greatest challenge for Muslims is ourselves. The greatest enemy of the Ummah are the emergence of misguided Muslims brothers and sisters, who think that anyone who does not subscribe to their interpretation of Islam is the enemy of Islam. These ignorant Muslims are the people who give Islam a bad name and therefore are a challenge to us all as leaders and followers. This kind of Muslims want to create sectarianism within Muslim society especially those who do not adhere to their ideology which has nothing to do with Islam. They may think they are good Muslims, but they're not.

Henceforth, Sheikh Ahmed Deedat, wrote quote, "The biggest enemy of Islam is the ignorant Muslim, whose ignorance leads him to intolerance, whose actions destroy the true image of Islam, and when the people look at him, they think that Islam is what he is," The true Islamic spirit can be seen in Madinah during the Prophet time and also during the four guided Caliphs were the helper (Ansar) gave sanctuary to Prophet Mohammad (PBUH) and his followers for the sake of Islam, not self-interest. This is self-evident to the extent that the Ansar were ready to divorce any of their wives so that the immigrants could marry them. How many of our brothers and sisters Muslims are refugees worldwide, and what have we done for them? They may receive blankets or food, but what they need is to be able to work and feed their families if possible. How many of our communities allow them to work for a living in our Muslim countries, societies, or communities, and why not?

To name a few, the Syrian crisis, the Gaza crisis and poverty in some Muslims communities is driving the migration of Muslims to Western world and not to Muslims nations or countries which is a challenge for us all and a concern. We can all see on our televisions every day whereby our Muslims brothers and sister are drowning in the Mediterranean sea trying to reach the shores of Europe.

We as the Muslims Ummah should try to find some solutions to some these crisis by giving refuges status to some of our brothers and sisters. Let learn from the example of Bilal who was a slave freed by the Muslims in Madinah and was made the one to call for prayers (Muazin) in the prophet Muhammad (PBUH) Masjid.

The author of this book strongly suggest that leaders and followers of the Muslim Ummah should create a Muslim Zakat organization whereby each of the Muslim nation should keep these Zakat that is collected to help Muslims Ummah to deal with problems of the Ummah instead of waiting for others like the UN to carry out such an important work for us all. Thus, the leaders of the Muslim communities or countries should rethink their strategy and understand that the Ummah was built on the foundation of shared brotherhood, not on nationalism but Al Deen Islam. King Salman Humanitarian Aid and Relief Centre is a great example and should be copied and coordinated by leaders' and followers of the Muslims Ummah.

Furthermore, as argued throughout this book, leadership from an Islamic perspective is examined against the background of the Quran and Sunnah of Prophet Muhammad (PBUH) and the Rightly Four Guided Caliphs and the Prophets. Therefore, leadership is selfless servitude purely for the pleasure of Allah/God alone. Leadership from an Islamic perspective is considered a trust (Amanah). Trust and accountability go hand in hand. Hence there are two levels of trust and accountability. First a leader is entrusted by Allah/God and he/she is accountable to Allah/God first and second to his followers.

The leader's efficiency here refers to the leader ability to accomplish a task or goal with minimal waste of resources, such as time, money, or energy of the people of the Ummah/Muslims communities and on the hand effectiveness means the degree to which a task or goal is achieved, regardless of the resources used for the better main of the Ummah/ Muslim communities. Secondly, the leader is also entrusted by his people and he/she is accountable to them. The leader is accountable to the people they serve whether in an organisation, group or even family they are accountable. The leader is held accountable on the Day of Judgement because he/she is entrusted by Allah/God to lead his people.

The role of leadership in Islam is at many levels. The state level, organizational level, community level and society level. The saying of Prophet Mohammad (PBUH), enhance the role of a leadership from an Islamic perspective for example "Each of you is a Shepherd, and each of you is responsible for his flock." A leader or ruler who has authority over people at any level of the organization or family is responsible for them. A woman is responsible for her house and family. A man is also a guardian and responsible for his family. Therefore, leadership from an Islam perspective emphasized the role of leadership at all levels, for example at institutions, organizations, or political level. Leaders and followers are all vicegerent of Allah/God on earth and should carry out Allah/God's will on earth. See Surah 2 Al Baqarah (2:30).

The importance of leadership from an Islamic perspective is that it enables followers and leaders to be accountable to one another, to be the gate keeper of one another and also to be a mirror to one another. We can see an example of Muslim brother being a mirror to his brother or Muslim sister from the saying of prophet(Hadith) as narrated by Abu Hurayrah (may Allah be pleased with him) reported that the Prophet (PBUH) said: "A believer is the mirror of his fellow believer." In this Hadith the Prophet Muhammad (PBUH) gives a beautiful description and an eloquent simile of the attitude of a Muslim towards his Muslim brother. He outlines the responsibility of a Muslim towards his fellow Muslim; directs him to good manners so that he would adopt them and warns him against evil manners so that he would avoid them. He is thus like a polished mirror to his brother in which the latter sees his true self. The Hadith indicates that giving advice to the believers is obligatory. If one becomes aware of a flaw in his Muslim brother or sister, or an error that he commits, he should bring it to his attention and guide him to rectify it. But this should be done privately, because such advice in public is tantamount to disgrace. There are many meanings to the above Hadith and one is that the believer sees good qualities in his brother so he attempts to emulate them, or he sees bad qualities in his brother so he knows that he possesses similar qualities and attempts to eradicate them. A second meaning is that the believer sees a fault in his brother so he tells him to remove it. He is thus like a mirror to his brother. That is why a true leader or follower is a mirror to one another and that should be done with discretion. This requires that continuous improve on the part of the leader and the follower.

Thus, accountability is taken very seriously in Islam, See Surah 9: Al Tawbah (9:105), Al- Hilali and Khan (1996, p.257), And say (O Muhammad), "Do deeds! Allah will see your deeds, and (so will) His Messenger and the believers. And you will be brought back to the All-Knower of the unseen and the seen. Then He will inform you of what you used to do."

The above verse shows the close link between accountability to Allah/God and accountability to people. That is why the Quran warns leaders and followers of their responsibilities towards their followers, Allah/God, and the Prophets. We can learn accountability lesson from the second Caliph Umar Ibn Al Khattab. Who know that his followers were there as his mirror to one another and they will not hesitate to correct him even though he was their leader.

Similar story of accountability as a leader is directed to prophet Yusuf

(Joseph) (PBUH) when asked to be given the task of organizing reserves in a time of plenty against the lean years to come in Egypt. See Surah 12: Al- Hilali and Khan (1996, p.301) (12:55-7). 55. [Yusuf (Joseph)] said: "Set me over the store-houses of the land; I will indeed guard them with full knowledge" (as a minister of finance in Egypt). 56. Thus did we give full authority to Yusuf (Joseph) in the land, to take possession therein, when or where he likes. We bestow of Our Mercy on whom We will, and We make not to be lost the reward of Al-Muhsinun (the good doers- See V.2:112). 57. And verily, the reward of the Hereafter is better for those who believe and used to fear Allah and keep their duty to Him (by abstaining from all kinds of sins and evil deeds and by performing all kinds of righteous good deeds)." Thus, Islam encourages accountability for those in leadership positions in Muslim communities while realizing that leadership is individual.

The Quran and the Sunnah (traditions) of Prophet Muhammad (PBUH) should be the guide and cornerstone of the content of leadership. If we believe that Allah/ God has created us and that the purpose of creation is to worship Him, then the Quran must have answers, guides, and solutions for leaders and followers who lead in our various communities or societies today. If we want to emulate someone who had lived the example of leadership as envisaged in this book, we should not look beyond the leadership of Prophet Muhammad (PBUH) and his Rightly Guided Khalifs.

The Prophet (PBUH) leadership qualities and deeds towards the uniting humankind with his Creator Allah(God) is very important for leaders and followers to learn from. Indeed, Allah(God) is the one who creates unity, as indicated in Surah Ali Imran (3:103-5), as translated in English by Al- Hilali and Khan (1996, p.93-4), 103. "And hold fast, all of you together, to the Rope of Allah (i.e., this Quran), and be not divided among yourselves, and remember Allah's Favour on you, for you were enemies one to another, but He joined your hearts together, so that, by His Grace, you become brethren (in Islamic Faith), and you were on the brink of a pit of fire, and He saved you from it. Thus Allah makes His Ayat (proofs, evidence, verses, lessons, signs, revelations, etc.) clear to you, that you may be guided." 104. Let there arise out of you a group of people inviting to all that is good (Islam), enjoining Al-Ma'ruf (i.e., Islamic Monotheism and all that Islam orders one to do) and forbidding Al-Munkar (polytheism and disbelief and all that Islam has forbidden). And it is they who are successful. 105. And be not as those who divided and differed among themselves after the clear proofs had come to them. It is they for whom there is an awful torment." As was the example of Prophet Muhammad (PBUH), the call for unity is central for any leader who wants to lead a united community as was in Madinah when he created the Islamic state. Therefore, the prophet Muhammad (PBUH) had to work harder as a leader of his community to create unity amongst his people, even though Allah/God was the one who created unity.

All the previous prophets, starting from prophet Adam (PBUH) to Abraham (PBUH), Jesus (PBUH), and Muhammad (PBUH), proclaimed the call to humankind to understand the purpose of Allah/ God creation, which is worshiping Him and also having unity amongst communities of followers. Therefore, in their leadership positions, they tried to unite their people within their communities towards worshipping Allah/God alone by submitting oneself to Islam. Thus, the consequence of disunity in Islam is not good at all.

See Surah 8 Al-Anfal (8:73),where Allah(God) warns Muslims of disunity, as translated by Al Hilali and Khan (1996, p.237), 73-"And those who disbelieve are allies of one another, (and) if you (Muslims of the whole world collectively) do not do so [i, e. become allies, as one united block under one Khalifah (a chief Muslim ruler for the whole Muslim world) to make victorious Allah's religion of Islamic Monotheism], there will be Fitnah (wars, battles, polytheism) and oppression on earth, and a great mischief and corruption (appearance of polytheism). Al Hilali and Khan (1996, p.237) made an observation on the interpretation of the above Verse based on Tafsir At-Tabari, Vol.10, page 56. [And those who disbelieve are allies of one another, (and) if you (Muslims of the whole world collectively) do not do so (i.e., become allies, as one united block-V8:73). Is "That if you do not do what We (Allah) have ordered you to do, [i.e., all of you (Muslims of the whole world) do not become allies as one united block to make Allah's religion (Islam) victorious, there will be a great Fitnah (polytheism, wars, battles, killings, robbing, a great mischief, corruption, and oppression, etc.). And it is Fitnah to have many Khalifah (Muslim rules), as it has been mentioned in Sahih Muslim by Arfajah, who said: I heard Allah's Messenger (PBUH) saying: "When you all (Muslims) are united (as one block) under a single Khalifah (a chief Muslims ruler), and a man comes up to disintegrate you and separate you into different groups, then kill that man."

There is also another narration narrated by Abu Said Al-Khudri (RA) Allah Messenger (PBUH) Said: "If the Muslim world gave the Bai'a (pledge) to two Khalifah (Chief Muslim ruler), the first one who was given the Bai'a (pledge) first would remain as the Khalifah, then kill the latter (the second) one. "The above Verse and the translated interpretation of the Verse discuss the consequences of disunity among Muslims. The unbelievers are protectors, one of the other, and also it is a legal obligation from the Quran and the Sunnah that there should not be more than one Khalifah (a chief Muslim ruler) for the whole Muslim world or otherwise, there will be a great Fitnah (mischief and evil) amongst the Muslims, the ultimate results of which will not be worthy of praise.

Yusuf Ali's (1992) commentary attests to the fact that Evil concurs with Evil. Therefore, the good has all the more reason for drawing together, living in mutual harmony, and being ready to protect each other. Otherwise, the world will be given over to aggression by unscrupulous people, and the good will fail in their duty to establish Allah's peace and strengthen all the forces of truth and righteousness. Allah/God always warns us as leaders and followers as it is in the Quran, through His Prophets, to be righteous and to be good people or leaders. The examples in the Quran can be drown from Allah/God prophets like Musa (Moses) the only Prophet of Allah/God who spoke to Allah/God directly and received the laws from Him, The Ten Commandments and all the Prophets from Israel followed the laws given to Musa (Moses) (PBUH).

Prophet Muhammad (PBUH) did not speak to Allah(God) directly but he received revelation from Allah(God) through Angel Gabriel, but he was the Prophet who expressed Allah/God words and those word is the Quran. Furthermore, Moses (PBUH), Jesus, and other Prophets created unity among their various communities by preaching to them on the oneness of Allah/God. Each nation was given the best person from among them to carry the message of Allah/God to their people. Each chosen person spoke the language of his people. See Surah 14 Ibrahim (14:4), Al Hilali and Khan (1996, p.317), 4. "And We sent not a Messenger except with the language of his people so that he might make (the message) clear for them. Then Allah misleads whom He wills and guides whom He wills. And He is the All-Mighty, the All-wise." In Surah 4 Al Nisa (4:163-165), Al-Hilali and Khan (1996, p.141), 163. "Verily, We have sent the revelation to you (Muhammad (PBUH) as We sent the revelation to Nuh (Noah) and the Prophets after him; We (also) sent the revelation to (Abraham), Ismail (Ishmael), Ishaq (Isaac), Ya'qub (Jacob), and Al- Asbat[theoffspringofthetwelvesonsofYa'qub (Jacob)], Isa(Jesus), Ayub (Job), Yunus (Jonah), Harun (Aaron), and Sulaiman

(Solomon); and to Dawud (David) We gave the Zabur (Psalms). 164. And Messengers We have mentioned to you before, and Messengers We have not mentioned to you, - and to Musa (Moses) Allah spoke directly. 165. Messengers are bearers of good news and warning that humankind should have no plea against Allah after the (coming of) of Messengers. And Allah is ever All-powerful, All-wise."

Thus, the previous Prophets did the same in leading their people and continuously warned them of the danger of not following the truth Islam. The four Rightly Guided Caliphs did the same with those they led. They warned them of the consequences of not worshiping Allah/God. Although leaders and follower of the Muslims Ummah today who occupy some leadership positions in their societies or communities may not be the same as previous Prophets for example Jesus (PBUH) or Prophet Muhammad (PBUH), whom Allah(God) choses to lead their various communities, but today leaders can learn from their experiences as model of leadership and strive to emulate such examples by being morally and ethically upright for their communities they lead. In other words, leaders and followers in Muslims communities should learn from the prophetic examples and also from the four Rightly Guided Caliphs and also follow the Hadith of Prophet Mohammad (PBUH), as narrated by Sahih Bukhari and Muslim: "Each of you is a shepherd, and each of you is responsible for his flock." Politics and religion go hand in hand in Islam. Therefore, today's leaders and followers should not be afraid of religion, especially if they do the right things for their people or community will follow them.

An excellent example of a leader who combined both politics and religion was Prophet Muhammad (PBUH), the Ummah (Islamic Community) leader, yet he was just and fair to all, irrespective of their creed. He used to invite Kings of other nations to accept Islam by writing to them.

There are many examples of these letters, and the author will examine some of them in this book. One earlier letter from Prophet Muhammad (PBUH) to Negus, the King of Abyssinia, carried by Amr ibn Umayyah al-Damri, stated the following; "In the name of Allah, the most Beneficent, the most Merciful. From Muhammad, the Messenger of Allah, to Negus, the King of Abyssinia: Peace on him who follows the path of Guidance. Praise to Allah besides Whom there is no other god, the Sovereign, the Holy One, the Preserver of Peace, the Keeper of the Faithful, the Guardian. I bear witness that Jesus, son of Mary, is a spirit of God and His word, which He conveyed to the chaste Virgin Mary. He created Jesus through His word, just like Adam with His hands. And now I call you to Allah, Who is One and has no partner, and to friendship in His obedience. Follow me and believe in what has been revealed to me, for I am the Messenger of Allah. I invite you and your people to Allah, the Mighty, the Glorious. I have conveyed the message, and it is up to you to accept it. Once again, peace on whoever follows the path of guidance".

Prophet Mohammad (PBUH) also sent a letter to Heraclius, carried by Duhayyah Ibn Khalifah Al-Kabi, a famous Meccan businessman who had accepted Islam. The letter reads: "In the name of Allah, the most Beneficent, and the most Merciful. From Mohammad, the slave and Messenger of Allah, to Heraclius, the Emperor of Rome. Peace be on him who follows the Guidance. After this, I invite you to accept Islam. Accept Islam, and you will prosper, and Allah will give you double rewards. But if you refuse, your people's sins will also fall on your shoulders. O People of the Book! Come to a word common between you and us: that we shall not worship anything save Allah, and that we shall not associate anything with Him, nor shall some of us take others for lords besides Allah. But if they turn back, then say: Bear witness that we are Muslims". (Ibid).

The Prophet (PBUH) also sent a letter to Khosrow II Parviz, son of Hormizd IV, the Sasanian Kisra of Persia. Abdullah Ibn Hudhafah carried this letter as recorded by the historian Al-Ya'qubi. The letter reads: "In the name of Allah, the most Gracious, the most Merciful from Mohammad the Messenger of Allah to Khosrow, son of Hormizd. Accept Islam so that you will be safe (from Allah's wrath); otherwise, be forewarned of war from Allah and His Messenger, and peace is with whoever follows the right guidance". (Ibid).

Prophet Muhammad (PBUH) sent a letter to Muqawqia, the then-Roman Viceroy, over Egypt. This letter was carried by Hatib Ibn Balta and had the following; "In the Name of Allah, the most Beneficent, the most Merciful. From Mohammad, the servant and Messenger of Allah, to Muqawqi, a Chief of the Copts: Peace be upon him who follows the path of Guidance. I invite you to accept the message of Islam. Accept it, and you shall prosper. But if you turn away, the sins (of misleading by your example) of the Copts shall fall upon you. O people of the book! Came to a word common between you and us: that shall worship none but Allah and that we shall ascribe no partners to Him and that none of us shall regard anyone as lord besides God. And if they turn away, then say: Bear witness that we are Muslims". (Ibid).

The above are four letters Prophet Mohammad (PBUH) sent to other leaders or emperors during his time were inviting them to Islam but not fighting them as always suggested by some scholars that the sword spread Islam. Therefore, the Prophet Mohammad (PBUH) only invited non-Muslim leaders into Islam without coercion.

Pharaoh, as shown in the Quran, subjugated their citizens, and Allah/ God requested Prophet Moses (PBUH) at the time to free them, in other words, Jews from Egypt. A great example of such a leader is the story of Pharaoh's encounter with Moses in freeing the people of Israel from

Egypt. The main issue was the enslavement of people as the Israelis were being held captive or enslaved by Pharaohs.

However, when Moses freed the people of Israel from Egypt, they did not obey Allah to enter the Promised Land and wandered in the Sinai desert for 40 years. This story of Moses (PBUH) is affirmed in Surah 5 Al Maidah (5:20-26), Al Hilali and Khan (1996, p.149), 20. "And (remember when Musa (Moses) said to his people: "O my people! Remember the favor of Allah to you: when He made Prophets among you, made you kings, and gave you what He had not given to any other among the Alamin (mankind and jinn, in the past)." 21. "O, my people! Enter the holy land (Palestine) which Allah has assigned to you and turn not back (in flight); for then you will be returned as losers." 22. They said: "O Musa (Moses)! In it (this holy land) are a people of great strength, and we shall never it till they leave it; when they leave, then we will enter." 23. Two men of those who fear (Allah and) whom Allah had bestowed His Grace (they were Yusha and Kaleb) said: "Assault them through the gate; for when you are in, victory will be yours; and put your trust in Allah if you are believers indeed." 24. They said: "O Musa (Moses)! We shall never see it as long as they are there. So go you and your Lord and fight you two; we are sitting right here." 25. He [Musa (Moses)] said: "O my Lord! I have power only over myself and my brother, so separate us from the people who are the Fasiqun (rebellious and disobedient to Allah)!" 26. (Allah) said: "Therefore it (this holy land) is forbidden to them for forty years; in distraction, they will wander through the land. So be not sorrowful over the people who are the Fasiqun (rebellious and disobedient to Allah)!" In additional comments, Yusuf Ali (Ibid) attests that the two men who had faith and courage were Joshua and Caleb and that Joshua succeeded Moses (PBUH) in leadership after 40 years. Thus, leadership requires the recognition of Allah as the originator of leadership and His laws. If disunited as the people of Israel or disobeying

Allah will face the consequences. The people of Israel were rebellious, and that is why Moses asked Allah/God to separate him and his brother Aaron from the rebellious people.

A similar story of Mosses (PBUH) and his people also happen to Prophet Muhammad (PBUH). The case of Prophet Mohammad (PBUH) is related to the first battle between the pagan Quraish and the Muslims. In facing this battle with the pagans of Makah in Medinah, Prophet Mohammad (PBUH) discussed the situation with their companions about the battle, and one of the companions by the name Al-Miqdad Ibn' Amr, then addressed the Prophet by saying that they should not repeat what the Children of Israel had said to Moses, "Go, you and your Lord, to fight while we sit here waiting. Rather, by God Who sent you to guide us, we should say: 'Go you and your Lord to fight, and we shall fight your foe on your right and on your left, in front of you and behind you, till the Lord grants you victory."

Hearing this speech of Miqdad, the Prophet Mohammad (PBUH) smiled and blessed him. Sa'ad Ibn Mu'ath from Ansar (Helpers) also supported Prophet Muhammad (PBUH) and said to the Prophet, "We had received you as the Prophet of God and had sworn allegiance to you, promising to obey you. We, therefore, are all ready to follow you, to do whatever pleased you, though it were to throw themselves into the sea. Prophet Muhammad (PBUH) respected this statement and made it known to them that he was ready and assured them of victory. See Surah 8 Al-Anfal (8: 5-8), Al Hilali and Khan (1996, p.228), 5. "As your Lord caused you (O Muhammad (PBUH)) to go out from your home with the truth; and verily, a party among the believers dislikes it, 6. Therefore, disputing with you concerning the truth after it was made manifest as if they were being driven to death while they were looking (at it). 7. And (remember) when Allah promised you (Muslims) one of the two parties (of the enemy, i.e., either the army or the caravan) that it should be yours; you wished that the one not armed (the caravan) should be yours, but Allah willed to justify the truth by His Words and to cut off the roots of the disbelievers (i.e., in the battle of Badr). 8. That he might cause the truth to triumph and bring falsehood to nothing, even though the Mujrimun (disbelievers, polytheists, sinners, criminals) hate it."

Allah warns us of transgressor leaders of every community. See Surah 2 Al Baqarah (2:81-82), Al Hilali and Khan (1996, p.24), 81. "Yes! Whoever earns evil and his sin has surrounded him; are dweller of the Fire (i.e., Hell); they will dwell therein forever. 82. And those who believe (in the Oneness of Allah-Islamic Monotheism) and do righteous good deeds they are dwellers of Paradise; they will dwell therein forever." Also in Surah (2:257) 2) in Al Hilali and Khan (1996, p.65), 257. "Allah is the Wali (Protector or Guardian) of those who believe. He brings them out from darkness into light. However, for those who disbelieve, their Auliya (supporters and helpers) are Taghut [false deities and false leaders]; they bring them out from light into darkness. Those are the fire dwellers, and they will abide therein forever."

Leaders should not seek gain in evil by subjugating their people or turning a blind eye to evil wherever they may be. We all have a shared purpose in life, irrespective of our color or creed. Unfortunately, today some leaders go to war for no reason other than national interest. National interest has been used as the weapon of choice to subjugate the weak and the vulnerable. Leaders should not focus on self-enrichment, self-glorification, or collusion with the rich and the powerful at the expense of their citizens. Instead, it should be seen as a selfless servitude purely for the pleasure of Allah/God.

Leadership today, either in the West or in Muslim communities, goes to those who are powerful, well-connected, rich, and influential to seek for power. The alienation of the middle class and the poor by those in leadership positions is a concern. In addition, there is a need for effective leadership and democracy within the Muslim communities and the lack of it is aiding the rise of what I term in this book misguided brothers who use the wrong method in fighting back the western influence and lack of democracy in Muslims communities or societies and the rise of radicalism by various extremist groups, who do not represent the genuine Islam taught by Prophet Muhammad (PBUH) which is a concern and the one of the reasons for writing this book. Prophet Muhammad (PBUH) used to invite Kings and Emperors of other nations to accept Islam by writing to them as a goodwill gesture, not by forcing them to become Muslims or by killing them. The kings that the prophet (PBUH) invited to Islam were not forced to accept Islam but were invited, this because there is no compulsion in Islam. See Surah 2 Al-Baqarah (2:256) as translated to English by Al Hilali and Khan (1996, p.65), 256. The Verse clearly states that "There is no compulsion in religion. Verily, the Right path has become distinct from the wrong path. Whoever disbelieves in Taghut and believes in Allah, then he has grasped the most trustworthy handhold that will never break. And Allah is All-Hearer, All-Knower."

In their complementary comment, Al Hilali and Khan (1996, p.65) argue that the word *Taghut* covers many meanings: It means anything worshiped other than the Real God (Allah), i.e., all the false deities. satan, devils, idols, stones, stars, angels, human beings, e.g., Messengers of Allah, falsely worshiped and taken as Taghut. Likewise, saints, graves, rulers, and leaders are falsely worshiped and wrongly followed. Sometimes Taghut means a false judge who gives a false judgment. See Surah 4 An-Nisa (4:60), in Al Hilali and Khan (1996, p.60 ,(122. Have you seen those (hypocrites) who claim that they believe in that which has been sent down to you and that which was sent down before you, and they wish to go for judgment (in their disputes) to the Taghut (false judges) while they have been ordered to reject them. But Shaitan (Satan) wishes to lead them far astray."

Today the best leaders and followers are those who take their leadership position as trust from Allah/God to selflessly lead their people for the pleasure of Allah/God a selfless desire to liberate their people and provide and protect them from harm and abuses. These leaders and followers may not be Muslims by proclamation but embody leadership spirit as envisage in the Islam. Some worldly examples of these leaders are Nelson Mandela in South Africa, Gandhi in India, Martin Luther King in the USA to name a few. Leaders who were selflessly serving their communities and transformed them into beacons of hope for their people and those who observed them from a distance.

Leadership is a trust and willingness to serve purposely for the pleasure of Allah/God alone. By selflessly serving their various communities these leaders demonstrated a great spirit of effective leadership and by so doing were able to liberate their people from institutional enslavement, impoverishment, and racial prejudice, especially in the case of South Africa were the apartheid government was subjugating the black South Africans.

Today Political leadership in many Muslim communities/Muslims Ummah main ambitions are about personal interest, power position, accumulating wealth for personal and family gain either directly or indirectly forgetting that during the Day of Judgement they will be accountable for their deeds. It is not too late to seek Allah/God forgiveness for their mistakes and do what is right and this is also one of the reason for writing this book so that those who are leaders now or are aspiring to be leaders understand that leadership is a trust (Amanah) and that on the Day of Judgment they will be accountable. It is also obvious that some citizens in Muslim and non-Muslim communities feel that their leaders do not represent their interests but rather the interest of the rich and powerful nations which is a concern and this need to be change.

This type of feeling that their leaders are serving the interest of other has led to voter apathy in Muslim communities and Western countries which shows that there is a political disconnect in some Muslim and non-Muslims communities between young and old, which is getting worse day by day which is a concern.

Leaders and followers in diverse Muslim communities should refrain from regarding poverty as a customary state, as it is not. Consequently, the distribution of national resources should be equitable among all citizens. A multitude of glaring disparities exist within certain Muslim and non-Muslim communities, and addressing this issue should be an urgent concern for leaders in Muslim communities. It is imperative that the welfare and interests of citizens take precedence. Regrettably, we have witnessed numerous individuals from some Muslim and some African communities losing their lives in the Mediterranean Sea while seeking a better future, and the global community has shown a lack of concern and solidarity.

We require individuals in Muslim communities to assume the roles of leaders and followers, fostering a sense of brotherhood and care for one another as brothers and sisters in Islam. Additionally, if feasible, it is important to extend support to these individuals by offering them refugee status and ensuring their protection. It is understandable why certain citizens in Western countries question why these individuals, who are seeking a better life, do not seek refuge in Muslim countries or communities. Their concern is valid. As members of the Muslim community, we have the capacity to accept and provide sanctuary to these individuals and also non-Muslims communities. However, it is disheartening that leaders and followers in some Muslim communities choose to ignore this issue, as if it is not their responsibility. It is imperative that we all acknowledge and address these concerns, working together to develop effective mechanisms to resolve these problems.

We can learn a Lesson from Khalifah Omar Ibn Abdul Aziz when he demonstrated an excellent example by using Baitul -Mal or public treasury to help those in need and it became obvious that everyone was fine and did not need money from Bitul Mal (public treasury) to leave or to eat food or for feeding. We as leaders and follower should establish Baitul- Mal to help others in time of distress. You can see what he said when he was first nominated to be the Caliph, he addressed his people, saying, "O people! The responsibilities of the Caliphate have been thrust upon me without my desire or your consent. If you choose select someone else as a Caliph, I will immediately step aside and will support your decision."

Caliph Umar Ibn Abdul Aziz (RA) mode of leadership is similar to that of the administration of Caliph Umar Ibn Khattab. He replaced corrupt and tyrannical administrators with accomplished and just ones. He restored confiscated properties to their rightful owners. He surrendered all his movable and immovable properties to the public treasury, including a ring given to him by Caliph Waleed. He was asked what he had left for his children as property he replied, Allah(God). Furthermore, his wife witnesses him weeping after his prayers. She asked for the reason for his grief, and he replied, "Oh" Fatima! I have been appointed as the ruler of Muslims. I am concerned about the poor that are starving, the sick that are destitute, the naked that are in distress, the oppressed that are stricken, the strangers that are in prison, the venerable elders, ones with large families and modest means, and the likes of them in countries of the earth and distant provinces, and I anticipate that my lord would hold me accountable for them on the Day of Resurrection. I fear that no defence would avail me, and I wept." Caliph Omar Ibn Abdul Aziz shows an excellent example of Islamic leadership. Most leaders in many Muslim countries or communities are mostly wealthy or supported by big lobbies and big businesses, and most government contracts are given to these wealthy individuals or groups, which is a concern.

We can derive valuable insights from the founding fathers of the American Federalist No. 52 Madison (1788), who emphasized the significance of a shared interest between the government and the people in order to safeguard liberty. They argued that the branch of government established by the constitution should maintain a close connection and understanding with the citizens. Presently, the influence of powerful interest groups and expansive corporations on leadership is a matter of concern not only in America, but also in the Western world and Africa, as well as globally. This concern serves as one of the motivations behind the writing of this book. The dominance of these influential entities holds the political elite captive, which raises apprehensions. The primary objective of individuals in leadership positions should be to serve humanity rather than accumulating personal wealth through various means. The next chapter focuses on the Causes and Rise of Misguided brothers/fundamentalist in Muslim Communities.

Chapter 5

The Causes and Rise of Misguided Brothers and Sister "Fundamentalism" in Muslim Communities

The emergence and proliferation of misguided brothers and sisters/ fundamentalist movements within Muslim communities is a concern and is one of the reason for writing of this book. This phenomenon has been attributed to a variety of factors, including political, social, educational and economic conditions, as well as religious and ideological beliefs. The rise of misguided brothers and sisters/fundamentalism has been characterized by a rejection of modernity from a western perspective and a return to a more traditional Islamic values and practices. In this chapter of the book the author aims to explore the causes and rise of misguided brothers and sister/fundamentalism in Muslim communities. This chapter try provide insights into the complex and multifaceted nature of this phenomenon, and its implications for Muslim societies and the wider global communities.

The rise of misguided brothers and sister/fundamentalism in the Muslim communities partly is due to the political situations in many Muslims communities. The rise of misguided brothers and sister /fundamentalism in Muslim communities as noted above can be attributed to political factors. This phenomenon is rooted in the historical context of the

Muslim world, which has experienced a series of political upheavals and socio-economic challenges. The rise of misguided brothers and sister using wrong methods to respond to these challenges, as it offers a sense of identity and purpose to individuals who feel marginalized and disempowered by the prevailing political order is a concern. Thus, it is argue in this book that one of the key political factors that has contributed to the rise of misguided brothers and sister/fundamentalism is the failure of secular government, elite classes and the so call democratic governments to deliver on their promises of social justice, economic development education and in the share of the national cake. This has led to a sense of disillusionment among many Muslims brothers and sisters, who have turned to misguided behaviours/fundamentalist ideologies or using the wrong method as a means of expressing their frustration and seeking alternative solutions to their problems.

The most important political factor that has contributed to the rise of misguided brothers and sisters/ fundamentalism is the role of external powers in shaping the political landscape of the Muslim world. The external powers collaboration with the so called democratic government that uses force and inhuman treatment of their citizen is one of the big political factor due to the fact that these government uses torture and all forms of in human abuses to their citizens and the external power turn a blind eye to those atrocities and inhuman treatment of their citizens.

The legacy of colonialism and imperialism has left a deep imprint with many Muslims countries and some citizens viewing the West as a source of oppression and exploitation. This has fuelled a sense of resentment and hostility towards Western values and institutions, which has been channelled into misguided behaviour and by using the wrong method to fight these challenges at their door step, hence the rice of misguided brothers and sisters. If we can understand some of these factors we can be able to address the root causes of the misguided brothers and sisters/ fundamentalism and promote greater social and political stability in the Muslim world and beyond.

One of the ways or strategy to address the root cause of the rise of the misguided brothers and sister in Muslims communities is for those who are in Leadership positions in the Ummah (Muslin communities) to serve the needs and the interest of their citizens first and the need and wants of those who reside in Muslims countries either for political or economic reasons irrespective of faith, colour, or race. In some Muslim countries today to run for a high office or to be presidential candidate for election as president of their nations they run to London, Paris, and Washington DC to get approval which is a concern.

This phenomenon is creating a problem for some youths in some Muslims countries who are questioning the legality of their leaders seeking approval from some western nations when they had their own independents and are free to govern their own people without the external powers interference.

The other political factor in the Muslim communities that lead to the rise of misguided brothers is money politics whereby to be a candidate for political position in their own countries they must be rich or must be wealthy before he/she is accepted or have those with big money businesses to endorse them for such a position, or have a government of superpower nation to endorse them as a candidate for election before he/she is accepted.

Similarly, the other political factor within the Muslim community is that of a candidate for presidency or higher position in government who have Western Education are there by supported easily over the locally educated candidate or a candidate who is educated in traditional Madrasah Islamic school.

The other political factor is that of a candidate with a military training in Western Educated nations are supported to be leaders in the Muslims Ummah, Muslim communities, and even in the extreme circumstance whereby the military western educated person deposed an elected leader who won an election through a democratic means. Some of these instances lead to some of our brothers to use the wrong method to want to get into power or fight against such injustices and favouritism by the external powers. And if brothers and sisters in the Muslims communities take the wrong step to fight against this kind of ploy they are all name or label terrorist or are then portrayed as being violent terrorists or fundamentalist ideologies, or jihadist. These name calling without addressing the root cause of the problems in the Muslims communities is a problem and a concern. In other words, when some of our brothers and sisters try to fight back these kinds of injustices, or the way some these leaders in Muslims communities are being supported by the external powers even though they don't serve the interest of their people then it became a problem and a concern that is needed to be address.

The emergence of Islamic fundamentalism or misguided individuals within the Muslim Ummah can be attributed to various factors, one of which is the education system in Muslim countries. In some Muslim nations, the education system still follows the colonial model, which fails to instil a sense of belonging and self-development, particularly in terms of Islamic education. The colonization of Muslim territories by European powers during the 19th and 20th centuries has had a profound and lasting impact on Islam and Islamic education. The influence of colonial powers on the educational system in Muslim countries is a matter of concern, as it not only challenged the dominance of Islam in state and society, but also imposed significant changes that had far- reaching consequences. Panjwani (2004, p.22) contends that Western colonialism had a profound impact on Muslim military, political, and intellectual life, resulting in a complete eclipse. These colonial powers introduced secular laws and Western-style education. According to Elmessiri (2002,p.70), secular education or secularism for Muslim countries implies a human-centred (anthropocentric) perspective where the mind, being self-referential and autonomous, requires no divine inspiration from above, as all knowledge comes from within and below. Keane (2002, p.29) also argues that secularism entails the separation of religion and politics. Furthermore, Keane (2002, p.29) explains that secularists believe that religious illusions have gradually vanished over the past few generations, which is fortunate since the removal of religious sentiments from domains such as law, government, party politics, and education - the separation of church and state - frees citizens from irrational prejudices and promotes open-minded tolerance, a crucial ingredient of a pluralist democracy. Thus, the Western powers' notion of secularism imposed on Muslim countries contradicts the Islamic concept of education. According to Cook (1999, p.340), secularism is incompatible with the Islamic principle of tawhīd (oneness), which emphasizes the integration of all aspects of life, both spiritual and temporal, into a cohesive whole. This suggests that the imposition of secular laws by colonial western powers was supported by foreign state apparatus, administrative methods, and social institutions. These colonial powers employed various strategies, such as direct assimilation used by the French and indirect assimilation employed by the British.

Tan (2017) acknowledges that the French, Italians, and Portuguese employed a direct assimilationist strategy, while the British pursued an indirect integrationist strategy. In both cases, the colonial governments replaced indigenous laws influenced by Islamic principles with secular ones. Tan (2017) also cites Janin (2005), who argues that the political dominance of European powers began prior to the 19th century. The signing of the Treaty of Carlowitz (1699) by the Ottomans marked a significant turning point, as it ended sixteen years of hostilities between the Ottoman Empire and the Holy League (Austria, Poland, Venice, and Russia). The defeat of the Ottoman Empire by Western powers hastened the spread of Western colonialism across numerous Muslim territories.

Cook (1999) further explains that the influence of secularism on Muslim education systems persisted even after colonialism. Many political leaders of newly independent countries, who themselves had received Western-style and non-religious education, sought to modernize their nations according to Western development paradigms, albeit to varying extents.

Turkey's education system underwent modernization efforts under Ataturk's leadership in the 1920s, as exemplified by Daun et al. (2004). Meanwhile, Esposito (2002) noted that Islamic law was replaced by Western secular codes in most Muslim countries, with the exception of family law. Despite this, Islamic matters were still included in the curriculum of state-run education systems in the Middle East, North Africa, and Pakistan, as summarized by Daun et al. (2004). In some countries, such as Egypt, Indonesia, and Pakistan, the secular and Islamic school networks coexisted. However, in countries with less influential Muslim traditions, such as those in Sub-Saharan Africa and some Asian countries, secular education systems were maintained, and Islamic educational arrangements were established outside of the state sphere.

Tan (2017) acknowledges the persistent obstacles faced by Muslims, including secularism, educational dualism, and the marginalization of Islamic education. In light of the various influences on Islamic education, a crucial inquiry arises: how do Islamic educational institutions confront these influences and navigate the array of demands and transformations in a post-colonial era? It is evident that until these challenges are recognized as a priority by Muslim communities worldwide, many Muslim countries will continue to grapple with them. Presently, the most significant challenge lies in establishing Islamic schools or Madrasah that integrate the teachings of Islamic religion with modern academic knowledge endorsed by diverse governments in Muslim communities, while simultaneously avoiding the perception of adopting a Westernized education system.

The schism among Muslims regarding their stance on Islamic education is a genuine issue that necessitates significant efforts from the scholars of the Muslim community to devise an alternative curriculum that can be embraced by all, particularly the parents of the Ummah's students. The Ummah must incorporate both secular and Islamic or religious subjects into their curriculum to meet the requirements of both government schools and Islamic schools, which is a significant challenge. This will enable us to have an integrated curriculum that encompasses both academic and Islamic education and science. As a result, many schools established in numerous Muslim countries, particularly in Africa, were missionary schools. These schools were established by colonial powers in the heart of many Muslim communities, and their impact on Muslim communities is a cause for concern. The influence of these schools in their respective localities is now being questioned by many young Muslims today. Different Muslim countries have taken various approaches to combat or confront the onslaught of colonialism or the colonial education system.

Ruthven (2006) identified four distinct responses to Western control among Muslims: the archaic, the neo-traditionalist, the reformist, and the modernist. The archaic response, exemplified by the revolts led by 'Abd alQādir (1808-1883) in Western Algeria, involved military struggles and attacks against Western dominance. Neo-traditionalists like Sayyid Abū al-'Alā' Mawdūdī (1903-1979) rejected modern Western civilization and advocated for a return to the traditions of early Muslims as sources of authority and emulation. Reformists, such as Muhammad 'Abduh (1849-1905) in Egypt, focused on internal reforms within Islam to strengthen its position against Western civilization. On the other hand, modernists like Sir Sayyid Ahmed Khan (1917-1998), founder of the Muhammadan Anglo-Oriental College at Aligarh in India, recognized the need for reform and aimed to rationalize Islamic thought and institutions to align them with Western paradigms. Additionally, Ruthven (2006: 291) argues that the key distinction between modernists and reformists lies in their approach: modernists sought to demonstrate that the Quran, when properly understood, did not hinder progress and could be harmonized with modernity, while reformists aimed to reconcile their cherished Islam with modernity by discarding aspects of Western reality that appeared incompatible with Islamic teachings and practices.

Numerous Muslim scholars held the belief that colonial education was a threat to their communities and attempted to counteract it. However, in certain African Sub-Saharan countries during the early stages of the establishment of Missionary schools, some students were coerced or convinced to convert to Christianity before being admitted, although this is no longer a common practice. This had an impact on those who lacked a strong foundation in their faith, particularly our Muslim brothers and sisters. As a result, the introduction of Western educational models and values has led to changes in the societal norms and behaviours of many Muslims. For example, the emphasis on individualism and critical thinking promoted by these schools has challenged traditional communal values and hierarchical social structures. Consequently, the establishment of missionary schools has contributed to the emergence of a more individualistic and egalitarian mind-set among certain segments of the Muslim populations worldwide. However, it is crucial to acknowledge that the influence of missionary schools in Muslim nations has not been universally beneficial, as contended throughout this publication, despite the presence of certain positive outcomes.

This has sparked debates among Muslim intellectuals regarding the appropriate course of action to take with regards to Western or colonial education systems within their own communities. Detractors argue that these institutions have frequently been utilized as instruments of cultural imperialism, aiming to erode local traditions, values, and the Islamic way of life. The imposition of Western educational models and religious ideologies has been perceived by some as a manifestation of cultural hegemony, thereby undermining the autonomy and identity of Muslim communities. Consequently, these concerns have contributed to the emergence of misguided individuals within these communities.

Therefore, the creation of Missions schools weather catholic or Protestant is a concern. Muslim Ummah or Muslims communities' leaders and followers are yet to understand the gravity of these concerns of the impact of these Missionary schools at the heart of Muslims communities worldwide. One of the greatest pre-occupation. Hence, the establishment of Catholic or Protestant Mission schools raises significant concerns. The leaders and followers of the Muslim Ummah, as well as Muslim communities worldwide, have yet to fully comprehend the gravity of these concerns and the potential impact of these Missionary schools. The unwavering dedication of Muslim leaders and followers to the construction of mosques for worship has overshadowed the significance of education in shaping Muslim citizens within their communities. This matter is of utmost importance, as both religious devotion and education are crucial for the comprehensive growth of individuals. Therefore, it is essential that we give equal importance to the educational aspect, recognizing its immense value. As responsible members and leaders of our communities, it is imperative that we thoroughly evaluate the quality of education imparted to our children and youth, as they are the driving force behind the development of the entire Ummah.

Muslim leaders and followers prioritize the construction of mosques for worship, but often overlook the crucial role that education plays in the development of Muslim citizens within their communities. This oversight is concerning, as both aspects are essential for the creation of well-rounded individuals, rather than solely focusing on religious rituals. It is imperative that we also emphasize the significance of education, as it plays a vital role in shaping the future of our communities. As followers and leaders, we must carefully consider the education of our children and youth, as they are the driving force behind the progress of the entire Muslim community. We in the Muslims Ummah have forgotten that the first part of revelation of Al Deen Islam to the prophet Mohammad (PBUH) started with read (Iqra). See Surah al-Aaq (96:1-5) as translated to English by Khan and Al Hilaili (p.779) 1.Read in the name of your Lord Who has created(all that exist) 2. He has created man from a clot (a piece of thick coagulated blood) 3.Read And your Lord is the Must Generous. 4. Who has taught (the writing) by the pen. 5. He has taught man that which he know not. We should establish good schools in various Muslims communities to teach them about everything they need to know and about their Deen. We as followers and leaders of Muslims communities should know that some of these schools established by the churches or missionaries by the church or western powers in Muslim communities worldwide are the source of some of the problems of the rise of misguided brothers in the Muslim Ummah and therefore there should be some strategies on how to mitigate the situation and not to use a wrong method in responding to all these challenges.

The presence of Western Educated Muslims, commonly referred to as the Muslim elite, has contributed to the emergence of misguided individuals within specific Muslim communities. These individuals have received their education from Western universities, which often leads them to adopt a condescending attitude towards their counterparts who have graduated from traditional educational institutions or Madrasas. Consequently, this attitude gives rise to confrontations and misunderstandings among community members. It is imperative for these individuals to acknowledge the significance of mutual respect and collaboration, as they possess unique areas of expertise and knowledge. By leveraging each other's strengths and abilities, a resolution can be reached to address the dichotomy between Western educated and traditionally educated Muslims.

These challenges are genuine and demand the attention of leaders and followers within the Muslim Ummah, particularly concerning the education of our children. A prime example of the complexities surrounding Missionary Education is my father, Mallam Inua Wirba. He was initially enrolled in a Catholic Mission school in Sop Jakiri subdivision, Bui Division, North West Province of Cameroon. However, he was unexpectedly withdrawn from the institution by his father, who replaced him with his half-brother from a different mother. Despite numerous attempts to comprehend the reasoning behind this decision, no explanation was ever provided before his father's demise. This sudden removal from school left my father with feelings of rejection and abandonment by his own father, Fai Tavire, a member of the warrior clan in upper Jakiri Subdivision, Bui Division, and North West Province of Cameroon. While in self-imposed exile from his family, he found refuge and acceptance among Muslim families and brothers. This encounter led him to embrace Islam and take the Shahadahh, a common experience for those in his father's generation who sought solace in the Islamic faith. As a result of his conversion, he became a Mallam, teaching Quran to children in his community and beyond. His journey is a testament to the transformative power of faith and the significance of seeking acceptance and support during difficult times.

In the 1960s, Mallam Inua Wirba, my father, not only imparted Quranic teachings to children but also took the initiative to establish the first Anglo-Arabic schools in Kumbo, Bui-Division, North West Province, and Cameroon. Mallam Inua Wirba is widely recognized as the pioneer of Anglo-Arabic schools in Cameroon due to his efforts. He personally visited each village where the Muslim population was dominant and successfully convinced them to establish schools that would provide education infused with Islamic values, while still following the government curriculum. This approach aimed to address the concerns raised by the author in this book, which had the potential to mislead fellow Muslims. These Anglo-Arabic schools function as community-based institutions, aligning with Mallam Inua Wirba's vision, and the parents of the students actively participate in managing the schools through the Parent Teachers Association (PTA).

It was a prudent decision on his part to delegate the responsibility of educating these children within his communities to the PTA, ensuring the preservation of the Islamic values, rather than allowing external entities such as the missionary schools to impose their own educational methods, as was the case with certain mission schools in his community. Furthermore, when the Cameroonian government began recognizing Anglo-Arabic schools as private educational institutions, similar to those established by the missionaries, my father was appointed as the manager of an Anglo-Arabic school by the authorities. He was affectionately known as "Pa Manager" for an extended period until his passing. In writing this book, I would like to express my gratitude to Allah/God for the guidance bestowed upon my father. I affirm that the divine guidance of Allah/God manifests in various ways, and my father's guidance is a remarkable blessing to all his descendants. I take great pride in acknowledging him as my father, and I and my brothers and sisters and grandchildren sincerely pray that Allah/God grants him the highest paradise, Jantul Firdaus.

During my father's generation, numerous Muslim families made the decision to convert to Christianity as a result of the educational institutions that were established within their communities. It is crucial to recognize and acknowledge the presence of these institutions, as their impact should not be underestimated. My father's personal experience serves as a testament to the fact that positive change can be achieved through both individual and communal efforts, without resorting to unethical means. While mosques undoubtedly play a vital role in our communities, it is equally important to establish Islamic schools that can effectively impart the principles of Islam to Muslim individuals, just as my father did within his own community. By following in his footsteps, we can prioritize our efforts accordingly, recognizing that we all serve as representatives of Allah/God on this earth. It is imperative that we do not overlook the existence of missionary schools within our communities, as some of these institutions may have the intention of converting Muslim youths to Christianity, which is a matter of concern.

The education of our young people is a shared responsibility, regardless of whether these schools have a religious agenda or not. It is crucial to prevent a situation where Muslim youths or communities are unjustly labelled as terrorists or fundamentalists simply because they employ misguided methods to address the issues within their own communities.

These young individuals may resort to direct or indirect confrontation with their respective governments, leading to them being branded as terrorists or, as the author refers to them in this book, misguided brothers and sisters or fundamentalists.

Instances have been observed where Muslims have been subjected to derogatory labels. One notable example of this phenomenon is the case of the young Muslim group in Nigeria that initiated a challenge against Western education, famously known as Borko Haram in Nigeria. Borko

Haram essentially signifies the prohibition of Western education. However, this approach to addressing an ongoing issue is erroneous and has the potential to exacerbate problems rather than resolve them. This particular group held a disdain for the Western education provided by Missionary schools in Nigeria. Instead, they could have pursued the establishment of Islamic schools imbued with Islamic principles, as seen in the example of the speaker's father in Cameroon. This would have offered a constructive solution to an existing problem.

In Cameroon, specifically in the city of Ngaundere, a Mission school was established within a predominantly Muslim community, which became a notable instance. Surprisingly, the presence of this missionary school did not initially raise any concerns among the Muslim parents residing in this community, as they failed to recognize the potential drawbacks associated with such an institution. However, the situation changed when a priest affiliated with this Missionary school decided to incorporate a cross as a symbol within the students' uniform. As a result, some influential members within the Muslim community began to voice their objections towards the imposition of this religious emblem on their children's attire. It became evident that the location of this school, situated at the heart of the Muslim community, had shielded them from comprehending the potential impact that these schools could have on their children.

Unfortunately, some elite members were unable to effect any meaningful change due to their lack of focus on their children's education and their failure to anticipate the influence of missionary schools within the Muslim communities. These are some of the problems that occasionally lead to misguided individuals within Muslim communities. Without government intervention and guidance, these situations could potentially escalate into chaos or result in the mislabelling of parents as terrorists or fundamentalists. It is crucial for Muslim leaders and followers to acknowledge these realities and actively seek solutions to address such issues. As members of Muslim communities, we must adopt a different approach in tackling these problems. One possible solution is the establishment of schools or education centres that promote Islamic values, while ensuring that they do not contribute to further complications. It is important to emphasize that with the willingness to take action, and by taking proactive measures, we can prevent such situations from occurring in the future.

It is crucial to highlight a reflection made by Moaddel (2002) in this book regarding the issue of education among Western-educated Muslims. Moaddel(2002) further, arguesthat Muslimswhohavereceiveda Western education are greatly influenced by Western ideologies. As a result, they attempt to devise alternative approaches to Islamic jurisprudence. This includes reinterpreting the Quran and Hadith, transforming the concept of shura into a parliamentary democracy, questioning the institution of polygamy, and associating Islam with civilization. Karcic (2001) also asserts that the failure of Muslim leaders to establish Islamic priorities is evident in contemporary Muslim societies. Examples of this can be seen in disputes and conflicts surrounding women's dress codes in Iran, political alliances in Malaysia, the production and distribution of liquor in certain Muslim countries, and the acceptance of interest, banking, insurance, and mortgages in many Islamic nations. Abu- Rabi (1997) further emphasizes the impact of Western influence on education, stating that Western powers have established educational and scientific institutions within the heart of Islam. This has led to a deviation from traditional Muslim traditions and beliefs, as Muslims are indoctrinated to view anything Western as sacred and worthy of emulation. Consequently, these Western-educated Muslims often attain influential positions in society, exacerbating the challenging situation faced by the Muslim Ummah.

The concerns raised by Muslim scholars regarding certain observations are significant, as they have the potential to cause violence and conflict within Muslim communities. It is imperative that leaders of the Muslim Ummah address these issues with sensitivity and provide effective guidance on how to manage them. Rather than resorting to the simplistic approach of labelling Western education as Haram, it is crucial to find peaceful and tactful solutions to prevent a clash of civilizations.

The issue of the rise of misguided individuals who associate themselves with Islam is a matter of great concern, and it is significantly influenced by Islamophobia and Western media bias. These factors are perpetuated through various media platforms, including social media, and their impact on Muslims globally cannot be underestimated. The Western Media, particularly following the September 11, 2001 terrorist attack at the World Trade Centre, has been marked by anti-Muslim sentiment, which has only increased and intensified over time. This has led to a distorted perception of Islam and Muslims in the Western world, with some individuals holding the belief that Islam is inherently violent and that Muslims possess a predisposition towards terrorism and violence.

In the study conducted by Chamber (2021) regarding Anti-Muslim rhetoric, a Canadian conservative author named Steyn was cited. Steyn claims that the majority of Muslims either desire or display indifference towards the demise of the societies in which they reside. Additionally, the Dutch politician and right-wing populist Geert Wilders referred to the Qur'an as a source that inspires and justifies hatred, violence, and terrorism across the world, Europe, and America. Furthermore, the British conservative political commentator Douglas Murray suggested that in order to mitigate terrorism, the United Kingdom should adopt a more limited presence of Islam. Lastly, the American neuroscientist and new atheist Sam Harris firmly asserts that there exists a direct correlation between the teachings of Islam and acts of terrorism committed by Muslims.

Bill Maher, an American comedian and television producer, asserts that there is a common thread of intolerance and brutality that links 1.6 billion Muslims to extremist organizations such as ISIS. Similarly, Ayaan Hirsi Ali, a Somali-born Dutch American activist and writer, argues that violence is an inherent aspect of Islamic doctrine. These views, however, are unfounded and can be categorized as Islamophobia. Certain Western media outlets propagate these ideas, contributing to the spread of ignorance and hatred towards Muslims and Islam. Such rhetoric is both dangerous and unacceptable. It is crucial for our Muslim brothers and sisters to remain patient in the face of these baseless claims originating from certain Western media sources.

Leaders in the Muslim Ummah have a crucial role to play in raising awareness among their fellow brothers and sisters, cautioning them against succumbing to the provocations presented by certain Western media outlets. It is imperative that we have competent leaders who can effectively guide their followers towards embracing a genuine Islamic ethos, one that emphasizes tolerance and coexistence even with individuals of different religious beliefs or ideologies. In the face of distorted misrepresentations of Islam, both our leaders and followers should seek guidance from Allah/God. It is essential for all of us to place our trust in Allah/God when confronting the challenges that the Ummah encounters, whether they originate from the Western media or elsewhere. This necessitates the presence of capable leadership and followership. As members of the Muslim Ummah, we must refrain from engaging in the practices that Mhd Omar (2022) argues have contributed to the rise of terrorism and violent extremism, due to the global failure in controlling the ideology of political Islam. Such actions adversely impact the perception of Islam as a religion of peace and security. We must exercise caution in employing misguided methods, as our adversaries exploit them for their own propaganda and resort to derogatory labelling. The Muslim Ummah is in dire need of exemplary leadership, as demonstrated during the time of Prophet Muhammad (PBUH) and the era of the Rightly Guided Khalifs/Caliphs/Vicegerents/Successors.

In the Islamic Ummah we also need leaders who build good schools and Masajids and to this effect Ahmed (2014), argues that Muslim institutions such as madrasas and institutions of higher Islamic learning should incorporate a well-informed study of current world issues in their curriculum so that their graduates, in their future careers as religious and community leaders have Islamic worldviews and values. Therefore, for that to happen, Muslim leaders should remember first that Allah/

God is the originator of Leadership and that their role as leaders and followers are of a caretaker or representative of Allah/God on earth. i.e., Khalifah of Allah/God on earth as it is affirmed in surah Quran (2:30); (6:166); (38:26).

Throughout history, Muslim communities have made efforts to distance themselves from being labelled as terrorists or what the author refers to as "misguided brothers." They have chosen to pursue the democratic route in order to attain power or ascend to power. However, many of these endeavours have ultimately failed. This failure can be attributed to the ruling minority elites within the Muslim countries who receive support from major powers or certain Western powers that have vested interests in these regions.

For instance, in Algeria in 1991, the Islamic Salvation Front (FIS) party emerged victorious in the elections but was prevented from assuming governance. Similarly, in Palestine, Hamas won the election through democratic means but faced rejection from certain countries. The question arises: why was Hamas, which sought power in Palestine through the democratic process and obtained a mandate from its people, denied representation? This double standard is a fundamental issue that leads some individuals to resort to inappropriate methods in their fight against injustice, resulting in them being labelled as fundamentalists or, as the author terms them in this book, "misguided brothers and sisters." The rejection of the choice made by the Palestinian people in Gaza and other parts of the Muslim community is a cause for concern. In Egypt, the Muslim Brotherhood won the election freely through the democratic process, only to be ousted from office by a military coup. Surprisingly, this coup was accepted by Western powers, some regional allies, and even certain Muslim countries. The fact that these actors speak about democracy while turning a blind eye to a military coup against a democratically elected president is deeply troubling. This kind of double standard undermines the principles of democracy and raises significant concerns.

Several factors contribute to the emergence of misguided movements like the Muslim brotherhood, which resort to violence as a means to combat injustice. These problems or reasons provide fertile ground for individuals to take up arms in pursuit of their objectives. It is crucial, however, to find alternative approaches and avoid resorting to violence. As Muslim leaders and followers, our unwavering faith should be solely placed in Allah/God. Additionally, we can draw inspiration from the exemplary conduct of Prophet Muhammad (PBUH), the Rightly Guided Khalifs/Caliphs/Vicegerents/Successors, and other righteous leaders who faced similar challenges in their time. By learning from their methods, we can navigate the complexities of our present circumstances. Several countries with a Muslim majority have demonstrated success in implementing democratic processes in their governance. One such example is the Turkish political model, which, although not without flaws, represents the will of the majority of Muslims in Turkey. Despite differing opinions from some Western powers, the Turkish political model has followed a democratic route to power.

In the modern era, the Malaysian model incorporates Islamic perspectives, which serves as a beacon of hope for those seeking peaceful co-existence with others. Malaysia, a predominantly Muslim country, is an exemplar of democratic processes that allow political parties with Islamic ethos, such as the Pan-Malaysian Islamic Party (PAS), to participate in elections. PAS is permitted to contest elections as a political party, and if they win, they govern the state. If they win the general election, they can govern Malaysia as a political party. In essence, if the citizens of Malaysia support PAS and vote them into power, they form a government. These examples are few but serve as models to emulate, avoiding situations where Islamic political parties are disbanded, forced underground, or labelled as terrorist organizations.

Once again, it is imperative for the Muslim Ummah to draw lessons from the exemplary model established by Prophet Muhammad (PBUH) when he founded the city-state of Madinah and formulated its constitution. Muslim leaders and followers should adopt the Madinah constitution as a blueprint for their governance, and this can be achieved by encouraging Muslim intellectuals to thoroughly study the Madinah constitution. By doing so, we can gain valuable insights and utilize it as a framework for governing our diverse communities, societies, and nation-states. It is crucial for majority Muslim countries to coexist harmoniously with non-Muslims and those who hold different ideologies or religious beliefs. During the time of Prophet Muhammad (PBUH) in Madinah, Muslims and non-Muslims coexisted peacefully, without any harm inflicted upon either party or their properties, including their places of worship such as churches and synagogues. Therefore, it is essential to engage in dialogue, even in the presence of ideological differences.

The challenges faced by Muslim communities, such as the Sunni-Shia divide, the Kurdish issue, the Yazidi predicament, and others, necessitate a thoughtful approach. The history of Islam teaches us that in Madinah, Jewish tribes lived in harmony and were protected by the Islamic city-state, without facing any harm. However, in contemporary times, some Muslims with misguided ideologies refuse to coexist with others, which is a cause for concern. These differences in faith have unfortunately contributed to the emergence of fundamentalism or misguided individuals within Muslim communities. During Prophet Muhammad's (PBUH) time in Madinah, there were ideological differences between the Muslim and non-Muslim countries or empires. One of the things the Prophet (PBUH) used to do was to invite other nations to accept Islam. If they refused because of different ideologies, he cooperated with them because there was no compulsion in religion. See Surah Al-Baqarah (2:256) as translated in English by Khan and Al Hilali (1996, p.65) 256 "There is no compulsion in religion. Verily the Right Path has become distinct from the wrong path. Whoever disbelieves in Taghut and believes in Allah, then he has grasped the most trustworthy handhold that will never break. And Allah is All-Hearer, All-Knower. The next chapter focuses on the Purpose of Creation and Influence Leadership from an Islamic Perspective.

Chapter 6

The Purpose of Creation and Influence Leadership from an Islamic Perspective

The significance of the purpose of creation in Islam cannot be overstated, as it profoundly impacts leadership within the Islamic context. Consequently, the Islamic perspective on the purpose of creation assumes a crucial role in religious discourse and leadership. This viewpoint serves to elucidate the foundational beliefs and principles that govern the lives of Muslims, shaping their comprehension of existence and the role of humanity within it. To fully grasp the purpose of creation from an Islamic standpoint, it is imperative to delve into the fundamental principles of Islamic theology and delve into the teachings of the Quran and the Hadith, which encompass the Sunnah of the prophet (PBUH).

In Islamic doctrine, the fundamental reason for existence is firmly grounded in the principle of tawhid, which denotes the conviction in the singular nature of Allah/God. Muslims hold a steadfast belief that Allah/God intentionally brought about the cosmos and all its constituents with a distinct objective. This objective is intricately intertwined with the concept of devotion, as human beings are regarded as Allah/God's representatives on Earth, bestowed with the duty of carrying out His instructions and faithfully following His guidance. The Quran, the holy book of Islam, emphasizes the purpose of creation by stating that Allah created human beings and jinn solely for the purpose of worshiping

Him. This act of worship encompasses various dimensions, including prayer, fasting, charity, and adherence to moral and ethical principles. By engaging in acts of worship, Muslims as leaders and followers seek to establish a deep connection with Allah/God, purify their souls, and attain spiritual growth.

Muslims are encouraged to actively contribute to society in a positive manner, with a focus on promoting justice, compassion, and the overall betterment of humanity. This entails fulfilling one's obligations towards their family, community, and the wider world, while upholding the principles of fairness, honesty, and kindness. From an Islamic perspective, the purpose of creation also includes the concept of accountability. Muslims firmly believe in the Day of Judgment, where every individual will be held responsible for their actions in this life. As both leaders and followers, Muslims should be mindful of these beliefs and take responsibility for their deeds. This belief serves as a motivation for Muslims to lead a righteous and virtuous life, as they strive to attain salvation and eternal happiness in the afterlife. Therefore, the purpose of creation, according to Islamic teachings, revolves around the belief in the oneness of Allah/God and the act of worship. Muslims perceive themselves as the representatives of Allah/God on Earth, as stated in Surah Al Baqarah (2:30), and they are entrusted with the responsibility of fulfilling His commands and following His guidance.

The purpose of existence encompasses both the individual and societal realms, underscoring the significance of making positive contributions to society and adhering to moral and ethical values. Moreover, the notion of accountability assumes a pivotal role, as adherents of Islam place their faith in the Day of Judgement. Consequently, the purpose of humanity's creation by Allah/God is unequivocally defined as the worship of Allah/God, a belief that finds affirmation in Surah 51.Adh- Dhariyat (51:56), and is translated into English by Al Hilali and Khan (1996, p.660), 56. "And I (Allah) created not the jinn and mankind except that they should worship Me (Alone). And also in Surah 21 Al Anbya (21:25), also as translated in English by Al Hilali and Khan (1996, p.410), 25. "And we did not send any Messenger before you (O Muhammad (PBUH) but We revealed to him (saying): La ilaha illa Ana [none has the right to be worship but I (Allah)], so worship Me (Alone and none else)." I have only created Jinns and men that they may serve Me."

Subsequently, Yusuf Ali (1989), also reflected on this very issue and affirm by the quote "Not a messenger did We send before thee without this inspiration sent by Us to him: that there is no God but I; therefore, worship and serve Me." The notion of creation for the leaders and followers of the Muslim Ummah is crucial in that they must lead their people knowing the purpose of creation and that guide them to be just and fair to those under their care as leaders of their own communities. By knowing how to serve Allah/God, leaders are bound to serve Allah/God and those under their authority very well indeed, hence the essence of this book which is to remind myself and those in authority in Muslims Ummah to be just faire and remember that whatever they do as leaders or followers they will be accountable in front of Allah/God on the Day of Judgement. Muslims leaders and follower must constantly remember the purpose of creation as part of their leadership and followership endeavours. Allah/God created humankind and gave him/her the mind to think with guidance to salvation throughout history, but many have rebelled. Of those who rebel, Allah/God salvation always goes astray.

Certain Muslim leaders and their followers hold the belief that their ascent to positions of power or leadership is solely attributed to their own capabilities and strength. However, it is crucial for them to acknowledge that these positions of authority are bestowed upon them by Allah/God.

They must bear in mind that they will be held accountable on the Day of Judgment, and if they have not acted righteously and sought forgiveness from Allah, they may face the consequences of hellfire (Jahannam). It is imperative for both leaders and followers within Muslim communities to strive for a state where there is no escape from the consequences of their actions. See Surah 23 Al-Mu'minun (23:99-100) as translated by Khan and Al Hilali (1996, p.440) 99, Until, when death comes to one of them (those who join partner with Allah), he says: "My Lord! Send me back, 100, "So that I may do good in that which I have left behind!" No! It is but a word that he speaks; and behind them is Barzakh (a barrier) until the Day of when they will be resurrected. Therefore we as followers and leaders must be very careful and take our duties carefully with diligent and tact.

Thus, the objective of leadership and followers and mankind in general is to worship Allah/God and to follow all the divine Laws that govern us all. If we all respect divine laws we will be in a position of leading others selfless purely for the pleasure of Allah/God which is the essence of this book. A Muslim is the mirror of his brother/sister and that is why I am writing this book as reminder for myself and other Muslims and non-Muslims brother of their obligation to Allah/God and that worshiping can be achieved by doing good deeds, refraining from evil, or indulging in unethical behaviour. Therefore, leader's and followers' activities can be an act of worship. Practicing simple things like being kind to neighbours, helping the elderly by assisting them even though they may not be part of immediate family, having good intentions, and sincerely seeking Allah's pleasure in all our undertakings. Prophet Muhammad (PBUH) said: "Greeting a person is charity. Helping a man onto his steed is charity. A good word is a charity. Every step taken on the way to performing prayers is charity. Removing an obstacle from the road is for others is charity. See Surah 14 Ibrahim (24-27) as translated in English by Khan and Al Hilali (1996, p.330) 24, See you not how Allah sets forth a parable? A goodly word as goodly tree, whose root is firmly fixed, and its branches (reach) to the sky (i.e. very high). 25Giving it fruit at all times, by the Leaves of it Lord, and Allah sets forth parables for mankind in order that they may remember. 26. And the parable of an evil word is that of an evil tree uprooted from the surface of earth, and having no stability. Allah Will keep firm those who believe, with the word that stand firm in this world (i.e. they will keep on worshiping Allah Alone and none else), and in the Hereafter. And Allah will cause to go astray those who are Zalimun (polytheists and wrong dowers), and Allah does what He wills.

Henceforth, it is imperative for the leaders and followers of the Muslim Ummah to embody the role of Khalif/Caliphs/Vicegerent/Successors and refrain from becoming Targut transgressors. Consequently, leadership within the Islamic context holds great significance, necessitating a comprehensive comprehension and adherence to divine laws, as well as recognizing the purpose behind creation.

Chapter 7

The Originator of Leadership from an Islamic Perspective

The concept of leadership in Islam is rooted in the belief that Allah/ God is the ultimate source of authority. The author strongly argues that the principles and teachings of leadership should be derived from the Quran, the Sunnah of the Prophet Muhammad, and the previous prophets sent by Allah/God. According to Islamic perspective, human beings are created by Allah/God to worship Him and to follow His Divine Laws. When discussing leadership from an Islamic standpoint, it is crucial to emphasize that Allah/God is the originator of leadership and that human beings are His representatives on earth.

The Prophets, starting from Prophet Adam (PBUH) to the final Prophet Muhammad (PBUH), serve as the best examples of Allah/God's representatives. They are all the best example of leadership from an Islamic perspective and a model to follow. They all demonstrated the highest standards of leadership through their teachings, actions, and character. Prophet Muhammad (PBUH) in particular exemplified a leadership style characterized by humility, compassion, justice, and wisdom. He serves as a role model for all Muslims to emulate. In this book, the author explores the various dimensions of leadership in Islam, including its spiritual, ethical, and practical aspects.

The author also highlights the significance of leadership in the Islamic tradition. Ultimately, the author strongly argues that the leadership legacy of Prophet Muhammad (PBUH) and the four Rightly Guided Caliphs continues to inspire and guide Muslims worldwide. Their examples provide a blueprint for effective and ethical leadership not only within Muslim communities but also for non-Muslim leaders who aspire to lead by example and serve as models for their respective societies. As Allah/God has granted mankind the responsibility of being His representatives on earth, it is imperative for individuals to emulate the examples set by the prophets and the four Rightly Guided Caliphs. By doing so, they can fulfil their role as leaders and contribute to the betterment of their communities and societies.

As Muslims worldwide, we believe that we are the Caliph or Vicegerent of Allah/God on earth. However, to truly represent Allah/God, we must follow the exemplary leadership of our beloved Prophet Muhammad (PBUH), the Messenger of Allah/God. His exceptional leadership qualities have had a transformative effect on the Muslim Ummah and are revered by all. He serves as a remarkable role model for us to emulate.

Numerous scholars from the Western world have reached a consensus regarding the unparalleled leadership exemplified by Prophet Mohammad (PBUH). For instance, De Lamartine (1854) expressed the utmost admiration for Prophet Muhammad (PBUH) when he asserted that, if the magnitude of purpose, the scarcity of resources, and the astonishing outcomes are the three criteria for human genius, no other historical figure can be compared to Muhammad. He was a philosopher, apostle, legislator, warrior, and conqueror of ideas. He restored rational beliefs and established a religion devoid of idolatry. Moreover, he founded twenty earthly empires and one spiritual empire.

Prophet Muhammad (PBUH) challenged prevailing beliefs in Makkah and Madinah during his time, even in the face of death threats, displaying unwavering determination. Despite numerous attempts to dissuade him from Islam by offering power, he never wavered. Thus, the Prophet of Allah/God possessed a clear vision and strategy for the advancement of Islam. He steadfastly upheld the truth while his followers faced the threat of death. One remarkable aspect of Prophet Muhammad's (PBUH) leadership qualities, shared by previous Prophets, is their continuous call for the worship of Allah/God alone. Additionally, Prophet Mohammad (PBUH) established an Islamic state in Madinah with a robust economic system, treating both Muslims and non-Muslims with fairness and justice. Regardless of their faith, he demonstrated impartiality towards all. The Prophet's duty was to convey the message of Allah/God to all of humanity, emphasizing the worship of Allah/God alone.

The Model of Leadership from an Islamic Perspective

The Islamic model of leadership is exemplified by Prophet Muhammad (PBUH), who was born in Makkah in the year 570 CE. According to Islamic tradition, Prophet Muhammad (PBUH) is considered the final prophet of the Abrahamic faith traditions, which include Judaism, Christianity, and Islam. He confirmed the monotheistic teachings of the prophets who came before him, such as Adam, Noah, Moses, and Jesus (peace be upon them). Prophet Muhammad's (PBUH) birth, known as the Mawlid, is celebrated by many on the 12th day of the third month of the Islamic lunar calendar, although the exact date of his birth is unknown. He was born in Mecca, which is now part of modern-day Saudi Arabia, on the 12th of Rabia' Ul-Awal, the third month of the Islamic calendar, in the year 570 of the Gregorian calendar.

According to the Quran, Allah has conveyed that Prophet Muhammed (PBUH) was sent to mankind as a source of mercy. The birth of Prophet Muhammed (PBUH) is considered to be the most significant blessing and favor bestowed upon our Ummah. It was an extraordinary event, and Allah sent numerous miraculous signs to the world, indicating the prophetic birth, many of which were unprecedented. The translation of Surah 21 Al Anbiya (21:107) by Khan and Al Hilali (1996, p.419) states that "107, And We have sent you, (O Mohammad (PBUH) not but a as a mercy for Alamin (mankind, jinn and all that exist).

Undoubtedly, the exemplary figure of leadership for the Muslim Ummah is none other than Prophet Muhammad (PBUH). In the face of adversity, including persecution and opposition from his adversaries, he made the momentous decision to migrate to Madinah, where he established the Islamic state. Nevertheless, his demise dealt a devastating blow to his followers, including the rightly guided Caliphs, who were left in a state of shock and disbelief, despite the Prophet Muhammad's (PBUH) repeated indications of his impending death. See surah Ali Imran (3:144) as translated into English by Khan and Al Hilali (1996, p.100) 144, Muhammad (PBUH) is not more than a Messenger, and indeed (many) Messengers have passed away before him. If he die or is killed, will you then turn back on your heels (disbelievers)? And he who turns back on his heels not the least harm will he do to Allāh; And Allāh will give reward to those who are grateful. This Surah show that Allah is the only one with eternal life. The death of the prophet was a shock to many of the prophet companions because the Prophet (PBUH) was their leader, guide, and above all, the Messenger of Allah/God. Umar Ibn Al-Khatab, along with other devoted followers, found it incredibly difficult to comprehend and process their emotions following the demise of the prophet. Umar, in particular, was overwhelmed with confusion and began addressing the people, vehemently denying the claims made by certain hypocrites who alleged that God's Messenger (PBUH) had passed away. Umar's inability to articulate his feelings stemmed from the realization that their esteemed leader and the Prophet of Allah/ God, Mohammad (PBUH), had departed from this world, leaving them without his invaluable guidance. In his distress, Umar even went as far as declaring that he would sever the head of anyone who dared to proclaim the death of the Messenger of Allah. Overwhelmed by his emotions, Umar drew his sword, using it as a means to intimidate those who spoke the uncomfortable truth about the prophet's demise. It is important to note that Umar was not the sole individual who experienced shock and disbelief upon learning of the prophet's passing. Abu Bakr, the prophet's father-in-law, also found himself in a state of astonishment, yet managed to maintain composure during this trying time.

Abu Bakr then went straight to his daughter Aisha the Prophet's wife, uncovered his face and knelt, and said; my father or my mother may be sacrificed for your sake. The one death God has decreed you shall experience; you now have had. You shall never die again." Abu Bakr then turned to Umar and others companions of the Prophet and said, "People, if any of you has been worshiping Muhammad, let him know that Muhammad is dead. He who worships God knows that God is always alive; He never dies." Abu Bakr remember the verse of the Quran they used to recite with the prophet which say that Allah is eternal and that death was a part for all the prophets who came before Prophet Mohammad (PBUH).

A strong leader who, when faced with the adversity of leadership, stands firm and that was the case with Abu Bakr. The loss of his spiritual leader and a Messenger of Allah was confusing yet a real as it is revealed in Surah 3 Ali Imran (3:144), Al Hilali and Khan (1996, p.100), 144. "Muhammad (PBUH) is no more than a Messenger, and indeed (many) Messengers have passed away before him. If he dies or is killed, will you then turn back on your heels (as disbelievers)? And he who turns back on his heels, not the least harm will he do to Allah; and Allah will give reward to those who are grateful." Abu Bakr recited the verse of the Quran above and it had some calming effect to some companions. But unfortunately, some Muslims who claimed to embrace Islam returned to vice and lawlessness after the passing of the prophet which was a significant challenges facing the leadership of Abu Bakr and other companions of the prophet. Abu Bakr dealt with those challenges with tact and diligent as the leader of the Muslim Ummah at the time.

Present leaders and followers of Muslim communities today should follow the example of the Abu Bakr and other guided Caliphs in facing challenges that are facing them today in their various Muslims communities. Leaders and follower of the Muslims Ummah today should take pride in the glorious history of Islam and also to follow the Quran and the Sunnah of our beloved prophet and they will not go astray. For example they should reflect on Surah 3 (Ali Imran (3:110), Al Hilali and Khan (1996, p.94), 110. "You [true believers in Islamic Monotheism, and real followers of Prophet Muhammad (PBUH) and his Sunnah are the best of people ever raised for humankind; you enjoin Al- Ma'ruf (i.e., Islamic Monotheism and all that Islam has ordained) and forbid Al-Munkar (Polytheism, disbelief and all that Islam has forbidden), and you believe in Allah. And had the people of the Scripture (Jews and Christians) believed, it would have been better for them;

among them are some who have Faith, but most of them are Al-Fasiqun (disobedient to Allah and rebellious against Allah's Command)." And also subsequently in Surah 2 Al Baqarah (2:143), Al Hilali and Khan (1996, p.37), 143. "Thus, We have made you [true Muslims-real believers of Islamic Monotheism, true followers of Prophet Muhammad (PBUH) and his Sunnah (legal ways)], a just (and the best) nation, that you be witnesses over mankind and the Messenger (Muhammad (PBUH) be a witness over you. And We made the Qiblah' (prayer direction) towards Jerusalem) which you used to face, only to test those who followed the Messenger (Muhammad (PBUH) from those who would turn on their heels (i.e., disobey the Messenger). Indeed, it was great (heavy) except for those whom Allah guided. And Allah would never make your Faith (prayers) to be lost (i.e., your prayers offered toward Jerusalem).

Indeed, Allah is full of kindness, the Most Merciful towards mankind." Thus, the model of leadership from the Islamic perspective is model on the Prophets, starting from prophet Adam (PBUH) right to the final Prophet of Allah/God prophet Muhammad (PBU) and the Rightly Guided Caliphs and some pious leaders. The Madinah constitution should also be model for Muslims leaders of the Ummah to learn, practiced and reflect upon for our various Muslim communities or societies.

Relationship between Caliphate and Monarchy from an Islamic Perspective.

The present chapter aims to explore the relationship between the Caliphate and Monarchy from an Islamic perspective. The Caliphate, as a political system, has been a significant feature of Islamic history, while Monarchy has been a prevalent form of governance in many parts of the world. This chapter discussion focus on the literature of Ibn Taymiyyah in his book translated by Adul-Haqq Ansari (2000), in which he discusses the relationship between Caliphate and the monarchy. In the translation of Ibn Taymiyah book by Adul-Haqq Asari (2000) he argued that the Caliphate as a system of governance would last thirty years, and then it would turn into a monarchy. That statement is affirmed by the narration that the "The Prophet said, "The Caliphate (Khilafah), on the pattern of the prophetic government (Khilafat an-Nubuwwah), will last for thirty years; after that, God will give His Kingdom or the government to whom he wills. The narration is supported by a Hadith from Abu Dawud, who recorded on the authority of 'Abdul-Warith and Al-'Awwam, "The Khilafah will last thirty years, then there will be a monarchy," or "The Khilafah will last thirty years, then it will turn to a monarchy."

According to Abdul-Haqq Ansari (Ibid), the duration of the rightly-guided Caliphate spanned thirty years and is widely accepted by various factions, including the 'fuqaha', the scholars of Sunnah, and the leaders of Sufism. Additionally, Ansari acknowledges that this belief is also held by the common Muslims. However, the author of this book presents an argument stating that even though the Caliphate concluded with the guiding caliphs, their exemplary leadership principles continue to resonate within the leaders and followers of the Muslim Ummah. The author emphasizes the importance of learning from their ideals and the principles set forth by the four guided Caliphs. The Caliphs served as the leaders of the Ummah, ensuring the implementation of Islamic state laws and the principles derived from the Quran, the Sunnah of the prophet, and the practices of the Rashidun Caliphs. According to Ridah (1922), it is argued that Islamic scholars should bear the responsibility of assisting the government in its tasks, while also possessing the authority to consistently assess and rectify the actions of the caliph, as well as provide moral guidance for the Islamic order. Ridah (1922) asserts that as long as the elected Caliph governs in accordance with Islamic principles and justice, it is the duty of all Muslims to comply and unite under his leadership. In the absence of an ideal Caliphate, Muslims are obligated to establish a "caliphate of necessity" – an Islamic state that may not fully meet the standards set by the four guided caliphs.

Muslim leaders and followers in our diverse communities should strive to embody the principles of the four guided Caliphs/Rashidun, regardless of our geographical location. The concept of the Islamic state transcends physical boundaries, as Muslims are part of the global Islamic community, known as the Ummah. Therefore, we should not wait for the establishment of a physical Islamic state to uphold the teachings of Islam, which emphasize the oneness of Allah/God, His prophets, and the guidance of the four Rightly Guided Khalifs.

Muslims, regardless of their location, should behave as if they are part of the Islamic community. This means that they should comply with the laws and regulations of their new country or society while maintaining their Muslim identity. It is essential for Muslim leaders and followers to actively promote harmony and prevent any form of chaos within the communities they coexist with. By doing so, they can create a sense of unity and make a positive contribution to the societies they are a part of. Given the diversity within Muslim communities and the presence of non-Muslim governments, it is not practical to establish an Islamic state or a unified Islamic nation. Therefore, it is necessary to follow the laws of the land. Nonetheless, it is crucial that we adhere to the principles and ideals of Islam, irrespective of whether we find ourselves in an Islamic state or Muslim communities. This commitment is exemplified by the practices during the era of the four guided caliphs. It is incumbent upon all of us to follow the principles derived from the teachings of the Quran and the Sunnah of the prophets, starting from Prophet Adam (PBUH) and culminating with the final prophet, Mohammad (PBUH), regardless of our geographical location. Those who hold positions of leadership within Muslim communities must acknowledge that their authority is a sacred trust bestowed upon them by Allah/God. They should exercise mindfulness in their actions and decisions, as they will be held accountable for them on the Day of Judgement.

According to Islamic beliefs, every individual is accountable for upholding social justice and eradicating exploitation as Allah/God has designated all of humanity as His Khalifs/Vicegerents on Earth. This responsibility extends to leaders and followers within the Muslim Ummah, who should seek guidance from knowledgeable and righteous Muslim scholars to fulfill their duties. These scholars have the responsibility to serve as moral guides to the Ummah, based on the Divine Laws (Shari'ah), and ensure that the Ummah remains united and follows the teachings observed during the era of the four guided caliphs. Despite the current divisions within the Islamic Ummah, it is important to remember the point made by Prophet Mohammad (PBUH) during his last sermon, which emphasizes the importance of unity and brotherhood among Muslims.

The prophet of Allah has reminded all Muslims of the two invaluable gifts he has left behind for us: the Quran and his Sunnah. As Muslims, it is our duty to firmly hold onto these two pillars, as emphasized by our beloved prophet Muhammad (PBUH), and not allow any religious differences to divide us. The Divine Laws, known as Sharia, should serve as our guiding principles in all aspects of our lives, whether we are leaders or followers within the Muslim community. It is crucial to understand that Sharia should not be solely entrusted to rulers or leaders of the Muslim Ummah, but rather, it should be supported by knowledgeable Muslim scholars (ulama) who can interpret and implement these laws appropriately wherever necessary. Despite the existence of various schools of thought within the Muslim Ummah, these differences should not create divisions among Muslims, regardless of their geographical location. Our challenge as Muslims lies in maintaining unity amidst our diverse perspectives, as our beloved prophet Muhammad (PBUH) warned us to adhere to the Quran and the Sunnah. It is important to recognize that there may be 72 or 73 sects (madhhab) within the Ummah, but the true followers are those who adhere to the Sunnah.

The enemies of Islam may attempt to exploit these divisions, making it even more crucial for us to follow the advice of our beloved prophet Muhammad (PBUH) and remain united despite our differences. Additionally, it is essential for us to select righteous leaders within our respective communities, regardless of whether we reside in an Islamic state or not. Any community where Muslims live, work, and pray becomes their own small Ummah or community. We should not wait for an exclusively Muslim community to label it as an Islamic or Muslim Ummah. Wherever we reside, it is already an Islamic Ummah or Muslim Ummah.

The significance of geographical location should not be overemphasized, but rather viewed as a means to an end. As such, the essence of Ummah should not be limited to a physical or geographical community, but rather a unifying spirit that binds us as Muslims regardless of our location. It is therefore imperative that our Muslim leaders in various communities exhibit honesty, truthfulness, loyalty, and empathy towards the vulnerable members of the society. Additionally, they should create a conducive environment, such as a mosque, where people can pray and offer charity to the less fortunate. Establishing prayer is a crucial aspect of the Muslim faith, as it provides an opportunity to worship Allah/God exclusively. See Surah 1 Al Fatiha (1:5), Al-Hilali and Khan (1996, p.12), "You (Alone) we worship, and you (Alone) we ask for help (for each and everything). Allah affirmed this in Surah 40 Ghafir (40:60), Al Hilali and Khan (1996, p.595-6), "And your Lord says: "Invoke Me, [i.e., Believe in My Oneness (Islamic Monotheism) and ask Me for anything] I will respond to your (invocation). Verily, those who scorn My worship [i.e., do not invoke Me, and do not believe in My Oneness (Islamic Monotheism)] they will surely, enter Hell in humiliation!"

In Surah 48, the Quran emphasizes the responsibilities of the leaders of the Muslim Ummah. These leaders are entrusted with the crucial tasks of establishing prayer and giving charity, while also placing their unwavering faith in Allah/God as their ultimate protector. It is imperative for these leaders to refrain from collaborating with evil forces in order to oppress their own citizens. Those who deny the truth and reject faith are akin to unbelievers. The Quran aptly describes such individuals or leaders as being lost in the depths of darkness within a vast ocean. See Surah 48, Al Fath (48:28-29), Al Hilali and Khan (1996, p.648), 28. "He is Who has sent His Messenger Muhammad (PBUH) with guidance and the religion of truth (Islam), that He may make it (slam) superior to all religions. And All-sufficient is Allah as a Witness. 29. Muhammad (PBUH) is the Messenger of Allah. And those who are with him are severe against disbelievers and merciful among themselves. You see them bowing and falling down prostrate (in prayer), seeking bounty from Allah and (His) Good Pleasure. The mark of them (i.e., of their Faith) is on their faces (foreheads) from the traces of prostration (during prayers). This is their description in the Taurat (Torah). But their description in the Injeel (Gospel) is like a (sown) seed which sends forth its shoots, then makes it strong, and becomes thick and it stands straight on its stem, delighting the sowers, that He may enrage the disbelievers with them. Allah has promised those among them who believe (i.e., all those who follow Islamic Monotheism, the religion of Prophet Muhammad (PBUH) till the Day of Resurrections) and do righteous good deeds, forgiveness, and a mighty reward (i.e., Paradise).

In a complementary commentary by Yusuf Ali (1989, p.1338), "The devotees of Allah wage war against evil, for themselves and for others; but to their brethren in the faith—especially the weaker ones—they are mild and compassionate: they seek out every opportunity to sympathize with them and help them."

Leaders in both Muslim and non-Muslim communities have a significant responsibility to act as vicegerents, serving their communities selflessly for the sake of Allah. To fulfill this role, they must first have faith in Allah and the Prophets who came before Prophet Muhammad (PBUH). They must also be prepared to fight against evil, establish prayer, protect the vulnerable, and show compassion towards those in need. By embodying these qualities, leaders can effectively serve their communities and fulfill their duty as vicegerents.

Prophet Mohammad (PBUH) warned his Ummah (Muslim communities) to be aware of what may happen after his death. In a Hadith, authentic (Sahih) and well-known (Mashhur), recorded in the Sunnah collections as cited in Abdul-Haqq Ansari (200, p.496), the Prophet said, "Those of you who live after me will see several controversies coming up, but you must follow my practice (Sunnah) and the practice of the right-minded and rightly-guided Caliphs after me. Stick to it and hold fast. Beware of innovations from a religious perspective; not every innovation is wrong, but that from a religious perspective is wrong. Allah knows everything, and his Deen is eternal, not for a specific time or place. The nest chapter is about the definition of leadership from an Islamic perspective.

Chapter 8

Definition of Leadership
from an Islamic Perspective

The concept of leadership in Islam is a comprehensive one that encompasses various dimensions and principles. It goes beyond mere exercise of authority or power, and instead emphasizes the responsibility entrusted to individuals who possess specific qualities and adhere to ethical standards. According to Islamic teachings, a leader is expected to demonstrate a strong sense of justice, wisdom, and integrity. These qualities are considered crucial for effective leadership as they ensure fairness, sound decision-making, and ethical conduct. Moreover, a leader in Islam is required to prioritize the welfare and well-being of their followers, as their main objective is to serve and guide them towards righteousness and truth.

The Islamic viewpoint on leadership places great emphasis on the value of consultation and collective decision-making. This approach encourages leaders to actively seek the opinions and advice of their subordinates, thereby fostering a sense of inclusivity and participation within the organization or community activities. Henceforth, involving others in the decision-making process, leaders can benefit from a diverse range of perspectives, ultimately enhancing the overall effectiveness of their leadership. It is important to note that the Islamic perspective on leadership extends beyond the mere pursuit of personal or organizational goals. Instead, it is regarded as a means to fulfill the greater purpose of serving humanity and promoting social justice.

Islamic leaders are expected to embody qualities such as compassion, empathy, and selflessness, as they strive to alleviate the suffering of others and contribute to the betterment of society as a whole. Consequently, the Islamic perspective on leadership encompasses a holistic approach that underscores the significance of ethical conduct, justice, consultation, and service to others. The Islamic perspective transcends the exercise of authority and power, highlighting the importance of character and values in effective leadership. By adhering to these principles, Islamic leaders have the ability to inspire and guide their followers towards the achievement of collective goals, thereby fostering a just and harmonious society.

Leadership, as viewed through an Islamic lens, is characterized by selfless devotion solely for the satisfaction of Allah/God. According to the Quran Surah Al Baqarah (2:30), the leader and the followers are considered as the Khalifah/Caliph/vicegerent/Imamah of Allah/God on this earthly realm.

The relationship between a leader and a follower is founded upon the willingness to carry out a selfless duty of servitude solely for the sake of Allah/God. As a result, this relationship is characterized by selflessness and reciprocity. The primary responsibility of the leader is to enforce the laws of Allah/God on Earth, and these Divine Laws (sharia) aid the leader in resolving the issues faced by the followers. Since their relationship is mutual, the leader becomes righteous in the eyes of the followers by fulfilling this duty, as leadership is considered a trust (Amanah). Failure to fulfill this duty will result in the leader being held accountable on the Day of Judgment. It is crucial to recognize that, from an Islamic standpoint, leadership is a trust and responsibility bestowed upon an individual within the Islamic Ummah, requiring them to exercise it with utmost care and diligence, while adhering to the laws and commandments of Allah/God as outlined in the Quran and Sunnah of the Prophet (PBUH).

Moten (2011) defines leadership in Islam as "A moral activity and a process of communication between equals directed towards the achievement of a goal. The leaders are primarily distinguished from the followers by their knowledge, commitment to the Islamic principles, and possession of superior moral values." He further states, "Neither party uses power to influence and gain an advantage over the other. Thus, the goal of leadership in Islam is selfless servitude and, simultaneously, a sense of worshiping Allah/God. Leadership position must be seen as a trust, privilege, and responsibility to serve, not as an opportunity to appropriate or enrich oneself for his close family and their allies or collaborators.

In Islam, both leaders and followers are considered as khalifah or vicegerents on earth. Their primary duty is to serve mankind selflessly, solely for the pleasure of Allah or God. This concept of selfless service can be traced back to the previous Prophets, starting from Adam (PBUH) and continuing through the final Prophet Muhammad (PBUH) and his guided Caliphs. It is important to note that these individuals did not assume the role of Caliphs with the intention of enriching themselves, but rather to serve the Muslim communities with sincerity and devotion to Allah/God as did Prophet Muhammad (PBUH) himself who was an exemplary figure, known for his inspiring manner and high moral standards. Even before his prophet hood, he was recognized by his tribe members as Al-Amin, meaning "the Trustworthy." So Allah says in Surah 68: Al-Qalam (68:4), as translated into English by Al- Hilali and

Khan (1996, p.719), "And verily, you (O Muhammad (PBUH) are on an exalted (standard of) character." Prophet of Allah/God Mohammad (PBUH), as being the final prophet of Allah/God on earth was sent (by Allah) to perfect sublime morals. Furthermore, when Aisha, the wife of the Prophet (PBUH) (May Allah be Pleased with Her), was asked to describe the manners and morals of the Prophet Muhammad (PBUH), she said, as noted earlier, "His morals were the morals of the Quran."

This means that all the Prophet's morals and manners are the actualizations of the precepts given in the Quran. Therefore, his daily life activities were an accurate picture of the Quranic teachings. That is why prophet Muhammad (PBUH) is a leadership model to follow by all irrespective of origin and faith. Hence, the meaning of the word 'moral' covers all human actions, man's behavior toward men, others, and his creator. The Prophet (PBUH) was a Messenger, father, and army general. He created a city-state in Madinah. The Prophet Mohammad (PBUH) ate with his companions and sought consultation from them when needed, as in the case of the battle of Uhud and other events in his life. He always seek consent from his companions. If Prophet Muhammad (PBUH) were not married, he would have left his one nation-state Ummah (Muslim communities) unguided on how to be a good and affectionate loving father. Thus, in the example of his life, we can follow a practical example as a perfect model to follow by all.

Prophet Muhammad (PBUH) was the leader of his community, a selfless servant, and a Messenger from Allah/God to his people and to all believers in Islam. He led by example and brought the truth to his people and the community he led. This is affirmed in Surah 17: Al Isra (17:81-2), as translated into English by Al Hilali and Khan (1996, p.365), 81. "And say: Truth (i.e., Islamic Monotheism or this Quran or Jihad against polytheism) has come, and Batil (falsehood, i.e., Satan or polytheism) has finished. Surely, Batil is ever bound to vanish. 82. And We send down of the Quran that which is a healing and a mercy to those who believe (in Islamic Monotheism and act on it), and it increases the Zalimun (polytheists and wrongdoers) nothing but loss." Only those who rebel against Allah's laws will suffer loss. The more they oppose the truth, the deeper down they will go into sin and wrath, which is worse than destruction. The Quran describes falsehood as darkness in the more bottomless ocean, where there is no light. Leadership from an Islamic perspective require to establish truth and shown falsehood because falsehood is bound to vanish. The Quran and Sunnah of the Prophet (PBUH) is enough for us all as it is a mercy for those who believe.

Background and Influence of the Definition of Leadership from an Islamic Perspective.

Background and influence of the definition of leadership from an Islamic perspective is the Quran and the Sunnah of the prophets starting from Adam (PBUH) on till the final prophet of Allah/God, prophet Mohammad (PBUH). This requires that leaders and followers from the Islamic perspective should follow the divine laws (sharia) since they are all Allah/God representative on earth, i.e. khalifas/vicegerent of Allah/God on earth.

Leaders and followers should have the willingness and selflessness to serve those they lead. Allah's willingness to appoint humankind as His representatives on earth is a great gift and honor to mankind. Therefore, a leader's and follower's action should reflect the gift, gratitude, and trust placed on them by Allah/God. One of the way Humankind has expressed his gratitude to Allah/God is affirm in Surah 1: Al Fatihah (1:5-7), as translated into English by Al Hilali and Khan (1996, p.9- 10), 5. "You (Alone) we worship, and you (Alone) we ask for help (foe each and everything). 6. Guide us to the Straightway. 7. The Way of those on whom You have bestowed Your Grace, Not (the way) of those who earned Your Anger (Such as the Jews), nor those who went astray (such as Christians)." We can also see in Surah AlBaqarah 2 (2:3) when Allah/ God had affirms his gift to us as being his representative on earth and even the Angels were surprised of such a gift to mankind to who they refers to as those who shed blood as if they deserve it more than mankind.

We can also learn a lesson from Surah 2: Al Baqarah (2:124), as translated into English by Al-Hilali and Khan (1996, p.32), "And (remember) when the Lord of Ibrahim (Abraham) [i.e., Allah] tried him with (certain) Commands, which he fulfilled. He (Allah) said (to him), "Verily, I am going to make you an Imam (a leader) for humankind (to follow you)."[Ibrahim (Abraham)] said, "And of my off spring (to make leaders)." (Allah) said, "My Covenant (Prophet Hood) includes not Zalimun (polytheists and wrongdoers)."

The covenant that humankind made with Allah/God also influences the definition of leadership in this book. This covenant with Allah is affirmed in Surah 7: Al A'raf (7:172-3), as translated into English by Al- Hilali and Khan (1996, p.223), 172. "And (remember) when your Lord brought forth from the Children of Adam, from their loins, their seed (or from Adam's loin his offspring) and made them testify as to themselves (saying): "Am I not your Lord?" They said: "Yes! We testify," (this), lest you should say on the Day of Resurrection: "Verily, we have been unaware of this." 173. Or lest you should say: It was only our fathers for time who took others as partners in worship along with Allah, and we were (merely they are) descendants after them; will You then destroy us because of the deeds of men who practiced Al-Batil (i.e., polytheism and committing crimes and sins, invoking and worshiping others besides Allah)?" (Tafsir At Tabari).

Prophet Muhammad (PBUH) explained that "when Allah created Adam, he took from him a covenant at a place called Na'maan on the 9th of the 12th month (Dhul Al Hijah). He then extracted from Adam all of his descendants who would be born until the end of the world, generation after generation, and spread them out before Him to take a covenant from them also. He spoke to them, face to face, making them bear witness that He was their Lord." Consequently, every human being is responsible for belief in God, which is imprinted on each and every soul, Bila Philips (1995, p.27). The covenant becomes innate in human nature, although he/she may disbelieve in Allah/God. So, for example, when something traumatic happens to even atheists, they will start to say, "O my God, O my God" why do they say that when they say they do not believe in Allah/God.

The purpose of creation is affirmed in Surah 51: Al Dhariyat (51:56), as translated in English by Al Hilali and Khan (1996, p.660), 56. "And I Allah created not the Jinn's and mankind except that they worship Me (Alone)." And in Surah 6: Al Anam (6:102), as translated into English by Al Hilali and Khan (1996, p.186), 102. "Such is Allah, your Lord! La ilaha illa Huwa (none has the right to be worshiped but He), the Creator of all things. So worship Him (Alone), and He is the Wakil (Trustee, Disposer of affairs or Guardian) over all things." In Surah 11: Hud (11:123), as translated into English by Al-Hilali and Khan (1996, p.294), 123. "And To Allah belongs the Ghaib (unseen) of the heavens and the earth, and to Him return all affairs (for decision). So worship Him (O Muhammad (PBUH) and put your trust in Him. And your Lord is not unaware of what you (people) do."

Allah/God say as in Surah 40: Al Ghaafir (40:57), as translated into English by Al-Hilali and Khan (1996, p.595), 57. "The creation of the heavens and the earth is indeed greater than the creation of mankind;

yet, most of mankind know not." In Yusuf Ali's (1989, p.1221) comment on the above verse 4431, he argues that "The heavens and the earth include humankind and all other creatures and millions of stars. Man is himself but a tiny part of creation. Why should he be egocentric? The whole is greater than a tiny part of it. Moreover, Allah, Who created the whole world, can do many more wonderful things than can enter man's imagination. Therefore, why should man be arrogant, doubt the Day of Judgement, and take it upon himself to doubt the possibility of Allah's Revelation? It is because he has made himself blind."

If leaders and followers do their duties and fulfill their responsibilities through worship or selfless servitude purely for the pleasure of Allah/ God, they will not be selfish or greedy. On the contrary, they will be responsible toward others, devote their attention to Allah, wage war against evil, and protect the weak within their communities, for they all know that they will face Allah and be accountable for all their deeds. Muslims accept that Islam is a way of life that provides them with guidance, such as cleanliness, trade rules, conflict resolution, politics and the structure of society, the role of law, and other issues in life. Islam cannot be separated from social, cultural, economic, and political life since religion offers moral guidance for every action a leader or a follower takes within society or community.

Thus, the critical act of faith in Islam is to implement Allah's will in both public and private life. The total submission of one will to Allah is Islam. Therefore, Muslims must do so by avoiding evil and enjoining what is right in their various communities. To avoid evil and believe in Allah is affirmed in Surah 3 Ali Imran (3:110), Al- Hilali and Khan (1996, p.94), 110. "You [true believers in Islamic Monotheism, and real followers of Prophet Muhammad (PBUH) and his Sunnah are the best of people ever raised for mankind; you enjoin Al-Maruf (i.e., Islamic Monotheism and all that Islam has ordained) and forbid (Munkar (polytheism, disbelief and all that Islam has forbidden), And had the people of the Scripture (Jews and Christians) believed, it would have been better for them; among them are some who have Faith, but most of them are Fasiqun (disobedient to Allah and rebellious against Allah's Commands)." Allah is the only sovereign in Islam, and his laws should be obeyed. See Surah 7 Al-Araf (7:54), as translated into English by Al Hilali and Khan (1996, p.207), 54. "Indeed your Lord is Allah, who created the heavens and the earth in Six Days, and then He rose over (Istawa) the Throne (really in a manner that suits His Majesty). He brings the night as a cover over the Day, seeking it rapidly, and (He created) the sun, the moon, and the stars subject to His Commandment. Blessed is Allah, the Lord of the Alamin (mankind, jinn, and all that exist)." In Islam, there is no distinction between religion and state authority.

Today some leaders fail to believe in Allah. To some, their powers are due to their efforts and nothing less than their powers. No! They shall be accountable for their deeds and their followers' deeds on the Day of Judgment, even if they do not believe. Allah made it very clear in verse (40:58, Ibid) "Not equal are the blind and those who (clearly) see; nor are (equal) those who believe and work Deeds of righteousness, and those who do evil. So little do ye learn by admonition!"

Chapter 9

Prophets/Leaders Who Were Sent To Various People By Allah/God On Earth And They Reject Their Prophets/ Leaders Send By Allah/God And Their Consequences As Revealed In Quran.

The focus of this chapter is on the prophets and leaders who were chosen by Allah/God to provide guidance and instruction to various communities on earth. This chapter delves into the unfortunate occurrence of those individuals facing rejection and disbelief from the very people they were sent to guide. Additionally, this chapter examines the consequences that result from such rejection, as outlined in the Quran.

There are numerous instances of individuals who refuse to accept the prophets or leaders sent by Allah/God to their respective communities. One such notable example is found in Surah 7: Al Araf (7:59), where the story of Nuh (Noah) and his people is recounted. This account, as translated into English by Al Hilali and Khan, serves as an excellent illustration of this phenomenon, (1996, p.207), 59. "Indeed, We sent Nuh (Noah) to his people, and he said: "O my people! Worship Allah! You have no other Ilah (God) but Him. (la iIaha illahah: none has the right to be worship but Allah) Certainly, I fear for you the torment of a Great Day!" The people of Nuh (Noah) rejected Him as a leader and Allah/God who send him to call to the oneness of Allah/God.

The account of the people of Nuh (Noah) serves as a poignant reminder to both leaders and followers that our responsibilities and obligations to others should be taken with utmost seriousness, akin to acts of worship. It is imperative to adhere to the teachings of the Quran and the Sunnah of the prophet. The story of Prophet Nuh (PBUH) (Noah) and his people holds significant value in the study of leadership from an Islamic perspective. Prophet Nuh (PBUH) called upon his people to worship Allah alone and abandon their polytheistic beliefs. He warned them of the dire consequences that would ensue if they persisted in their rejection of his message and continued to engage in wrongdoing. Despite his unwavering efforts to guide them, only a handful of individuals, including his family members, embraced his message and followed him. Eventually, Allah/God commanded Noah to construct an Ark to safeguard those who believed, as a great flood was unleashed to punish the disbelievers. See Surah 11 Hud(11:36-37) as translated into English by Al Hilali and Khan (1996, p.283), 36, "And it was revealed to Nuh (Noah): "None of your people will believe except those who have believed already. So be not sad because of what they use to do. 37, "And construct the ship under our Eyes and with Our Revelation, and call not upon Me on behalf of those who did wrong; they are surely, to be drowned. Also see Surah 71 Nuh (71-1-4), as translated into English by Al Hilali and Khan (1996, p.730), 1, Verily, We send Nuh (PBUH) Noah to his people (saying): "Warn your people before there comes to them a painful torment." 2, He said: "O my people! Verily I am a plain warner to you, 3, "That you should worship Allah (alone), be dutiful to Him, and obey me. 4, He (Allah) will forgive you of your sins, and respite you to an appointed term. Verily, the term of Allah when it comes, cannot be delayed, if you but knew." The above Quran verses show to us as leaders and followers how the people of Prophet Nuh (PBUH) (Noah) rejected his message of Allah/God and the consequences of their rejection.

Islam is not limited to the Arab nations alone; it is a global religion that encompasses believers from all walks of life. The universality of Islam is evident in the fact that the Holy Qur'an does not solely address the Quraysh or the Arab nation, but rather it speaks to all individuals, regardless of their nationality or background. This affirmation further solidifies the inclusive nature of Islam, emphasizing its universal appeal and relevance to all people and it is affirmed in Surah 7 Al-A'raf (7:158) as translated into English by Al Hilali and Khan (1996, p.220), 158, Say (O Muhammad (PBUH): O mankind! Verily, I am sent to you all as the Messenger of Allah-to Whom belongs the dominion of the heavens and the earth. La ilaha illa Huwa (none has the right to be worshiped but He). It is He who gives life and causes death. So believe in Allah and His Messenger (Muhammad (PBUH), the prophet who can neither read nor write (i.e. Muhammad (PBUH) who believe in allah and His Words [(this Quran), the Taurat (Torah) and the Injeel (Gospel) and also Allah's Words: "Be!"-and he was, i.e. Isa (Jesus) son of Maryam (Mary) (AS), and follow him so that you may be guided.

The above verse show that the Holy Prophet declaration that his mission was a universal is true even though he was from the Quraysh tribe and Arab. See Surah 34 Saba (34:28), as translated into English by Al Hilali and Khan (1996, p.542), 28, And We have not sent you (O Muhammad (PBUH) except as a giver of glad tidings and a warner to all mankind, but most of them know not. Also see Surah 2 Al-Baqarah (2:252), as translated into English by Al Hilali and Khan (1996, p.62), These are the Verse of Allah, We recite them to you (O Muhammad (PBUH) in truth, and surly, you are one of the Messenger (of Allah). See Surah 68Al-Qalam (68:52), Surah 36 Ya-Sin (36:69-70). Surah 9 Al-Taubah (9:33), Surhah 21 Al-Ambiya (21:107), as translated into English by Al Hilali and Khan (1996, p.419), And We have sent you (O Muhammad (PBUH) not but as a mercy for all the Alamin (Mankind, jiin and all that exist).

The revelation of these Holy verses occurred in Mecca, serving as evidence that the call to Islam was extended from its earliest stages, emphasizing its universal nature for all of humanity rather than being exclusive to Arabs. Despite this, there were numerous individuals who rejected these undeniable truths. Recognizing the universal essence of Islam, the Prophet took the initiative to send letters of invitation to various kings, urging them to embrace the faith. Among the recipients of these letters was al-Najashi, the ruler of Abyssinia, which is present- day Ethiopia.

The subsequent discussion pertains to those individuals who, in addition to the aforementioned, declined to embrace Islam and consequently faced the repercussions of rejecting the divine message of Allah/God to humanity. The people of Ad, under the guidance of the esteemed prophet Hud (peace be upon him), similarly turned away from both him and Allah/God, ultimately experiencing a fate akin to that of Noah (peace be upon him). Their narrative serves as a testament to the consequences of their refusal. See Surah 7: Al Araf (7:65-67), as translated into English by Al Hilali and Khan (1996, p.208), 65. "And to Ad (people, We sent) their brother Hud. He said: "O my people! Worship Allah! You have no other Ilah (God) buy Him. (la ilaha illalah: none has the right to be worshiped but Allah). Will you not fear (Allah)?" 66. The leaders of those who disbelieved among his people said: "Verily, We see you in foolishness, and verily, we think you are one of the liar." 67. Hud said: "O my people! There is no foolishness in me, but (I am) a Messenger from the Lord of Alamin (mankind, jinn, and all that exists)." Thus, the people of Ad, rejected prophet Hud and Allah/God message to them.

The story of the Thamud people with their Prophet Salih is also affirmed in Surah 7: Al A'raf (7:73-75), as translated into English by Al Hilali and Khan (1996, p.209). 73 And to Thamud (people, We sent) their brother

Salih (Saleh). He said: "O my people! Worship Allah! You have no other Ilah (God) but Him. (Lailaha illalaha: none has the right to be worshiped but Allah). Indeed, there has come to you a clear sign (the miracle of the coming out of a huge she-camel from the midst of a rock) from your Lord. This she-camel of Allah is a Sign unto you; so you leave her to graze in Allah's earth, and touch her not with harm, lest a painful torment should seize you. 74. And remember when He made you successors after Ad (people) and gave you habitations in the land, you build for yourselves palaces in plains and carve out homes in the mountains. So remember the grace (bestowed upon you) from Allah, and do not go about making mischief on the earth. 75. The leaders of those who were arrogant among his people said to those who were counted weak – to such of them as believed: "Know you that Salih (Saleh) is one sent from his lord." They said: "We indeed believe in that with which he has been sent." 76. Those who were arrogant said: "Verily, we disbelieve in that which you believe in." 77. So they killed the she- camel and insolently defied the Commandment of their Lord and said: "O Salih (Saleh)! Bring about your threats if you are indeed one of the Messengers (of Allah)." 78. So the earthquake seized them, and they lay (dead), prostrate in their homes." 80. Then he, Salih (Saleh), turned from them and said: "O my people! I have indeed conveyed to you the Message of my Lord and have given you good advice, but you like not good advisers."

The purpose of this book is to convey these narratives in order for both leaders and followers of the Muslim Ummah, as well as non-Muslims, to derive valuable lessons from them. It is crucial for us, as leaders and followers, to understand that we must wholeheartedly obey Allah/God and all the prophets chosen by Him, without any discrimination. These stories shed light on the prophets who were sent by Allah/God to guide their respective communities, and highlight the repercussions faced by those who rejected Allah/God's message and failed to comply with the teachings of these prophets.

The primary objective of this book is to serve as a constant reminder, both for myself and others, about the repercussions that arise from rejecting Allah/God. It emphasizes the notion that Allah/God has created us with the sole purpose of worshiping Him, particularly when we hold positions of leadership or are part of various communities. This book serves as an exceptional tool to reiterate the significance of adhering to the teachings of Allah/God and obeying the messages conveyed by all the prophets. Consequently, dedicating oneself solely to the worship of Allah/God is a virtuous path to follow. It is evident that adversaries of Islam are exerting immense pressure on Muslim leaders, urging them to embrace practices that are incompatible with Islamic principles. In light of this, it is crucial for our leaders and followers to exercise utmost caution and constantly remember Allah/God and the esteemed prophets, particularly Prophet Muhammad (PBUH). The truth should be followed by leaders and followers.

This book serves as a poignant reminder to both our leaders and followers, urging them to avoid the pitfalls faced by the prophets and their people who rejected Allah/God, and the dire consequences that followed. Whether within the Muslim Ummah or beyond, leaders and followers alike should exercise their rationality to steer clear of situations that compromise their faith and religious beliefs. While the allure of embracing other cultures may be strong, it is imperative for leaders and followers to remain steadfast in their adherence to the principles of Islam.

The renunciation of faith is a fallacy that holds no merit for any leader or follower, regardless of their location. An enlightening interview with

Egypt's Mufti in 1998 shed light on this matter, emphasizing the need for Muslims to be cautious in safeguarding themselves from the adverse effects of such expansion, while remaining cognizant of the peril of losing their distinct identity in the globalized world. We must not forsake our identity in our pursuit of interaction and coexistence with the Western world. As Muslim leaders and followers, we should not fear globalization, but rather strive to harness its potential for progress in the realms of science, economics, and wealth, all the while propagating the virtues of Islam.

There will always be those who endeavor to sow division among us by propagating negative narratives about Islam and the Muslims, and it is incumbent upon all of us to actively work towards changing these narratives. The writing of this book represents a personal endeavor to promote the noble virtues of Islam to those who are unaware, as well as to serve as a reminder to those who are already acquainted with the truth. Muslims in diaspora and those residing in various Muslim communities have a duty to make their voices heard, without feeling the need to apologize for Islam.

It is important for both leaders and followers within the Muslim Ummah to understand that those who reject Islam, regardless of their location, have no regard for the religion. This is evident in the Quranic verses that describe those who reject Allah/God and his prophets. These people did not heed the clear warnings given to them by Allah/God and their prophets. These disbelievers may worship various entities, such as money, power, false deities, or even membership in a cult or society. Allah has warned us about these disbelievers, as is affirmed in the Quran. See Surah 31: Luqman (31:7-8), as translated into English by Al Hilali and Khan (1996, p.512)7. "And when Our Verse (of the Quran) are recited to such a one, he turns away in pride, as if he heard them not – as if there were deafness in their ear. So announce to him a painful torment. 8. Verity, those who believe in Islamic Monotheism) and do righteous good deeds, for them are Gardens of Delight (Paradise)." Those who reject Allah, mock, or laugh will be responsible for their deeds. We should be aware of the tactics of the disbelievers towards our religion Islam.

These stories of those people who rejected Allah/God and their Prophets are many and in this book the author tried to share as many stories from the Quran as many as possible so that we can lean lessons from those stories. Hence the story of Lud (Lot) and also the story of the Madyan (Midian) people who rejected their Prophet Shu'aib as is confirmed in Surah 7: Al Araf (7:85-90), as translated into English by Al Hilali and Khan (1996, p.210), 85. And to (the people of) Madyan (Midian), (We sent) their brother Shu'aib. He said:"O, my people! Worship Allah! You have no other Ilah (God) but Him. [la illaha illallah (none has the right to be worship but Allah)." Verily, a clear proof (sign) from your Lord has come unto you; so give full measure and full weight and wrong not men in their things, and do not do mischief on the earth after it has been set in order, that will be better for you, if you are believer. 86. "And sit not on every road, threatening, and hindering from the path of Allah those who believe in Him, and seeking to make it crooked. And remember when you were but few, and He multiplied you. And see what was the end of the Mufsidun (mischief-maker, corrupters, liars). 87…

90. The chiefs of those who disbelieved among his people said (to their people): "if you follow Shu'aib, be sure then you will be the losers!" But as Verse (7:91), Stated, "So the earthquake seized them and they lay (dead), prostrate in their homes."

The story of Moses and Pharaoh as narrated in the Surah 28: Al Qasas (28:3-5), as translated into English by Al Hilali and Khan (1996, p.486),

3. "We recite to you some of the news of Musa (Moses) and Fir'aun (Pharaoh) in Truth, for a people who believe (in this Quran, and in the Oneness of Allah). 4. Verily Firaun (Pharaoh) exalted himself in the land and made its people sects, weakening (oppressing) a group (i.e., Children of Israel) among them: killing their sons and letting their female live. Verily, he was of the Mufsidun (i.e., those who commit great sins and crimes, oppressors, tyrants). 5. And we wished to do a favor to those who were weak (and oppressed) in the land, and to make them rulers and to make them inheritors."

The repercussions of Pharaoh's rejection of Allah are evident and serve as a valuable lesson for all. In contemporary times, numerous leaders engage in acts of violence against their own people or initiate wars without valid justifications, solely relying on their superpower status to act with impunity and no one condemn such an act as being inhumane and barbaric, but rather they use such crudity as an act of self-defense. How could leaders of the world be indifference when it come to the killings of children's and caped bombing of the civilian in the name of self-defense? Shockingly, these leaders often escape condemnation and remain untouched by the international court of justice. Astonishingly, some of these leaders even manage to secure re-election despite their heinous crimes against humanity and lack of respect for the international laws.

Presently, some leaders resort to warfare as a means to showcase the might of their military machinery and how strong is their army and the intelligence service. However, it is crucial to acknowledge that Allah/God is not oblivious to these actions, even if we, as followers, may be blinded by our own biases. It is imperative for both our leaders and their followers to deeply contemplate and draw insights from the accounts of those who rejected Allah/God and the Messengers, Prophets, or leaders sent by Allah/God.

Leaders and followers should understand that good leaders and followers are those who adheres to Surah 6: Al Anam (6:162), as translated into English by Al-Hilali and Khan (1996, p.198), 162. "Say (O Muhammad (PBUH) "Verily, my Salat (prayer), my sacrifice, my living, and dying are for Allah, the Lord of the Alamin (mankind, jinn, and all that exist)." These are verses that we want our leaders and followers to adhere to. To this effect Allah/God reassured all of us in Surah 2: Al Baqarah (2:286), as translated by Al-Hilali and Khan (1996, p.74), that 286. "Allah burden not a person beyond his scope. He gets reward for that (good) which he has earned, and he is punished for that (evil) which he has earned. "Our Lord! Punished us not if we forget or fall into error, our Lord! Lay not on us a burden like that which You did not lay on those before us (Jews and Christians); our Lord! Put not on us a burden greater than we have strength to bear. Pardon us and grant us Forgiveness. Have mercy on us. You are our Maula (Patron, Supporter and Protector) and give us victory over the disbeliever people."

Allah/God does not burden a soul beyond its capacity. And that with difficult situations which humans face in life will not be without intervals of rest. See, Surah 94: Al Sharh or Ash-Sharh (94:5-6), Al- Hilali and Khan (1996, p.778), 5. "Verily, along with every hardship is a relief, 6. Verily, along with every hardship is relief." (I.e., there is one hardship with two reliefs, so one hardship cannot overcome two reliefs). Allah/God reassures us all as leaders/followers that whatever difficulties or troubles we encounter as humankind, He always provides a solution and a way out, a relief and a way to happiness if they only follow His path and show faith by patience. See Surah 94. Ash-Sharh (94:8) as translated into

English by Al Hilali and Khan (1996, p.778), Allah Said: 8. "And to your Lord (Alone) turn (all your) intentions and hopes." In Allah/God we trust. Therefore good leaders should be those who believe and do deeds of righteousness and understand that the original leader is Allah/God and that we are only Allah/God representatives on earth.

It is imperative for any leader or follower of an institution or organization, regardless of its nature, to be a devout believer in Allah/God and to prioritize selfless servitude solely for the pleasure of Allah/God. A good leader/follower is a representative of Allah/God on earth and should possess qualities such as humility, trustworthiness, honesty, and justice. Their obedience should first and foremost be to Allah and the Prophet Muhammad (PBUH), while simultaneously dedicating their services to Allah/God and the people they serve. A responsible leader/follower will utilize their power and position for the greater good, rather than to exert control over others. They will establish places of worship and education systems that bring people closer to Allah/God. The duties and responsibilities of leaders and followers should be carried out solely for the pleasure of Allah/God, and not for personal gain or recognition.

A true leader or vicegerent is one who possesses the ability to give and receive love, and whose devotion is towards the glorification of Allah/God. This is why Allah/God affirms our vicegerent status in the Quran. See Surah 2: Al Baqarah (2:30), as translated into English by Al Hilali and Khan (1996, p.16), 30. "And remember when your Lord said to the angels: "Verily, I am going to place (mankind) generations after generations on earth." They said: "Will You place therein those who will make mischief therein and shed blood, while we glorify You with praises and thanks and sanctify you." He (Allah) said: I know that which you do not know." In this Surah 2 Al Baqarah (2:30) Allah/God addressed humankind in general without distinction as vicegerent of Allah/God on earth. Therefore being Allah/God representative on earth is a noble course and should be seen as leading humanity toward the truth of believing in the oneness of Allah, for the originator of leadership is Allah/God and made us all his representatives. The prophets, especially prophet Mohammad (PBUH) is known as one the "Best of Creation" (Khayru-l-Khalq) as this assertion is affirmed in Surah 3: Ali Imran (3:110), Yusuf Ali (1989, p.155), "Ye are the best of peoples, evolved for mankind, enjoining what is right, forbid what is wrong, while also believing in Allah. If only the people of the Book had faith, it were best for them: among them are some who have faith, but most of them are perverted transgressors."

As the representative of Allah/God on earth, we are the finest creation tasked with promoting righteousness and prohibiting wrongdoing while also having faith in Allah/God alone. This is why Allah has bestowed upon all Muslims the honour of being the best nation, community, and group of people. As one nation, the Ummah (Islamic/Muslim communities) holds a unique position. This perfect Ummah is blessed with the wisdom of Allah/God's laws (Sharia). The worship of Allah/God alone is the ultimate goal of all Muslim communities, regardless of their location. However, this does not mean that Muslims should not strive to create an Islamic state where they are the majority. This was evident in Medina, where an Islamic state was established despite the presence of non-Muslims. In situations where Muslims are a minority and cannot establish an Islamic state, they should live their lives normally and abide by the laws of the land they reside in. However, this does not mean that they should abandon their Muslim way of life. For instance, the recent ban on Hijab for Muslim students in France highlights the need for Muslim communities to establish their own schools where their children can receive a good education while also functioning normally in their country of residence. Rather than fighting against a system that is prejudicial to their way of life, Muslims should learn how to function within it. Allah/God is All-Seeing and All-Knowing.

The challenge of constituting an Ummah, or a community of Muslims, in one place is well-known. This is due to various factors, including the creation of nation-states among Muslims, which has made it difficult to establish a vast piece of land designated solely for Muslims. These barriers pose a significant challenge to the concept of Ummah, as each nation seeks to provide for its own and may not want to share resources with other Muslim communities. Despite these challenges, Allah/ God has shown His gratitude to His Ummah by creating the cities of Makkah and Madinah as the only lands or cities where all Muslims can come together and experience the brotherhood of Islam. It is important to note that wherever Muslims may be living, working, studying, or engaging in any activities, they are still part of the Islamic Ummah. What unites us all is our belief in Allah/God as the one true God and that Muhammad (PBUH) is His Messenger. We all follow Divine laws and are representatives of Allah/God on earth. Regardless of our location in the world, we are all brothers and sisters because our vision, missions, and goals are the same: to worship Allah/God alone.

In order to become the best version of ourselves, we must follow the example set by Prophet Muhammad (PBUH). As Yusuf Ali (1989, p.155) explains, Islam is about submitting to the will of Allah/God, which involves having faith, doing what is right, setting a positive example for others, and actively working to promote justice and defeat injustice. As Allah's vicegerent, whether we are leaders or followers in our communities, it is our responsibility to be accountable and act in a noble and responsible manner. Allah has given us the gift of emotions, thoughts, and reflection, and it is through these abilities that we are able to do good, discourage evil, and maintain our faith in Allah/God. This concept of vicegerency is not unique to humans, as it is also confirmed in the story of David. See Surah 38: Sad (38:26), as translated into English by Al-Hilali and Khan (1996, p.572), 26. "O Dawud (David)! Verily, We have placed you as successor on the earth, so judge you between men in truth (and justice) and follow not your desire, for it will mislead you from the path of Allah. Verily, those who wander astray from the path of Allah (shall) have a severe torment because they forget the Day of Reckoning." Thus, these great gifts that Allah/God bestowed to Mankind is not to be a matter of self-glory by those who are in the position of leadership, but to use such a position to be just to others and not for them to follow their desires and because they will be judge on the Day of Reckoning. These means that leaders and even followers should be faithful, doing good, being right, being an example to others to follow and do right, having the power and will to see that right prevails, and also having powers to make sure that justice prevails, and injustice is defeated.

To be Allah/God representative on earth means to live a life of a Muslim, worship, and be just to other fellow human beings. That is why this trust should be maintained with sincerity. See Surah 6: Al Anam (6:123), as translated into English by Al-Hilali and Khan (1996, p.123), 123. "And thus, We have set up in every town great ones of its wicked people to plot therein. But they plot not except against their own selves, and they perceive (it) not." See also Surah 6: Al Anam (6:165), as translated into English by Al-Hilali and Khan (1996, p.198), 165. "And it is He who made you generations coming after generations, replacing each other on the earth. And He has raised you in ranks, some above others that He may try you in that which He has bestowed on you. Surely, your Lord is swift in retribution, and certainly, He is Oft-forgiving, Most Merciful." All these Surah/verses of the Quran show the importance of being a vicegerent of Allah/God on earth.

The inheritors of Allah/God on earth cannot become the owner and, therefore, leaders/followers must follow the laws laid down by the owner Allah/God on earth for us to follow period. See Surah 3: Ali Imran (3:33), as translated into English by Al-Hilali and Khan (1996, p.79) "Allah choose Adam, Nuh (Noah), the family of Ibrahim (Abraham) and the family of 'Imran above the Alamin (mankind and jinn) (of their times)."

Similarly, in Surah 15: Al Hijr (15:23), as translated into English by Al-Hilali and Khan (1996, p.328), 23. "And certainly, We! We it is who give life, and cause death, and we are the Inheritors." We as leaders and followers are inheritor only and that is why we have been made the vicegerents of Allah/God on earth only. Also See Surah 3: Ali Imran (3:180), Al-Hilali and Khan (1996, p.107), 180. "And let not those who covetously withhold of that which Allah has bestowed on them of His Bounty (wealth) think that it is good for them (and so they do not pay the obligatory Zakat). Nay, it will be worse for them; the things which they covetously withheld shall be tied to their necks like a collar on the Day of Resurrection. And to Allah belongs the heritage of the heavens and the earth; and Allah is Well-Acquainted with all that you do." Therefore, being a leader or a follower is a gift. Therefore, we as leaders and followers should not impede with the authority entrusted to us by Allah/God. See Surah 4 Al Nisa (4:58), as translated into English by Al-Hilali and Khan (1996, p.122), 58. "Verily, Allah commands that you should render back the trusts to those, to whom they are due; and that when you judge between men, you judge with justice. Verily, how excellent is the teaching which He (Allah) gives you! Truly, Allah is Ever All-Hearer, All-Seer."

Furthermore, the notion of Khalif/Caliph/Vicegerent/Successor in Islam is very clear as is affirmed in Surah Al Baqarah (2:30). It is a decree from Allah/God, even though the angles were with the view that they were the one who deserves such a great gift from Allah/God. But Allah/God explain to them why He Allah/God grant such a gift to Mankind.

The great thing that vicegerent as leaders and followers should do is to establish truth by establishing regular prayers and giving charity at the same time to forbid wrong doing as affirmed in Surah 22: Al Hajj (22:41), as translated by Al-Hilali and Khan (1996, p.426-7), 41. "Those (Muslim rulers) who, if We give them power in the land, (they) enjoin Iqamat-Salat [i.e. to perform the five compulsory congregational Salat (prayers) (The males in mosques)], to pay Zakat and they enjoin Al Ma'ruf (i.e. Islamic Monotheism and all the Islamic orders one to do), forbid Al-Munkar (i.e. disbelief, polytheism and all that Islam has forbidden) [i.e. they make the Quran as the laws of their country in all the spheres of life]. And with Allah rests the end of (all) matters (of creatures)." Also See Surah 21: Al Anbiya (21:73-4), as translated by Al- Hilali and Khan (1996, p.414), 73. "And We made them leaders, guiding (mankind) by Our Command, and We revealed to them the doing of good deeds, performing Salat (Iqamat-as-Salat), and the of Zakat and of Us (Alone) they were the worshippers." 74. "And (remember) Lut (Lot), We gave him Hukm (right judgement of the affaires and Prophethood) and (religious) knowledge, and We save him from the town (folk) who practiced Al-Khaba'ith (evil, wicked and filty deeds). Verily, they were a people given to evil, and were Fasiqun (rebellious, disobedient, to Allah)." The verses of the Quran offer valuable lessons for both leaders and followers. By upholding righteousness and refusing to compromise with evil, we can protect our way of life from those who seek to destroy it.

Muslim leaders and followers must not be swayed by attempts to modernize their societies, as this may lead them away from the path of righteousness. Instead, we must focus on fulfilling our duties as leaders and followers, which include performing good deeds, praying regularly, giving to charity, and worshipping Allah/God alone. By doing so, we can ensure the preservation of our way of life and uphold the teachings of the Quran. See Surah 35: Fatir (35:39), as translated into English by Al-Hilali and Khan (1996, p.551), 39. "He it is Who has made you successors generations after generation in the earth, so whoever disbelieves (in Islamic Monotheism) on him will be his disbelief. And the disbelief of the disbelievers adds nothing but hatred of their Lord. And the disbelief of the disbelievers adds nothing but loss." Also see Surah 3 Al-Imran (3:85), Al-Hilali and Khan (1996, p.90), 85. "And whoever seeks a religion other than Islam, it will never be accepted of him, and in the Hereafter, he will be one of the losers."

Khalif/Caliph/Vicegerent/Successor is a trust from Allah/God and we all must obey it, or be like those who reject Allah and were made to see consequences of their transgressions, for example as seen by those previous nations and people of the Pharaohs, the people of Noah, the Ad and Thamud, the Madyan people; and Moses, see Surah 22: Al Hajji (22:42-44). How can we not learn from the history of earlier nations that were destroyed for their evil deeds and the following of Targut? Yet, we still keep repeating past mistakes by following our desire and lust for power and personal enrichment.

Nowadays, certain political leaders engage in warfare under the pretext of national interest, nationalism, and the display of power. They also do so to gain sympathy from their citizens during elections. However, Islam teaches us that war should only be waged against evil, not for the sake of national interests, pride, prejudices, or the benefit of nation states. Those leaders who commit atrocities against other nations or their citizens will be held responsible and accountable for their crimes before Allah/God on the Day of Judgement. Regardless of their location, they will be answerable for their actions against humanity. We have witnessed wars where lives were lost and blood was shed without any sense of shame, all in the name of the state and its superior powers. The same was true for the Pharaohs in Egypt, and the same pattern continues today. This is precisely why I am writing this book – to remind myself and those in positions of authority in their respective nations or communities, particularly the leaders and followers in the Muslim Ummah, of their responsibility towards Allah/God and those they govern or lead. Therefore, in this book, I define leadership as selfless servitude solely for the pleasure of Allah/God. Consequently, Allah/God warns and assures the righteous that they should not lose hope, for they are the Khalif/Caliph/Vicegerent/Successor on earth. In other words, they are the representatives of Allah/God on earth.

Chapter 10

Obedience to Leadership

The notion of obedience to leadership holds great significance within the Islamic framework of leadership. Islamic teachings place a strong emphasis on the importance of adhering to and obeying those in positions of authority, whether it be within the religious or secular domains. This obedience is deeply rooted in the belief that leadership is divinely ordained and serves as a means of upholding order and harmony within society. In Islamic ideology, obedience to leadership extends beyond mere blind submission, encompassing a comprehensive understanding of the responsibilities and rights of both leaders and followers. Leaders are expected to discharge their duties with justice, fairness, and compassion, while followers are obligated to pledge their allegiance and provide support. This reciprocal relationship between leaders and followers is deemed essential for the overall well-being and progress of the community as a whole.

The Quran and Sunnah of the prophet (PBUH) serve as a crucial guide for leadership, with the primary requirement for any leader being their obedience to Allah/God and the prophet. Additionally, leaders are urged to obey those in authority, as long as their commands align with the principles of Islam. Prophet Muhammad (PBUH), who embodies Islamic teachings, emphasized the importance of obeying leadership by stating,

"Whoever obeys me, obeys Allah, and whoever disobeys me, disobeys Allah." It is essential to note that obedience to leadership does not imply blind adherence to unjust or oppressive rulers. Islamic teachings encourage individuals to speak out against injustice and tyranny, and to actively work towards establishing just and righteous leadership. This principle is supported by historical examples of Islamic scholars and leaders who actively opposed oppressive regimes and advocated for social justice. Therefore, obedience to leadership in an Islamic context is a multifaceted concept that encompasses the responsibilities and rights of both leaders and followers. It is based on the belief that leadership is divinely ordained and serves as a means of maintaining order and harmony in society. However, this obedience is not absolute and should not be extended to unjust or oppressive rulers. Islamic teachings encourage individuals to actively oppose injustice and strive for the establishment of just leadership.

It is crucial to highlight within this book that the primary allegiance of both leaders and followers is to Allah/God and the prophets, commencing from Adam (PBUH) and extending to the ultimate prophet of Allah/God, Mohammad (PBUH). This allegiance serves as the cornerstone for successful leadership. Consequently, adherence to Allah's laws and the teachings of Prophet Muhammad (PBUH) holds utmost significance for all leaders and followers within the Islamic Ummah. See Surah 3: Ali Imran (3:132), as translated into English by Al-Hilali and Khan (1996, p.98), 132. "And obey Allah and the Messenger9 Muhammad (PBUH) that you may obtain mercy." Also see Surah 4: Al Nisa (4:13-14), as translated into English by Al-Hilali and Khan (1996, p.113), 13. "These are the limits (set by) Allah (or ordainments as regards laws of inheritance), and whoever obeys Allah and His Messenger (Muhammad (PBUH) will be admitted to Gardens under which rivers flow (in

Paradise), to abide therein, and that will be a great success. 14. And whoever disobeys Allah and His Messenger Muhammad (PBUH), and transgress His limits, He will cast him into the Fire, to abide therein; and he shall have a disgraceful torment."

In Surah 9: Al-Tawbah (9:71), as translated into English by Al-Hilali and Khan (1996, p.250), 71. "The Believers, men, and women, are Auliya' (helpers supporters, friends, protectors) of one another; they enjoin (on the people) A-Ma'ruf (i.e., Islamic Monotheism and all that Islam orders one to do), and forbid (people) from Al-Munkar (i.e., polytheism and disbelief of all kinds, and all that Islam has forbidden); they perform As-Salat (Iqamat-as-Salat), and give the Zakat, and obey Allah and His Messenger. Allah will have His Mercy on them. Indeed, Allah is All-Mighty, All-Wise."

Again in Surah 24: Al Nur (24:52), as translated into English by Al- Hilali and Khan (1996, p.450), 52. "It is such as obey Allah and His Messenger, and fear Allah and do right, that will win (In the end)." In Surah 24: An-Nur (24:54), also as translated into English by Al- Hilali and Khan (1996, p.450), 54. "Says: "Obey Allah, and obey the Messenger, but if ye turn away, he (Messenger Muhammad (PBUH) is only responsible for the duty placed on him (i.e., to convey Allah's Message) and you for that placed on you. If you obey him, you shall be on the right guidance. The Messenger's duty is only to convey (the Message) in a clear way (i.e., to preach in a plain way." Similar to the above Verse is in Surah 64: Al-Taghabun (64:12), Al-Hilali and Khan (1996, p.709), 12. "Obey Allah, and obey the Messenger Muhammad (PBUH); but if you turn away, then the duty of Our Messenger is only to convey (the Message) clearly." Here the Message is clear from Allah/God that the Messenger comes to guide and teach, not to force and compel. There is no compulsion in religion see Surah Al Baqrah 2(2:256). The Messenger's teaching are clear and unambiguous and is open and free to all.

Allah/God promises those who obey Him and the Prophet Muhammad (PBUH), and it is affirmed in Surah 24: Al-Nur (24:55), Al-Hilali and Khan (1996, p.450), 55. "Allah has promised those among you who believe and do righteous good deeds, that He will certainly grant them succession to (the present rulers) in the land, as He granted it to those before them, and that He will grant them the authority to practice their religion which He has chosen for them (i.e., Islam). And He will surely, give them in exchange a safe security after their fear (provided) they (believers) worship Me and do not associate anything (in worship) with Me. But whoever disbelieved after this, they are the Fasiqun (rebellious, disobedient to Allah)." Subsequently, in Surah 4: Al Nisa (4:59), Al-Hilali and Khan (1996, p.122), 59. "O you who believe! Obey Allah and Obey the Messenger (Muhammad (PBUH), and those of you (Muslims) who are in authority. (And) If you differ in anything amongst yourselves, refer it to Allah and His Messenger Muhammad (PBUH), if you believe in Allah and in the Last Day. That is better and more suitable for final determination".

Additionally, Yusuf Ali (1992, p.203) provided additional insights regarding individuals entrusted with the responsibility of making decisions or resolving matters. According to him, ultimate authority lies solely with Allah. The Prophet of Allah, in turn, derived his authority from Allah/God. Consequently, Islam does not draw a clear distinction between matters of religious significance and worldly affairs. It emphasizes the importance of governments embodying righteousness. Similarly, Islam expects Muslims to honor and acknowledge the authority of the government they are subject to, as without such recognition, chaos and disorder would prevail. See Surah 4: Al Nisa (4:69), Al-Hilali and Khan (1996, p.124), 69. "And whoso obey Allah And the Messenger (Muhammad (PBUH), then they will be in the Company of those on whom Allah has bestowed His Grace of the Prophets, the Siddiqun (those followers of the Prophets who were first and foremost to believe in them, like Abu Bakr As-Siddiq (RA)), the martyrs, and the righteous. And how excellent these companions are!"

The veneration for authority in Islam is profound, as evidenced by the early days of the religion when Prophet Muhammad (PBUH) advised certain Muslims to leave Makkah due to religious persecution and migrate to Abyssinia. Despite the fact that the King of Abyssinia was a Christian and not a Muslim, he was known for his fairness and impartiality. As a result, Muslims everywhere hold the authority of the government in high regard, regardless of where they reside or work. When the Muslims arrived in Abyssinia and were received by King Negus, who was known for his benevolence and justice towards his people, Ja'far ibn Abi Talib, the leader of the Muslim delegation that had fled persecution in Makkah, spoke on behalf of the Muslims and their religion, Islam, as well as their Prophet Mohammad (PBUH)," O King! We have been a people of ignorance, worshiping idols, eating the flesh of dead animals, committing abominations, neglecting our relatives, and doing evil to our neighbours, were the strong among us would oppress the weak. We were in this state when Allah/God sent us the Messengers from among us whose descent, sincerity, trustworthiness, and honesty were known to us.

The Prophet Muhammad (PBUH) called upon us to worship the One True God and abandon the worship of stones and idols that our ancestors had practiced. He emphasized the importance of speaking the truth, fulfilling our responsibilities, showing kindness to our relatives and neighbors, and abstaining from forbidden food and the consumption of blood. He prohibited us from engaging in immoral behavior, stealing from orphans, and defaming married women. The Prophet commanded us to worship only one God, to pray and fast. We believe in his honesty, accept the message he brought from Allah/God, and consider him to be truthful. This account of the Prophet Muhammad (PBUH) conveying the message of Islam to Negus, the King of Abyssinia, who was not a Muslim at the time, demonstrates the respect that Islam holds for non-Muslim leaders. It also highlights the idea that Islam does not draw a strict line between religious and secular matters. Therefore, promoting justice is a crucial aspect of leadership. When Negus, the King of Abyssinia, learns about the Prophet Muhammad (PBUH) from his companions who had migrated to Abyssinia and embraced Islam, he converts to Islam.

The story of King Negus and earlier Emigrants of Muslims to Abyssinian shows that Islam is the religion of love, love for justice, unity, and moderation of humankind. See Surah 4: Al Nisa (4:64, 80- 81), as translated into English by Al-Hilali and Khan (1996, p.123), 64. "We sent no Messenger, but to be obeyed by Allah's Leave. If they (hypocrites), when they had been unjust to themselves, had come to you (Muhammad (PBUH) and begged for Allah's Forgiveness for them. Indeed, they would have found Allah All-Forgiving (One who forgives and accepts repentance), Most Merciful." Again see Surah 4: Al Nisa (4:80-81), as translated into English by Al-Hilali and Khan (1996, p.125), 80. "He who obeys the Messenger (Muhammad (PBUH), has indeed obeyed Allah, but he who turns away, then We have not sent you (O Muhammad (PBUH) as a watcher over them. 81. They say: "We are obedient," but when they leave you (Muhammad (PBUH), a section of them spend all night planning others than what you say. But Allah records their nightly (plots). So turn aside from them (do not punish them), and put your trust in Allah. And Allah is Ever All-Sufficient as a Disposer of affairs."

Those who obey Allah/God and the Prophet (PBUH) are doing so to seek Grace. We can also see from the speech made by Abu Bakr when he was chosen as the first Caliph of the Islamic state after the death of Prophet Muhammad (PBUH) who is a great testimony to how important obedience to Allah/God and Prophet Muhammad (PBUH) is to Islamic perspective of a leader. In this speech Caliph Abu Bakr said: "Obey me as long as I obey Allah/God and His Prophet (PBUH). If I do not obey them, you owe me no obedience." This story sheds light on the importance of obeying Allah/God the originator of leadership, and his Prophet, Muhammad (PBUH).

The follower is obedient to his leader if he/she obeys Allah/god and his Messenger. Thus, those who disobey Allah/God on earth are cursed. The example of those who disobeyed Allah on earth is affirmed in Surah 5: Al Maidah (5:78-79), 78. "Those among the Children of Israel who disbelieved were cursed by the tongue of Dawud (David) and 'Isa (Jesus), son of Maryam (Mary). That was because they disobeyed (Allah and the Messengers) and were ever transgressing beyond bounds. 79. They used not to forbid one another from the Munkar (wrong, evil-doing, sins, polytheism, and disbelief) which they committed. Vile indeed was what they used to do."

Chapter 11

Challenge to Leadership

The challenge to leadership from an Islamic perspective today is not new. Challenges faced by Islamic Leaders are many and this is due to the fact that leadership from an Islamic perspective is rooted in the religious and cultural aspects of the community. One of the primary challenges faced by Islamic leaders is striking a balance between adhering to religious principles and adapting to the changing needs of the community. This requires a deep understanding of Islamic teachings and the ability to interpret them in a manner that is relevant to contemporary circumstances of the Muslims communities.

Additionally, Islamic leaders may face resistance or opposition from various factions within the community, making it crucial for them to navigate these conflicts while upholding their responsibilities as leaders. Thus, leadership from an Islamic perspective encompasses a distinct set of qualities, responsibilities, accountabilities and challenges. The leaders from an Islamic perspective should adhere to the principles of integrity, justice, humility, and compassion. The challenges that Muslims leaders and followers in the various communities are facing are not new and were also faced by the prophets and more importantly prophet of Allah/ God prophet Mohammad (PBUH) and the rightly four guided caliphs. Prophets were challenged by their followers and those who seek to reject

Allah/God message in their various societies and in various periods. Many of their people rejected Allah/God and disobey their prophets and the consequences that followed them.

The great example of these people are the people of prophet Nuh (PBUH) (Noah), the Pharos of Egypt and the list goes on and on. Prophet Mohammad (PBUH) faced the same challenges when his people in Makkah challenge him to give up Islam and promise him the worldly powers if he could give up Islam. These disbelievers were ready to provide the prophet whatever he needed for him to give up Islam, the promise him wealth and power and when he refuses to do so they even plan to kill him, especially when prophet Muhammad (PBUH) received divine direction to depart from Makkah to Madinah. When the Prophet receive revelation to migrate, he then started preparing for his journey to Madinah and he informed Abu Bakr (RA) of his plan to migrate to Madinah of which the two of them departed together.

On the night of his departure, the prophet (PBUH) house was besieged by men of the Quraysh who planned to kill him in the morning. At the time, the prophet possessed property of the Quraysh given to him in trust, so he handed it over to Ali Ibn Abi Talib (RA) and directed him to return it to its owners, and asked him to lie down on his bed assuring him of Allah/God's protection. Soon as the prophet joined Abu Bakr (RA), left the city, and the two took shelter in a cave outside the city. Next morning, the besiegers were frustrated to find Ali(RA) in the prophet (PBUH) place in his bed. They were being fooled and thwarted by the prophet (PBUH) plan, they rummaged the city of Makkah in search for the prophet (PBUH), and some of them eventually reached the threshold of the cave, but success eluded them. They did not enter the cave because there was an unbroken spider's web at the entrance of the cave.

When the Quraysh came to know of prophet (PBUH) escape, they announced heavy reward for bringing the prophet back to them, alive or dead. Unable to resist this temptation, pursuers scattered in all directions. After staying for three days, the prophet (PBUH) and Abu Bakr (RA) resumed their journey and were pursued by Suraqa bin Malik. But each time he neared the prophet (PBUH), his horse stumbled and he finally abandoned his desire of capturing the prophet of Allah Muhammad (PBUH. After eight days' journey, the prophet (PBUH) entered the outskirts of Medina on 24 May 622, but did not enter the city directly. The prophet stopped at a place called Quba', a place some miles from the main city, and established a mosque there which known now as Majid Quba. After a four-day stay at Quba', the prophet of Allah Muhammad(PBUH) with Abu Bakr(RA) continued their migration to Medina, participated in their first Friday prayer on the way, and upon reaching the city, were greeted cordially by its people according to Prophet Mohammad Hijira (2016). These challenges that were faced by prophet Muhammad (PBUH) in preaching about Islam to his people is not new.

The same challenge is faced by many leaders and followers in the Muslim communities today. There are many pressures from especially the west on Muslims leaders and followers to modernise their system of governance, education and even their way of life in order to be accepted by them which is a concern. Leaders and follower should be very careful about such demands. The Quran warn the Ummah and this is affirmed in Surah Al Baqarah 2 (2:120-123) as translated into English by Al-Hilali and Khan (1996, p.31), 120, Never will the Jews and the Christians be pleased with you (O Mohammad (PBUH) till you follow their religion. Say: "Verily, the Guidance of Allah (i.e. Islamic Monotheism) that is the (only) Guidance. And if you (O Mohammad (PBUH) were to follow their (Jews and Christians) desires after what have received of knowledge (i.e., the Quran), then you would have against Allah neither any Wali(protector guardian) nor any helper.121, Those (who embraced Islam from Bani Israel) to who We gave the Book [the Taurat (Torah)] [or those (Muhammad's companions) to whom We gave the Book (the Quran)] recite it (i.e. obey its order and follow its teaching) as it should recited (i.e. followed), they are the ones who believe therein. And whoso disbelieve in it (the Quran), those are they who are the losers. (Tasir Al-Qutubi. Vol.2.page 95). 122, O children of Israel! Remember My favour which I bestowed upon you and that I preferred you to the Alamin [Mankind and jinn (of your time period, in the past)]. 123, And fear the Day (of Judgement) when no person shall avail another, nor shall intercession be of use to him nor shall they be helped. These Verse 120-123 of the Quran are a decree from Allah/God to us all leaders and followers of the Muslims Ummah not to yield to those pressures from those who seek to destroy our way of life in the name of modernisation because if you do so as a leader or follower you have gone against the will of Allah/God and will end up being a loser.

The Quran is clear on this matter and I have brought here in this book to warn those who think that if they yield to these pressures they will be accepted as modernisers. Please do not fall for it. Do not as leaders as well as follower to fall for these scam. They are all false. All these tricks are not new and therefore must be avoided at all time.

Let us learn the lesson from our beloved Prophets Mohammad (PBUH) when he was at such situation whereby his tribe men will promise him the world to give up Islam and his way of life he would categorically reject those advances and would tell them firmly that he would not give up his religion and his way of life for anything. The prophet would respond to those who challenged his faith Islam in an affirmation in Surah Al Kafrun 109 Al Kafirun (109:6) as translated into English by Al-Hilali and Khan (1996, p.788), 6. "To you be your religion, and to me my religion (Islamic Monotheism)." And also translated into English by Yusuf Ali (1992, p.1708). These is the way for us all to respond to these disbelievers who want to change our way of life by hiding behind modernisation. We should be aware of these terms and avoid going against the warning of Allah/God as in Surah Al Baqarah (2:120-123) as noted above.

The Prophethood of Prophet Muhammad (PBUH) was revealed to him one night while he was in a cave in Mount Hira. He had an encounter with Angel Gabriel as affirmed in Surah 96 Al Alaq (96:1-5), as translated into English by Al-Hilali and Khan (1996, p.779), 1. "Read! In the name of your Lord who has created (All that exists). 2. He has created man from a clot (a piece of thick coagulated blood). 3. Read! And your Lord is the Most Generous. 4. Who has taught (the writing) by the pen. 5. He has taught man that which he knew not." Yusuf Ali's (1992, p.1672) also made a complimentary comment (6204), which state that "The declaration or proclamation was to be in the Name of Allah the Creator. It was not for any personal benefit to Prophet Muhammad (PBUH); to him, there was to come bitter persecution, sorrow, and suffering. It was the call of Allah/God for the benefit of erring humanity. After receiving this truth, Prophet Muhammad (PBUH) and his followers faced persecution and hardship from the majority of the Quraysh who refused to follow the truth, Islam as it is affirmed in Surah 5: Al Maidah (5:3), as translated into English by Al-Hilali and Khan (1996, p.144), 3. "...This day, I have perfected your religion for you, completed My Favour upon you, and have chosen for you Islam as your religion."

Yusuf Ali (1992, p.245) also commented on this verse and attested that "the last verse revealed chronologically, making the approaching end of

Mustafa's ministry in his earthly life and it is also affirmed in Surah 15: Al Hijr (15:9), Al-Hilali and Khan (1996, p.326), 9. "Verily, We, it is We who have sent down the Dhikr (i.e., the Quran) and surely, We will guard it (from corruption)." The above Surah affirmed Allah's assurance to Mankind that Allah/God truth is guarded through all ages, even though some may mock it or be bent on destroying it. Thus, the requirement of the leaders and followers of the One Nation (Ummah), wherever they may be, is to respect the Quran and teach the Quran to others and simultaneously be the ambassadors of Islamic Ummah, forbid evil and worship Allah alone.

Leadership from an Islamic perspective holds immense significance for the overall welfare of humanity, as extensively emphasized in the aforementioned literature. Consequently, individuals entrusted with the role of a leader within a community or any other position must acknowledge that leadership is synonymous with trust (Amanah), encompassing both responsibility and accountability. The author of this book defines leadership as an altruistic act of servitude, driven solely by the desire to please Allah/God. The prophet leadership was selfless purely for the pleasure of Allah/God alone if not he could have given up on Islam when he was challenge and even try to kill him and his followers. He would have given up and save his life and enjoy the good life but he rejected all those advances from his tribe men who were very powerful and resourceful like our current super powers. Many leaders and followers when faced with such difficulties would have given up when the big powers come knocking at their doors. Thus, leadership is very important for the Muslim Ummah and these require sacrifices and resilient against pressures that my come their ways and also remember that the prophets and the rightly four guided Caliphs went through many pressures but they did not give in because they have Allah/

God on the side and that they are Allah/God representative on earth. Henceforth, leadership from Islamic perspective adhere to the Prophet Muhammad (PBUH) advised or saying that even when three people are on a journey, they should appoint one as a leader, so that if there is any misunderstanding or disagreement the leader should be the one to be listen to.

Islam is a way of life; therefore, leaders have to be the embodiment of that way of life by being role model and also submissive to the laws and will of Allah/God. Prophet Mohammad (PBUH) exemplified that kind of leadership in Makkah and Madinah. Thus, leadership from an Islamic perspective is vicegerent, whose willingness and selflessness servitude is purely for the pleasure of Allah/God. A leader and a follower is a vicegerent of Allah/God and Allah/God has made them His representative on earth who exercises delegated power on behalf of Allah/God on earth. In other words, a leader and a follower is a person regarded as an earthly representative of Allah/God on earth and it is affirmed in Surah Al-Baqarah (2:30). Hence, leaders are only obeyed if they Obey Allah/God and the Prophet Muhammad (PBUH), as in the case of Caliph Abu Bakar, who said in his acceptance speech as the first caliph "Obey me if I obey Allah/God and His prophet (PBUH). If I don't obey them do not obey me."

Furthermore, the exemplification of vicegerency on earth is that of the life of Prophet Muhammad (PBUH) and his four Rightly Guided Caliph (Hulafah Al-Rashidun) who work tirelessly to build the first Islamic city-state in Madinah. Prophet Muhammad (PBUH) and other Prophets before him led exemplary lives that a leader and followers alike can follow. Prophet Mohammad's (PBUH) life in Makkah and Madinah provides a practical example of leadership from an Islamic perspective.

Prophet Muhammad (PBUH) followed the laws of Allah/God and created the great city-state of Madinah, in which the Muslims and non-Muslims lived in harmony without any disturbance. He knew there was no compulsion in Islam. However, not everyone believed him, including Abu Jahal, whose actual name was Amr Ibn Hisham, commonly known as Abu Hakam (Father of Wisdom), one of the Prophet Muhammad (PBUH) relatives. He was a wise man among the Quraish but the worst enemy of Islam. His relentless hostility and belligerence towards Islam earned him the name of Abu Jahal (Father of Ignorance) among the Muslims. Today there are many scholars and professionals of high calibre but are still acting like the likes of Abu Jahal by not accepting Islam as a way of life.

There are many professors in their field of studies but have yet to believe in Islam. Therefore, the model for leaders and followers is Prophet Muhammad (PBUH), whom Allah/God described as the best of character. See Surah 33: Al Ahzab (33:21), as translated into English by Al-Hilali and Khan (1996, p.528), 21. "Indeed, in the Messenger of Allah (Muhammad (PBUH), you have a good example to follow for him who hopes for (the Meeting with) Allah and the Last Day and remembers Allah much." Yusuf Ali (ibid) comments, "We now have the psychology of the Believers-God fearing men, led by that pattern of men and a leader of Muhammad (PBUH)." See Surha 61 As-Saff (61:6) as translated into English by Al-Hilali and Khan (1996, p.702-3), 6, And (remember) when Isa (Jesus), son of Maryam (Mary), said :(O children of Israel! I am the messenger of Allah unto you, confirming the Taurat [(Torah) which came] before me, and giving glad tidings of a Messenger to come after me, whose name shall be Ahmed. But when he (Ahmad i.e. Mohammad (PBUH) came to them with the clear proofs, they said:" This is plain magic. See Surah 48 Al-Hujurat (48: 29) as translated into

English by Al-Hilali and Khan (1996, p.648), Mohammad (PBUH) is the Messenger of Allah. And those who are with him are sever against disbelievers, and merciful amongst themselves. You see them bowing and falling dawn prostrate (in prayer), seeking Bounty from Allah and (His) Good pleasure. The mark of them (i.e. of their Faith) is on their faces (foreheads) from the traces of prostration (during prayers).

This is their description in the Taurat (Torah). But their description in the Injeel (Gospel) is like a (sown) seed which sends forth its shoot, then make it strong, and becomes thick and it stands straight on it stem, delighting the sowers, that He may enrage the disbelievers with them. Allah has promise those among them who believe (i.e. all those who follow Islamic Monotheism, the religion of Prophet Mohammad (PBUH) till the Day of Resurrection) and do righteous good deeds, forgivingness and a mighty reward (i.e. paradise). Also see Surah 47 Mohammad (47:2), as translated into English by Al-Hilali and Khan (1996, p.639), 2, But those who believe and do righteous good deeds and believe in that which I sent down to Mohammad (PBUH) for it is the truth from their Lord-He will expiate from them their sins, and will make good of their state.

Furthermore, there many references to Prophet Muhammad (PBUH) as "Messenger", "Messenger of God", and "Prophet" as can be seen in these Quran verses 2:101, 2:143, 2:151, 3:32, 3:81, 3:144, 3:164, 4:79–80, 5:15, 5:41, 7:157, 8:1, 9:3, 33:40, 48:29, and 66:9). There are also other terms are used referring the prophet of Allah which, including "Warner", "bearer of glad tidings", and the "one who invites people to a Single God" (12:108, and 33:45–46), "Seal of the Prophets" (Khatam an-Nabiyyin) 33:40 i.e. there will be no more prophets after him), a "Summoner unto Allah" and "a Lamp that gives bright light" 33:46. Thus, prophet

Mohammad (PBUH) was a prophet and a statesman in Madinah and the Ummah. Hence during his leadership in Madinah and the Prophet Muhammad's (PBUH) he did not discriminate against people he lead and no man had superiority over others based on caste, colour, nationality, or gender. No man was superior to a woman. Each of them undertook to care for their duties without any transgression. Thus, Islam teaches the sanctity of humanity and equal rights to all without distinction of race, sex, or colour. Thus, the lack of leaders in Muslims Ummah who follow the definition of leadership in this book, as one whose willingness and selfless servitude purely for the sake of Allah on earth and Mankind is because we as leaders and followers have abandoned the Islamic way of life. Hence our primary motivation for leading or doing any duty as a leader or follower is to serve Allah/ God alone.

How many of us assume our duties or responsibilities purely for servitude to Allah/God and praising Him? Let us take an example from the Prophet Muhammad's (PBUH last sermon in Arafat as advice for anyone who aspires to serve purely for the sake of Allah/God. Our Beloved Messenger Prophet Muhammad (PBUH) has this to say to his people:

"O people, just as you regard this month, this day, this city as Sacred, so regard the life and property of every Muslim as Sacred trust. Return the properties entrusted to you to their rightful owners. Hurt no one so that no one may hurt you. Remember that you will indeed meet your Lord and that He will indeed reckon your deeds. Allah has forbidden you to take Usury (interest); therefore, all interest obligations shall henceforth be waived. Your capital, however, is yours to keep. You will neither inflict nor suffer any inequity. Allah has judged that there shall be no interest and that all the interest due to Abbas Ibn Mutalib (Prophet's Uncle) shall henceforth be waived... Beware of Satan for the safety of your religion. He has lost all hope that he will ever be able to lead you astray in big things, so beware of following him in small things."..." Finally, I leave behind me two things, the Quran and my example, the Sunnah, and if you follow these, you will never go astray." After praising and thanking Allah, Prophet Muhammad (PBUH) said:

"O people, lend me an attentive ear, for I know not whether, after this year, I shall ever be amongst you again. Therefore, listen to what I am saying to you very carefully and take these words to those who could not be present here today.

"O people, just as you regard this month, this day, this city as Sacred, so regard the life and property of every Muslim as Sacred trust. Return the goods entrusted to you to their rightful owners. Hurt no one so that no one may hurt you. Remember that you will indeed meet your Lord and that He will indeed reckon your deeds. Allah has forbidden you to take Usury (interest); therefore, all interest obligations shall henceforth be waived. Your capital, however, is yours to keep. You will neither inflict nor suffer any inequity. Allah has judged that there shall be no interest and that all the interest due to Abbas Ibn Mutalib (Prophet's Uncle) shall henceforth be waived.... Beware of Satan for the safety of your religion. He has lost all hope that he will ever be able to lead you astray in big things, so beware of following him in small things.

"O People, it is true that you have certain rights concerning your Women, but they also have rights over you. Remember that you have taken them as your wives only under Allah's trust and with His permission. Do treat your women well and be kind to them, for they are your partners and committed helpers. And it is your right that they do not make friends with any one of whom you disapprove, as well as never to be unchaste.

O People, listen to me in earnest, worship Allah, say your five daily prayers (Salah), fast during the month of Ramadan, and give your wealth in Zakat. Perform Haj if you can afford to. All Mankind is from Adam and Eve, an Arab has no superiority over a non-Arab, nor a non- Arab has any superiority over an Arab; also, a white has no superiority over a black nor does a black has any superiority over a white except by piety (taqwa) and good action. Learn that every Muslim is a brother to every Muslim and that the Muslims constitute one brotherhood. Nothing should be legitimate to a Muslim which belongs to a fellow Muslim unless it was given freely and willingly. Do not, therefore, do injustice to yourselves. Remember, one day you will appear before Allah and answer your deeds. So beware, do not stray the path of righteousness after I am gone.

O People, No Prophet or Apostle, will come after me, and no new Faith will be born. Reason well, therefore, O People, and understand the words which I convey to you. I leave behind me two things, the Quran and my example, the Sunnah, and if you follow these, you will never go astray. All those who listen to me shall pass on my words to others and those to others again, and may the last one understands my words better than those who listen to me directly. Be my witness, O Allah, that I have conveyed your message to your people." The above sermon should act as a guide to us all. This book is written with the hope we can revive the spirit of Islam and be good leaders for ourselves and our communities.

Furthermore, the responsibilities and duties of a leader is clarified in a Hadith (2942) reported in Sunan Abu Dawud by Abu Maryam al-Azadi; the Prophet (PBUH) said: "If Allah puts anyone in the position of authority over the Muslims' affairs and he secludes himself (from them), not fulfilling their needs, wants, and poverty, Allah will keep Himself away from him, not fulfilling his need, want, and poverty." Subsequent Hadith on leadership in Islam states, "Behold! Every one of you is a leader, and you shall be asked about those you lead. Imam is a leader over the people and shall be asked about them; a woman is a leader over her children and shall be asked about them." Reported by Abdullah Ibn Omar in Bukhari and Muslim.

Prophet Muhammad (PBUH) said the following regarding leadership in Islam, "Whosever obeyed the leader, he obeyed me, and whoever disobeyed the leader, he disobeyed me." Reported by Muslim. The Hadith also from the Prophet Mohammad (PBUH) is, "Each one of you is a shepherd, and all of you are responsible for your flocks." Narrated by Saheeh Al-Buhari and Muslim.

The final Sermon of the Prophet Muhammad (PBUH) delivered in the Uranah Valley of Mount Arafat serves as an inspiration to both leaders and followers. It is a guide that teaches us to apply Allah's qualities and attributes, such as knowledge, mercy, appreciation, forgiveness, benevolence, justice, love, grandeur, beauty, and power, to our daily lives and activities. Additionally, we can learn from Salahadeen's letter of advice to his son, which emphasizes the importance of winning the hearts of the people and watching over their property. This exemplifies the leadership qualities that have been present throughout Islamic history. As leaders, we should strive to follow these teachings and lead humanity and our communities with gentleness and kindness.

Chapter 12

Consultation of Leaders in Islam

Consultation of Leaders in Islam from an Islamic Perspective is very important because consultation of leaders holds significant importance in the Islamic faith, as it is deeply rooted in the teachings and principles of Islam. This practice is based on the belief that consultation is a fundamental aspect of decision-making and governance within the Islamic Ummah. Henceforth, leaders are encouraged to seek the opinions and advice of others before making important decisions that affect the community as a whole.

The concept of consultation from an Islamic perspective is known as "Shura" in Arabic, which is derived from the Quran and the teachings of the Prophet Muhammad (PBUH). The Quran emphasizes the importance of consultation in several verses, highlighting its role in fostering unity, justice, and effective governance. See Surah Al-Imran (3:159), as translated into English by Khan and Al-Hilaili (1996), 159, "And consult them in the matter. And when you have decided, then rely upon Allah. Indeed, Allah loves those who rely [upon Him]." Again from the Islamic perspective, consultation is not limited to a specific group of individuals but rather encompasses a broad range of stakeholders in the Muslims communities, for example leaders, scholars, experts, and members of the community who possess knowledge and expertise in relevant areas.

The aim of consultation is to ensure that decisions are made collectively, taking into account diverse perspectives and expertise, thereby promoting inclusivity and fairness, whether these is practiced or not in many Muslims communities or not is an ideals that should be followed and practice. Furthermore, the consultation process in Islam is characterized by certain principles and values. These include mutual respect, open-mindedness, and the willingness to listen to differing opinions. It is essential for leaders to create an environment that encourages constructive dialogue and allows for the expression of diverse viewpoints. This fosters a sense of ownership and participation among community members, as they feel their voices are heard and valued. Consultation of leaders in Islam is not merely a formality but rather a genuine effort to seek guidance and wisdom from others. Leaders are expected to actively engage in the process, carefully considering the opinions and advice put forth by others. This demonstrates humility and a recognition of the fact that no individual possesses all the knowledge and wisdom required for effective decision-making. Thus, consultation of leaders in Islam is a practice deeply rooted in the teachings and principles of the faith. It emphasizes the importance of collective decision-making, inclusivity, and the recognition of diverse perspectives. By adhering to the principles of consultation, leaders in Islam can foster unity, justice, and effective governance within the Islamic community wherever they may be.

Furthermore, Consultation in Islam is very essential for leaders and even followers in the Muslim Ummah. The leadership model for all Muslim to follow is that of our beloved prophet Mohammad (PBUH) who in his dealing used to consult his companions in all affairs and even affaire related to battles war faire. Consulting is very important for all the leaders and followers from the Islamic perspective due to the fact that Prophet Muhammad (PBUH) made consulting a Sunnah and he set up an example for his companions to follow.

The practice of consulting others has many benefits from an Islamic perspectives. Consultation (Mushawarah) stimulates thought, enhances self-esteem, strengthens relationships, and binds society together irrespective of their differences. Consultation is to sooth other people hearts, strengthen your opinion, and raise high their self-esteem and create an atmosphere of trust. Consultation is very crucial in Islam and is affirmed in Al-Shurah 42 (42:38) as translated into English by Al- Hilali and Khan (1996, p.613), And those who answer the call of their Lord[i.e. to believe that He is the only One Lord (Allah), and to worship none but Him Alone], and perform As Salat (Iqamat-as-Salat), and who (consult) their affairs by consultation, and who spend of what We have bestowed on them. It is therefore very important to note that consultation is very critical and that the prophet (PBUH) used to encourage his companions to consult each other's. It also important to note that as consultation is very important, the consultant should be trustworthy, respectful, adviser, steadfast, non-self-absorbed, non-hesitant, not liar. Therefore consultation is of great important and progressive for both the individual as well as the society when members seek the opinion of others who are trustworthy before making a decision that affect their lives or society at large.

In Islam if we do not have any to consult, we can consult Allah/God directly by performing Istikharah Salah (seeking guidance from Allah by performing two Rak'ahs), of prayers and ask seek Allah/God guidance in the affair we want to do or a decision we want to perform. Thus Istikharah is all about seeking aid from Allah/God, whereas consulting is sought from experts among believers and those who are trustworthy. Thus, the necessity of consultation is also that we should consult those worthy of it, not consultation for consultation sake and eventually make the final decision based on what seems most appropriate. If we look at the life of our beloved prophet Mohammad (PBUH) we can see that he use to consult others, especially if Allah/God did not send him revelation about things he needed to make decisions about it. Thus, consultation was always the practice of the Holy Prophet Mohammad (PBUH) and other previous prophets before him. However, things that was revealed to him by Allah/God regarding the laws by Allah he would only implement them. That is why things that were not revealed to him by Allah/God he would put aside his own view and opinions on a matter and go along with a suggestion from his companion. The best example of the prophet Mohammad (PBUH) consulting others can be seen during the battles of 'Uhud and Khandaq, where the Prophet accepted suggestions of military tactics from the companions.

Thus consultation is very important in Islam and it is affirmed in Surah 42: Ash- Shura (42:38), as translated into English by Al-Hilali and Khan (1996, p.613), 38. "And those who answer the call of their Lord [i.e. to believe that He is the only One Lord (Allah), and to worship none but Him Alone], and perform As-Salat (Igamat-as –Salat), and who (conduct) their affairs by mutual consultation, and who spend of what We have bestowed on them. See also Surah 3: Ali Imran (3:121-148), as translated into English by Al-Hilali and Khan (1996, p.97), 121. "And (remember) when you (Muhammad (PBUH) left your household in the morning to post the believers at their stations for the battle (of Uhud). And Allah is All-Hearer, All-knower…148. "So Allah gave them the reward of this world and the excellent reward of the Hereafter. And Allah loves Al-Muhsinun (the good-doers). Also, see V.3.134 and V.9.120.

Furthermore, mutual consent and consultation are very important even when others disobey your order and this example is affirmed Surah 3: Ali Imran (3:159), Al-Hilali and Khan (1996, p.102), 159. "And by the Mercy of Allah, you deal with them gently. And had you been severe and harsh-hearted, they would have broken away from about you; so pass over (their faults), and ask for (Allah's) forgiveness for them; and consult them in affairs. Then when you have taken a decision, put thy trust in Allah. Certainly, Allah loves those who put their trust (in Him)." The above surah to the prophet of Allah/God is great lesson of leadership of the prophet Mohammad (PBUH) during the battle of Uhud, especially when the Muslims disobeyed his command and their victory became a failure. Many great Muslims companions were killed, including Hamzah. But Allah/God decree to the Prophet Muhammad (PBUH) to be gentle with those who did not follow his instructions in the battle field. If he the prophet was harsh with their companions they could have abandoned him and dispersed like broken glass which cannot never be assembled as in it originality.

Queen Bilqis was another female leader of the Islamic history that had use consultation as a cornerstone of her leadership and this affirmed in Surah 27: Al Name (27:32-44), as translated into English by Al-Hilali and Khan (1996, p.478), which related to consultation, 32. "They said: "O chiefs! Advise me in (this) case of mine. I decide no case till you are present with me (and give me your opinions). 33. They said: "We have great strength and great ability for war, but it is for you to command: so think over what you will command. 34. She said: "Verily, Kings, when they enter a town (country), they despoil it and make the most honourable amongst its people the lowest. And thus they do. 35. "But verily, I am going to send him a present and see with what (answer) the messenger return." With regard to consultation by Queen Bilqis in the Quran as seen in the verse above Yusuf Ali (1989, p.945) made a complementary comment on it and concluded that the characteristic of Queen Bilqis was that of a ruler who enjoyed great wealth and dignity and the complete confidence of her subjects. She did nothing without consulting her council, and her council was ready to carry out her command in all things. Her people are manly, loyal, contended, and ready to take the field against any enemy in their country. But their Queen is prudent in policy and unwilling to embroil her country in war."

These example of consultations as required by leaders and followers in the Quran are very important for those in leadership position to learn and draw lessons. Another good example to follow from the Quran is the encounter of our beloved prophet Mohammad (PBUH) when the blind person or handicap was at one of his gathering with the leaders of the Qureshi and his attentions was with those leaders and not the disable person and Allah/God reminded the Prophet of Allah/God to paying attention to the disable or the blind person as those who are able as it is affirmed in Surah 80: Abasa (80:1-4), as is translated into English by Al- Hilali and Khan (1996, p.754), 1. "The Prophet (PBUH) frowned and turned away. 2. Because there came to him the blind man (i.e., Abdullah bin Umm-Maktum, who came to the Prophet (PBUH) while he was preaching to one or some of the Quraish chiefs). 3. And how can you know that he might become pure (from sins)? 4. Or he might receive admonition, and the admonition might profit him?" The above Verse narrates an incident of reflection and we can all learn from it in our daily lives. The prophet was interrupted by a blind man Abdullah bin Umm-Maktum, who was also poor and whom everyone could have ignored, but Allah/God decree that the prophet should take note of those who are with him irrespective of their background or imperfection. The lesson from the blind man story in the Quran is that as leaders and followers we should be open to listening to all kinds of people around us irrespective of their background whether poor or rich, blind or handicapped.

However, unfortunately in many Muslims Ummah today what concerns many leaders and followers is their personal interest above all things their financial gains above all things, not the interest of the nation or others, but only their immediate families, cronies and their friends. There are many benefits of consultation as noted from the above verses of the Quran and the prophet lives experiences and those of the Queen Bilqis as affirmed in the Quran is that consultation add to intelligence and wisdom of others to the one who have to make the final decision rather than relying on your own self. Consultation reduces by far likelihoods of mistakes. We can all learn from Ali when he said that the Messenger (s) sent me to Yemen and advised me, 'the one who consults does not regret'. Ali also said that: He who acts solely according to his own opinion gets ruined, and he who consults other people shares in their understanding. (Saying No.161).

Chapter 13

Comparison between Leadership from a Western and Islamic Perspective

This chapter compare between leadership from and Islamic and western perspective and analysing the similarities and deviations that exist between the two perspectives. Additionally, it investigates the commonalities and divergences between these two perspectives, aiming to shed light on the concept of leadership and compare it in both contexts. In essence, the objective of this chapter is to emphasize the shared elements and disparities, ultimately contributing to the existing knowledge on leadership from both Western and Islamic perspectives.

Furthermore, the contrast between Western and Islamic leadership can be observed in various aspects. While Western leadership is often characterized by individualism, competition, and a focus on achieving personal goals, Islamic leadership emphasizes collectivism, cooperation, and the pursuit of communal objectives. Additionally, Western leadership tends to prioritize rationality and pragmatism, whereas Islamic leadership values spirituality and morality. These differences in leadership styles can be attributed to the distinct cultural and historical contexts in which they have developed.

Common Points

Leadership from both perspectives involves influence relationship between the leaders and the followers who have mutual interest that bind them. Leadership from both perspective have followers and communities or nation state they serve. Leadership from both perspective in the history of humankind has always been the pivotal factor in setting up, designing and shaping up the event in their given communities, societies or nations states.

The rise and fall of leadership from both perspective have always been attributed mainly to the absence or the presence of an effective leadership. The rise and fall of leadership from both perspective is when the fear of Allah/God is absent from leaders and followers alike. Secondly, when leaders and followers disobey Allah/God and by so doing start to believing in their own powers and strength.

Great leaders arouse the curiosity of their followers and have the courage to confront abuses and assumes responsibility and at the same time articulate the vision for his people and avoid evil dealings only to win elections stay in power and create laws that affect the less privilege in society or nation state. The other common ground or point between Westernand Islamicperspectiveistheimportanceofleadershipachieving success and progress. Both perspectives recognize the importance of ethical and moral values in leadership. Both perspectives emphasize the importance of communication, teamwork, and collaboration in achieving common goals. Both perspective of leadership emphasise the importance of education and continuous learning. Both perspective also emphasise the need for higher level of education and to continuously update their knowledge and skills as a means of achieving personal and societal development for their citizens.

Divergence

There are many differences or divergence between the Islamic perspective of leadership and the Western perspective of leadership as argue throughout this book. As noted above in the Western culture, leadership is often associated with individualism, competition, and achievement. Leaders are expected to be charismatic, visionary, and decisive. They are also expected to be accountable for their actions and to take responsibility for the success or failure of their organizations.

In Islamic culture, leadership is based on the principles of justice, compassion, and humility. Leaders are expected to be honest, trustworthy, and to serve the common good. They are also expected to be accountable to God and to the community they serve. The centrality of the divergence between western and Islamic perspective of leadership is based on the notion of the originality of leadership as argue very strongly in this book.

The originator of leadership from the Islamic perspective is Allah/ God. Allah/God created mankind to be His representative on earth not claiming sovereignty of the people who he/she lead but accountable for their collective well-being. See Surah 2 Al-Baqarah (2:30). Therefore the content of leadership is and should be from the Quran and Sunnah of Prophet Mohammad (PBUH), previous Prophets, the four guided Caliphs, and other great pious leaders in Islam. That content of leadership from and Islamic perspective above all is and should reflect the reason of creation which is to worship Allah/God alone and follow Divine Laws (Sharia).

Mankind being the creation of Allah/God cannot simply abandon the laws of his creator and assume that his own laws are superior to those of his creator Allah/God and that is why leadership from an Islamic perspective take the central stage as argue throughout this book that the originator of leadership is Allah/God. And we as leaders and followers are His representative on earth.

How can the Khalifah, the Caliph, the Vicegerent, or the Successor on earth fulfil their responsibility without feeling accountable to the creator, who is the ultimate source of leadership? In the Islamic perspective, leadership is considered a trust (Amanah) bestowed upon mankind by Allah/God, with the purpose of caring for and preserving the earth, making it a liveable place for all, regardless of their affiliations. This book defines leadership as an act of selfless servitude, solely driven by the desire to please Allah/God. A true leader serves their people with the intention of pleasing Allah, rather than pursuing personal or selfish interests. Throughout history, Allah/God has sent prophets, starting from Adam (PBUH) and culminating with the final prophet Muhammad (PBUH), to guide mankind and warn them against associating anything with Allah, emphasizing the importance of worshipping Allah/God alone.

Therefore the model of leadership from Islamic perspective is prophet Mohammad (PBUH) and his Rightly four Guided Khalifs(Khulafah Al-Rashidun). In other words, leadership from the Islamic perspective starts from the premise that the originator of leadership is Allah/God and that humankind is Allah/God representative on earth. The representative of Allah/God on earth therefore have to follow the laws of the originator of leadership who have given mankind legitimacy to represent Him and also the reason for the creation of mankind which is to worship Allah/God only. That is why the definition of leadership in this book is selfless servitude purely for the pleasure of Allah/God alone.

The leader role is to serve Allah/God and by so doing he/she is serving his followers the way Allah/God want him to serve his people by implementing the divine laws (sharia) of Allah/God which has the best practices leaders and follower can use to serve them. The Quran have lay for us all countless ways to behave either with our friends, families and foes which is a great guide to mankind and also how those leaders who trance grace His order or authority end up in their lives. The good example of those people in the past civilizations, are for example the people of prophet Hud, the people of Madiyan, the Pharos in Egypt and many other examples. These example of those leaders and followers who reject Allah/God Message through the prophets that were send to guide their people and give them good tightness speak to us today more than ever before as leaders and follower, especially those of the Muslim Ummah and the western world for Prophet Muhammad(PBUH) was send as mercy to mankind. Some today may not believe in Islam but they will be ask in the Day of Judgement whether they did receive the preaching of Prophet Muhammad (PBUH) to worship Allah/God alone.

We have read how those leaders and followers who reject faith as preached by the prophets send to them end up with their lives, we as leaders and followers are not far away from committing the same mistakes committed by the past people when it come to the rejection of Allah/God and His prophets. Thus, leadership or leadership position is a trust (Amanah) given to us mankind by Allah/God as his representative on earth to serve humanity and not to trans grace our authority. We are now witnessing one of the greatest catastrophe in human history for a long time whereby some leaders in the world are being given the blank check to bomb a people into obeys, carpet bombing with no regard for human being and suffering of children and elderly. How could such a thing happen when we all have the fear of Allah/God and the Day of Judgment and the sense of responsibility as Allah/God vicegerent on earth?

The story of Musa (Moses) remind us of the ancient Egypt was a super-power, with totalitarian government or Pharos who had absolute control over the life and death of its residents and no one could escape from their bondage or their apartheid system whereby their in slave people could not escaped to. The Israelites lived in Egypt for 210 years. They lived a genocide, throwing all the baby boys into the Nile, and continued with over eight decades of sadistic torture and oppression and they were freed by Moses at the burning bush, that generation of Israelites had lived their entire lives under the whip. The most important thing here is that Allah/God send Musa (Moses) to liberate Israelites from the Pharos who had tortured them killed their children and keep them in bondage for a long time and they realised that their only hope was God, and "they cried out" to God in despair and Musa (Moses) was send to liberate them from Egypt. In other words, Allah/God then charged Moses to lead the Israelites out of bondage and bring them to the Promised Land and Moses asked Allah/God to make his brother Aaron as his spokesman, because "he can speak fluently" and then Moses and Aaron dutifully set out for Egypt, where they requested an audience with Pharaoh so that they could be able to liberate their people from the tyrant superpower of the time the Pharaoh of Egypt. These stories here are written as a reminder to mankind to learn lessons from history.

Have we forgotten history and can we as human being learn a lesson from these stories and realise that leadership position is not about political power but servitude for the pleasure of Allah/God only. We cannot claim to be a the only democracy in the region and yet act as a totalitarian government or Pharos who had absolute control over the life and death of its residents and no one could escape from their bondage or their apartheid system whereby others where enslaved and besieged and they could not could not escape. These stories are good reminders to us all irrespective of political affiliation and faith.

Henceforth, where is the international laws of engagement not respected even if we do not follow Divine Laws (Sharia) in passing judgment and safeguarding life. The international community cannot be silence and advocate self-defence when there is war to avoid a situation of some of the above historical events in the history of mankind.

Leadership from Islamic perspective also accept man-made laws that does not contradict the Quran and the Sunnah of the prophet (s). Man-made laws have their limitations, and when these man-made laws goes against Allah/God's laws, they should not be implemented and this also requires the assistance from the Islamic scholars who understand the Islamic theology and not hand stamp scholars who cares about themselves but the Ummah and have the fear of Allah/God and the prophet (s). Therefore, leaders and followers from Islamic perspective should adhere to the core principles of 'Tawheed' or oneness in Allah/God, worship (Ibadah) and be guided by Divine Laws (Shariah, the Islamic laws).

The other key element of the differences between the Islamic perspective of leadership and Western leadership perspectives concerns the role of Parliament in making the laws of the land as noted above with regard to man-made laws. Man-made laws or secular laws cannot be above Divine Laws (sharia). Therefore Divine laws (sharia) are above the laws made by a parliament especially if they go contrary to the sharia. In other words, Divine laws (Sharia), from the Islamic perspective of leadership, should be supreme over the laws of the land that are created through the parliament or any institutions that the law makers make laws. Divine Laws are not comparable to man-made laws as in the case of laws made in the Western parliaments and non-Western parliament democracies. Hence is a problem or a concern.

The fact that the Islamic perspective of leadership negates Parliamentary Democracy does not mean that an Islamic perspective of leadership is against all aspects of democracy, such as the rights of citizens, the right to life, freedom of expression, freedom of assembly, right to protest and other aspects of democracies that are universal in nature. The international laws that prevent genocide are important from an Islamic perspective and that is why prophet Muhammad (PBUH) used to invite Kings of other nations to accept Islam and sign treaties with them.

The most significant conflict between Divine Laws and Parliamentary democratic laws is that divine laws are sacred, and man-made laws are not. Since Divine laws are sacred, Parliament may pass some laws which are against Divine laws, for example, same-sex marriage, or constant coercion or indoctrination of western nations on African and some countries in the south to accept laws with regard LGBTQ. All these laws or man-made laws cannot be compatible with Divine Laws (sharia) and therefore is not acceptable from the Islamic perspective of leadership.

Islam as a way of life and does not divide spiritual and progressive activities. There is no separation between the leader and his religion as the case with the west who argue for the separation of religion from the state.

Prophet Mohammad (PBUH) served as a prophet and as a statesman in Madinah and the Ummah. The prophet (PBUH) made a tremendous changes as a leader and a Prophet of Allah/God in Madinah as noted by Armstrong (1992) who argue that the spread and acceptance of Islam during his time reflect the unique message of Islam and was clearly a reflection of the genius of Mohammad (PBUH). Furthermore, Armstrong (1992) argue that Muslim scripture, the Qur'an, gave them a mission: to create a just and decent society, in which all members were treated with respect. The political well-being of the Muslim community was, and is, a matter of supreme importance.

Armstrong (2006) further ascertain that the life of the Prophet Muhammad (c. 570–632 CE) was as crucial to the unfolding Islamic ideal as it is today. His career revealed the inscrutable God's activity in the world, and illustrated the perfect surrender (in Arabic, the word for "surrender" is Islam) that every human being should make to the Divine. Beginning during the Prophet's lifetime, Muslims had to strive to understand the meaning of his life and apply it to their own. A little more than a hundred years after Muhammad's death, as Islam continued to spread to new territories and gain converts, Muslim scholars began to compile the great collections of Muhammad's sayings (a hadith) and customary practice (Sunnah), which would form the basis of Muslim law.

The Sunnah taught Muslims to imitate the way Muhammad (PBUH) spoke, ate, loved, washed, and worshipped, so that in the smallest details of their daily existence, they reproduced his life on earth in the hope that they would acquire his internal disposition of total surrender to God. Thus, Islam is a way of life; the leader and follower from an Islamic perspective are urged in their various activities and persuasions or reflections to respect the ones and sovereignty of Allah/God and this is affirmed in Surah 3: Al-Imran (3:189), as translated into English by Khan and Al –Hilali (1996, p. 108), 189. "And to Allah belongs the dominion of the heavens and the earth, and Allah has power over all things." Thus, a leader in Islam does everything for the sake and pleasure of Allah/God, and whatever he/she does for his/her followers is distinctively for Allah/God pleasure. It is therefore forbidden for the leader to do injustice to his/her follower. The only thing distinguishing the leader from the follower is their faith, knowledge, and commitment to Islamic values and principles. The central point and reason for creation in Islam is to serve Allah/God and follow His laws, as revealed in the Quran and the Sunnah of the Prophet Mohammad (PBUH) as a practical example for us all to follow.

Leadership from Islamic perspective is to speak the truth because leadership is a trust that Allah/God has bestowed on us and we are not in these position of leadership without the will Allah/God and that leaders should know that they will be accountable for their deed during the Day reckoning.

Leadership from Islamic perspective is affirmed in Surah 21, Al Anbiya (21:73), as translated into English by Khan and Al Hilali (1996, p. 414), "And we made them leaders, guiding (mankind) by Our Commad, and We revealed to them the doing of good deeds, performing Salat (Iqamat-as –salat), and the giving of Zakat and of Us (Alone) they were the worshipers."

Leadership from an Islamic perspective does not stop with the leader alone only as the Quran affirmed in Surah Al Baqarah 2 (2:30). Leaders and followers are all vicegerent of Allah/God on earth but followers chose to give bayah (allegiance) to one leader to take care of their affaire and protect them and serve them as prescribed in the Quran.

All the prophets of Allah/God especially the final prophet of Allah/God Mohammad (PBUH) always follows the will of Allah/God revelations. Allah/God affirmed the finality of His prophet in Surah Al-Ahzab (33:40) as translated into English by Khan and Al Hilali (1996, p. 533),40, Mohammad (PBUH) is not the father of any of your men, but he is the Messenger of Allah and the last (end) of the prophet. And Allah is Ever All-Awear of everything. You can also see Al Baqarah (2:252) as translated into English by Khan and Al Hilali (1996, p. 63). In this verse of the Quran (2:252) as narrated by Jbir bin Abdullah (RA): The prophet (PBUH) said: "I have been given five (things) which were not given to anyone else before me:a) Allah made me victories by awe, (by His frightening my enemies) for a distance of one month's journey; b) The earth has been made for me (and my followers) a place for praying and a thing to purify (perform Tayammum), therefore anyone of my followers can pray whenever he is, at time of prayer; c)The booty have been made Halal (lawful) to me yet it was not lawful to anyone else before me; d) I have been given the right of intercession (on the Day of Resurrection); e) Every prophet used to be sent to his nation only, but I have been sent to all mankind" (Sahih Al-Bukhari, vol.1, Hadith No.331).

Also as narrate by Aisha (RA) and Ibn Abbas (RA): On his deathbed Allah Messenger (PBUH) put a sheet over his face and when he felt hot, he would remove it from his face. When in that state (of putting and removing the sheet) he said:, "May Allah's Curse be on the Jews and the Christian for they built places of worship at the graves of their Prophets" (By that) he intended to warn (the Muslims) from what they (i.e. Jews and Christians) had done. (Sakhih Bukhari, Vol. 4, Hadith No.683). Also see Khan and Al Hilali (1996, p. 63).

Abu Hurairah (RA) also narrated the Prophet (PBUH) said, "The Israelis used to be rulea and guided by Prophets. Whenever a Prophet died, another would take over his place. There will be no Prophet after me, but there will be caliphs who will increase in number." The people asked. "O Allah Messenger? What do you order us (to do)?" He said, "Obey the one who will be given the Bai'ah-pleage first, Fulfil their (i.e., the caliphs') right, for Allah will ask them about (any shortcomings) in ruling those whom Allah has put under their guardianship." (Sakhih Bukhari, Vol. 4, Hadith No.661). It should be noted here as in the English translation of Quran by Khan and Al Hilali (1996, p. 63) is that If the Bai'ah (pledge) is given to a caliph and after a while another caliph is given the Bai'ah (pledge) by some members of the society, the common Muslims should abide by the Bai'ah (pledge) given to the first caliph, for the election of the second is invalid.

Leadership from Islamic perspective is trust (Amanah) and there is a story of one companion of the prophet Muhammad (PBUH0 who wanted to be given a post as a governor of a region and Prophet Mohammad (PBUH) warned him against it and said to him do not to ask for authority for you will be accountable for such a responsibility and I am not sure you are ready for it.

This story is affirmed by the narration of Abu Dhar, who said: "I said: "O Messenger of Allah, will you appoint me as a governor? Prophet Muhammad (PBUH) struck my shoulder with his hand and then said: O Abu Dharr, you are weak, and it is a trust (Amanah). On the Day of Judgement, it will be a disgrace and regret except for the one who took it by its right and fulfilled his duty in it." This Hadith is so powerful and send a strong message to some of us who spend their wealth and powers to be leaders of their various communities for self-enrichment, prestige or the power to control others and create for himself, his family and his cronies. The hadith teaches us all that seeking power for the sake of power is not right. We can see around us either in the Muslim Ummah or in the Western world how people are chasing power by all means and at all cost possible even if means death and destruction of others.

Leadership from an Islamic perspective, as seen from the creation of the Islamic city state in Madinah, emphasizes succession. It is observed from the Madinah period and through the righteous Caliph that they did not lay down the foundation for heredity or assume power by force rather than through election and then govern through consultation according to the Shariah (Divine law). The first Caliph, Abu Bakr, had a similar passage and became the first Caliph. He said, I have been entrusted with your affairs, although I am not the best among you. Help me if I do well, and correct me if I do wrong. Obey me if I Obey Allah and His Prophet Mohammad (PBUH). The second Caliph, Umar, also went; through a similar process and said to his people that he is one among them.

The third Uthman, Caliph, and the fourth Caliph, Ali, all used consultation and upheld Sharia or (Divine law). This was quite evident after the death of Prophet Mohammad (PBUH). The death of the Prophet (PBUH), Caliph Abu Bakr, was nominated after some consultation by the representatives of the Muslim communities at that time. Abu Bakr was very close to Prophet Muhammad (PBUH). Even during the Prophet's time, he had allowed Abu Bakr Sidiq to lead the prayer. Umar and the other close companions were there, and they gave him allegiance, and Abu Bakr became the first Caliph. The Caliphs who followed Abu Baker were also chosen or nominated by other companions. This principle of succession, as noted in the Caliphs' case after the Prophet Mohammad's death (PBUH), was stimulated by the Quranic value of 'Shura' or (consultation). However, in the Western leadership perspective, leaders are voted into high office by their citizens.

Leadership is seen either in the West or non-Western countries as an opportunity to gain privilege and prestige. Big lobbies and big businesses are now endorsing many leaders to serve their future interests, crippling Democracy. From an Islamic perspective, leadership is about servitude purely for the pleasure of Allah. From an Islamic perspective, leadership focuses on establishing prayers, giving charity, and forbidding evil. The Western perspective focuses on the worldly life. This dichotomy is evident that the Islamic leadership perspective draws its core values from faith, while in the West and some other countries, leaders call for the separation of religion from politics altogether. The author strongly argues in this book that the two perspectives are the core differences between the Quran, Sunnah, and 'Sharia,' the laws that guide leadership.

The above had been some of the divergence of leadership from the Islamic perspective. Thus, the nature of leadership from an Islamic perspective is conceived primarily in the Quran and that differs from leadership from the Western perspective which does not derived from the scripture but from the literature, theory, practice and writings of many Western scholars and practitioners. Thus, what is leadership from a western perspectives that defers from the Islamic perspective as examine above?

Leadership from a Western perspective content is not derived from a biblical or the Ten Commandments or religions principles and that is a concern. Leadership from a western perspective is based on western cultures which is often associated with individualism, competition, and achievement. Leaders are expected to be charismatic, visionary, and decisive. They are also expected to be accountable for their actions and to take responsibility for the success or failure of their organizations. That is good but not good enough. Allah/God should be put at the centrality of leadership. In other words, the content of leadership in the western perspective content should be the Bible, Ten commandments, and other religious principles to avoid a situation that mankind think that he/she is the centre of the universe. When there are many scandals in the west you start hearing people talking about ethical leadership. Those ethical principles of leadership are in the Quran and the Bible, let those in leadership refer to them to avoid all these scandals. The Bible contains a vast amount of guidance from Allah/God to humanity on leading a spiritual life and interacting with one another. If the leaders and followers of the Western world were to adhere to the teachings of the Bible, the world would not be plagued by incessant wars and the exploitation of individuals for economic purposes. Some Western powers have perpetuated various ills, such as the slave trade and colonization. These acts are carried out by individuals who deviate from the teachings of religious texts such as the Quran, the Sunnah of the Prophet (PBUH), the Bible, the Ten Commandments, and other religious principles.

Let's look at the Tent Commandment as commented and written uploaded by Hain (2023)'s as a block for Sysop Catholics' Resources Network CompuServe ID 76711, 1340: 1) 1. I AM THE LORD THYGOD: THOU SHALT NOT HAVE STRANGE GODS BEFORE ME. COMMANDS: faith, hope, love, and worship of God; reverence for holy things; prayer. FORBIDS: idolatry; superstition; Spiritism; tempting God; sacrilege; attendance at false worship; 2. THOU SHALL NOT TAKE THE NAME OF THE LORD THY GOD IN VAIN.COMMANDS: reverence in speaking about God and holy things; the keeping of oaths and vows. FORBIDS: blasphemy; the irreverent use of God's name; speaking disrespectfully of holy things; false oaths and the breaking of vows; 3. KEEP THE SABBATH HOLY.COMMANDS: going to church on Sundays and holy days of obligation. FORBIDS: missing church through one's own fault; unnecessary servile work on Sunday and holy days of obligation. 4. HONOUR THY FATHER AND THY MOTHER. COMMANDS: love; respect; obedience on the part of children; care on the part of parents for the spiritual and temporal welfare of their children; obedience to civil and religious superiors. FORBIDS: hatred of parents and superiors; disrespect; disobedience; 5. THOU SHALT NOT KILL. COMMANDS: safeguarding of one's own life and bodily welfare and that of others. FORBIDS: unjust killing; suicide; abortion; sterilization; duelling; endangering life and limb of self or others; 6. THOU SHALT NOT COMMIT ADULTERY. COMMANDS: chastity in word and deed. FORBIDS: obscene speech; impure actions alone or with others. 7. THOU SHALT NOT STEAL. COMMANDS: respect for the property of rights and others; the paying of just debts; paying just wages to employees; integrity in public office. FORBIDS: theft; damage to the property of others; not paying just debts; not returning found or borrowed articles; giving unjust measure or weight in selling; not paying just wages; bribery; graft; cheating; fraud; accepting stolen property; not giving an honest day's work for wages received; breach of contract;

8. THOU SHALT NOT BEAR FALSE WITNESS AGAINST THY NEIGHBOR.COMMANDS: truthfulness; respect for the good name of others; the observance of secrecy when required. FORBIDS: lying; injury to the good name of others; slander; talebearing; rash judgment; contemptuous speech and the violation of secrecy; 9. THOU SHALT NOT COVET THY NEIGHBOR'S WIFE.COMMANDS: purity in thought. FORBIDS: wilful impure thought and desires; 10. THOU SHALT NOT COVET THY NEIGHBOR'S GOODS. COMMANDS: respect for the rights of others. FORBIDS: the desire to take, to keep, or damage the property of others.

The above Ten commandment are critical to adhere to by those at leadership and followers with regards t western perspective of leadership. If those in leadership and followers adhere to these commandment we would not have these problems we have today as the care takers of Allah/God representatives on earth. There would not have been slavery or colonisation in both perspectives. Thus this book is written as a reminder for those in leadership position to remember that Allah/God is seeing and is All Knowers and that you will be accountable for all your deed during the Day of Resurrection. In other words, leadership from a western perspective content should be influence by the Bible and the Ten Commandment as well as I argue here that leadership from the Islamic perspectives should be derived from the Quran and the Sunnah of the Prophets, starting from prophet Adam (PBUH) to the final prophet of Allah/God prophet Mohammad (PBUH) and the four rightly guided caliphs to avoid man-made laws that goes contrary to the Divine Laws (sharia).

Today leadership from a Western perspective have some of its origins in the early theory of leadership, starting from the Great Man theory of leadership. This theory stipulates that confident individual leaders have innate qualities of leadership that enable them to lead. To this effect Northouse (2010) argue that to the traditional trait theories, certain individuals possess innate qualities that enable them to lead. Thus in the traditional trait approach of leadership as argue by Gill,(2006), leaders are born, leaders born with some characteristics due to their psychological personality and Northouse (2010) identifies intelligence these traits as , self-confidence, determination, integrity, and sociability as the five traditional traits associated with effective leadership and that it is these traits that distinguish leaders from followers. There is evidence to suggest that some of the traits thought to be important to leadership are culturally determined. Yukl (2002) identify some traits that facelifted an effective leadership as, traits of intelligence, honesty, understanding, verbal skills and determination. Since these theories could not delaminate trait approach to leadership, behavioural theory emerged. The Behaviral theory of leadership main assumption is that a leaders is judge base on his/her behaviour and not his or her characteristic as the trait theory. Situational theory of leadership is also very important to understand western perspective of leadership. The situational approach emphasizes contextual factors influencing leadership processes. The basic argument of this approach is that different situations warrant different kinds of leadership. Leadership effectiveness is enhanced only when leaders pick up cues in the environment and adapt their policies, behaviours, and actions accordingly.

The leaders must adjust their leadership style (delegative, supportive, directive, coaching) to match the varying level of religious, personal and psychological maturity of their followers. Northouse (2004) argue that for a leader to be able to shape events, the leaders must recognize the situation and the needs of the employees. This gives rise to considerations about factors that help a leader transform the behaviour of followers. Transformational theory of leadership is also vital for the understanding of leadership from a western perspective. Transformational theories focus on how leaders motivate followers to pursue goals that transcend their immediate self- interest.

According to Bass (1997) Transformational theories mainly promote desirable attitudes, values, and beliefs which affect the culture. They attach considerable importance to such values as relative equality of power between leaders and the led, high tolerance of ambiguity, high levels of trust and openness and a desire to share feelings and emotions. They also emphasize values such as trust, teamwork, rationality, delegation, productivity and customer service, among others. Transformational leaders mobilize their followers through "idealized influence" (charisma), "inspirational motivation", intellectual stimulation, high-performance expectations and effective articulation of a vision. On the other hand transactional theory of leadership focuses on a notion of transaction, which means give and take.

Servant leadership theory developed by Greenleaf (1977), is based on four main principles of moral authority, specifically a) the leader's sacrifice, b) the leader's commitment to a worthy cause, c) the leader's teaching whose ends and means are inseparable, and, d) leader's relationships. Servant leadership has some commonality with the Islamic leadership perspective because the core notion of servant leadership is that the leader is a servant first. The leader is not a master to his people but a good Shepard. Hence, there has been some criticism about servant leadership by Whinstone (2002) whereby he argue that servant leadership is being too good to be true. Johnston (2001), on the other hand, argues that servant leadership is associated with the negative term servant (or slave). Others like Hunter (2000) also argue that servant leadership focuses on services' biblical and religious context. Nonetheless, there are some Western scholars who call for leadership to be more ethical and moral, for example Cuilla (1995 Brown and Trevino (2004). Thus, leadership from ethical and moral dimension is centered to those scholars and writer who argue that leadership is a trust and privilege to serve humanity. Cuilla (1995) advocate for ethical and moral leadership from a Western perspective of leadership, however these kind of western scholars and practitioners who calls ethical and moral leadership are in a minority.

Moral and ethical leadership arguments usually grasp the attention of most Western leadership scholars and practitioners when there are many scandals facing the politics, business, or others spheres in life. There are many of those scandals that are starting to create awareness in the western political arena and business calling for moral leadership which is still a minority.

The definition of Leadership from a western perspective tend to focus on the ability of individuals to influence organization members toward the. Accomplishment of goals (Yukl, 1994b). Bums (1978) on the other insisted that an understanding of "the nature of leadership requires the understanding of the essence of power, for leadership is a special form of power".

The definition of leadership from an Islamic perspective define leadership as selfless servitude purely for the pleasure of Allah/God alone. Even though the ability of individual is recognized but it is also limited and therefore requires the Quran and the Sunnah of the prophets as a source of guide in attaining the best decisions in serving mankind and the Bible and also the Ten Commandments to guide both leaders and followers in leading others.

Chapter 14

The Sources of Islamic Leadership Principles and the Example of Islamic Leadership

This chapter examines the source of Islamic leadership principles and the example of Islamic leadership using the Quran, the Holy prophet Muhammad (PBUH), the four Rightly Guided Caliphs (Khulafah Al-Rashidun), and pious leaders and some followers. The source of Islamic leadership principles differs from a Western perspective on leadership because leadership from the Islamic perspective content is and should be guided by the Quran and Sunnah of Prophets and more importantly prophet Muhammad (PBUH). Therefore, some of the Islamic leadership principles is very important because of its content is and should be from the Quran and the Sunnah of the prophet Muhammad (PBUH).

The prophet said in one of his Hadith Sahih/Authentic in (Al-Bukhari and Muslim) as narrated by Abdullah Ibn 'Umar (may Allah be pleased with him) reported: I heard the Messenger (PBUH) say: "All of you are shepherds and every one of you is responsible for his herd. A leader is a shepherd, a man is the shepherd over his family and a woman is the shepherd over her husband's house and his children. So all of you are shepherds, and every one of you is responsible for his herd." In another wording: "All of you are shepherds and every one of you is responsible for his herd. A leader is a shepherd and is responsible for his herd. A man is the shepherd over his family and is responsible for his herd. A woman is the shepherd over the house of her husband and is responsible for her herd. A servant is the shepherd over the wealth of his master and is responsible for his herd. So all of you are shepherds, and every one of you is responsible for his herd."

Thus it is clear from the above Hadith that everyone is entrusted with the protection and care of those under him, and will be held accountable for them. For instance, a ruler will be asked about his subjects on the Day of Judgment. Likewise, a man is responsible for his family, and he should obey Allah/God, forbid them to disobey Him, and fulfil their due rights. He will be asked about these duties on the Day of Judgment. Also, a woman is responsible for keeping her husband's house and for caring for the children, and she will be questioned about this on the Day of Judgment. A servant is also a protector of his master's wealth and will be questioned about that on the Day of Judgment. So everyone is invested with the responsibility of protecting those under their care and they will be questioned about this on the Day of Judgment. Therefore, leadership from an Islamic perspective can be understood as a sacred duty, wherein both leaders and followers are bound by their obligations to Allah/God and the prophet (PBUH). It is crucial for leaders to recognize that they will be held accountable on the Day of Judgement for the protection and well-being of those under their authority. It is disheartening to witness the lack of seriousness displayed by certain individuals in positions of power, such as husbands, servants, women, and leaders, who fail to fulfil their responsibilities. These individuals will undoubtedly face questioning and be held accountable for their actions on the Day of Judgement.

In Islamic teachings, the leader is likened to a shepherd, responsible for the welfare of their entire flock. Despite not owning the flock, the shepherd diligently cares for it, assuming full responsibility. Hence, a true leader is one who is deeply connected to their people, understands their needs, communicates effectively, and empowers them to reach their full potential. In his lecture on prophetic leadership, Qadhi (2014) discusses the teaching methods employed by the Prophet (PBUH). Qadhi highlights that the Prophet (PBUH) would often utilize parables or diagrams drawn in the sand to effectively convey his message to the people. This approach allowed him to elucidate complex concepts and ideas in a manner that was easily comprehensible to his audience. Furthermore, Qadhi emphasizes that the Prophet (PBUH) possessed the remarkable ability to bring out the best qualities in even the most challenging individuals. Of particular significance is the Prophet's (PBUH) choice to begin his teachings by drawing a parable of a leader as a shepherd.

This analogy served to underscore the importance of leadership qualities such as guidance, protection, and care for those under one's charge. Additionally, the Prophet (PBUH) extended this analogy to encompass the roles of Imman/Khalifah/Caliph, as well as that of a father and mother. By doing so, he emphasized the vital responsibilities and duties associated with these positions of authority and influence. The beauty of the analogy is that the shepherd take care of the flock he does not own, he know what is beneficial for the flocks, and he know how to nature the animal and he is satisfied when the flocks are healthy and breading well. Furthermore, the shepherd is regarded as a symbol of guidance, protection, and care. This role encompasses not only the physical act of tending to a flock of sheep but also extends to the spiritual and moral responsibilities associated with leading and nurturing a community. The shepherd does not own the sheep/camel he is taking care of, rather he or she is accountable to somebody else for that flocks, he know what is better for the flock better than the flocks. Subsequently, as a shepherd diligently watches over and tends to his flock, a leader in the Islamic context is expected to exhibit similar qualities of vigilance, compassion, and responsibility towards those under their care.

This includes providing guidance, protection, and support to ensure the well-being and growth of the community. Qadhi (2014) argue in his lecture that the prophet started the Hadith with the example of the Immam/khalif, who is the shepherd because he is responsible for the entire people under his care because he know that he is not above the law and no matter how grand his palace is and how much money he owns, still he is a shepherd and that there is a master above him and the master will question him about his flocks, the entire Muslim Ummah, and his master will ask him for there is only one Allah/God and everyone is under Allah/God. After the Immam/Khalif the next analogy was that of a father/husband and mother/wife who the very building block of every society. If the family is sound all will be sound, engineer, teacher, CEO are under the two and therefore a successful shepherd should lead the way and also be a role model.

The Holy Quran as a Primary Source of the Islamic Leadership Principles.

The Quran is the Word of Allah, not speech by any human being or Angels, and it is uncreated. See Surah 69: Al Haqqah (69:40-3), Al-Hilali and Khan (1996, p.726), 40. "That this is verily the Word of an honoured Messenger [i.e., Jibael (Gabriel) or Muhammad (PBUH), which he has brought from Allah]. 41. It is not the Word of the poet: little is that you believe! 42. Nor it is the Word of a soothsayer (or a foreteller): little is that you remember! 43. This is the Revelation sent down from the Lord of the Alamin (mankind, jinn, and all that exist)." The Messenger referred to here is Muhammad (PBUH). Also see Surah 81: (19-21), Al- Hilali and Khan (1996, p.757), 19. "Verily, this is the Word (this Quran brought by) a most honourable Messenger [Jibrael (Gabriel), from Allah to Prophet Muhammad PBUH)]. 20. Owner of power (and high rank) with (Allah), the Lord of the Throne, 21. Obeyed (by the angles in the heaven) and trustworthy." The Messenger here is Gabriel. Here the message is evident in both verses that Prophet Muhammad (PBUH) and Angel Gabriel were not the writers of the Quran and that the Quran is uncreated by any human being but is the Word of Allah/God alone.

Allah/God has challenged those who think the Quran is not from Him by stating in Surah 10 Yunus (10:38), as translated into English by Al-Hilali and Khan (1996, p.269), 38. "Or do they say: He (Muhammad (PBUH) has forged it?" Say: "Bring then a Surah (chapter) like unto it, and call upon whomever you can besides Allah, if you are truthful!" See also Surah 11 Hud (11:13), as translated into English by Al-Hilali and Khan (1996, p.280), 13. "Or they say, "He (Prophet Muhammad (PBUH) forged it (the Quran)." Say: "Bring you then ten forged Surah (chapters) like unto it, and call whomever you can, other than Allah (to your help), if you speak the truth!" Subsequently, in Surah 9: Al Tawbah (9:6), as translated into English by Al-Hilali and Khan (1996, p.239), 6. "And if anyone of the Mushrikun (polytheists, idolaters, pagans, disbelievers in the oneness of Allah) seeks your protection, then grant him protection so that he may hear the Words of Allah (the Quran)- and then escort him to where he can be secure, that is because they are men who know not."

These Verses clearly shows that the Messenger conveys is Allah's true Word, not the Messenger's Word as is in Surah 5 Al Maidah (5:15), as translated into English by Al-Hilali and Khan (1996, p.148), 15. "O people of the Scripture (Jews and Christians)! Now has come to you Our Messenger (Muhammad (PBUH) explaining to you much of that which you used to hide from the Scripture and pass over (i.e., leaving out without explaining). Indeed, there has come to you from Allah a light (Prophet Muhammad (PBUH) and a plain Book (this Quran)." The Quran is the most straightforward, beautiful, unambiguous, self-evident Book, and it is a privilege for humankind to recite. The Quran is a shining light by which we recite to guide us in all our endeavours, and the Quran makes things clear for us and distinguishes truth from falsehood. The Quran is the Word of The Almighty Allah/God, the Originator of everything and The One Who encompasses everything with His knowledge and kindness. See also Surah 4: Al Nisa (4:82), as translated into English by Al-Hilali and Khan (1996, p.126), 82. "Do they not then consider the Quran carefully? Had it been from other than Allah, they would have found many a contradiction therein." Every piece of information in the Qur'an is the secret miracle of this divine Book. Thus, the Holy Quran is the primary source of leadership and success principles. Revealed by a supreme author, Allah, its message has universal and eternal relevance to all humanity. See Surah 2: Al Baqarah (2:23), Al-Hilali and Khan (1996, p.15), 23. ""And if you (Arab, Jews, and Christians) are in doubt concerning that which We have sent down (i.e., the Quran) to Our slave (Muhammad (PBUH), then produce a Surah (chapter) of the like thereof and call your witnesses (supporters and helpers) besides Allah, if you are truthful."

This Verse is vital for those who doubt the Quran. Allah challenges those who doubt the Quran to produce a Surah like thereunto or even with helpers. They cannot do so because the Quran is the word of Allah. The

Quran is a complete code of life that contains guidelines on all aspects of life, spiritual, social, economic, and political. Nevertheless, some people do not believe it. Nevertheless, the Quran is the last and complete revelation of divine guidance. It is the source of leadership principles that can guide leaders and followers towards success and the highest attainment in their endeavours as leaders and good citizens of the one Nation Ummah (Islamic communities), wherever they may be.

Hence, the notion of a unified Ummah, or Islamic community, does not imply that all inhabitants of a particular land are all Muslims, they could be majority Muslims. Rather, it signifies a scenario where Muslims constitute a majority and the governing authority chooses to implement Sharia Divine Laws, with the primary objective of worshipping Allah, prohibiting wrongdoing, promoting righteousness, establishing prayers, and fostering acts of charity. The Quran's magnificence lies in the universal nature of its teachings, which are intended for all of humanity, regardless of their geographical location, community, or political jurisdiction. The Quran addresses all mankind and also share the stories of the people of the past history of the prophets, the people of Madyan, The people of Hud, and the people of Noah so that we can learn lessons from their mistakes and be better leaders and followers. See Surah 6: Al Anam (6:19), as translated into English by Al-Hilali and Khan (1996, p.172), 19. "Say (O Muhammad (PBUH): "What thing is the greatest in witness" Say: "Allah (the Greatest!) Is witness between you and me; this Quran has been revealed to me that I may in addition to that warn you and whomsoever it may reach. Can you verily bear witness that besides Allah, there are other aliha (gods)?" Say: "I bear no (such) witness!" Say: "But in truth, He (Allah) is the only one Ilah (God). And truly, I am innocent of what you join in worship with Him." Also, see Surah 17: Al Isra (17:88-9), Al-Hilali and Khan (1996, p.365), 88. "Say: "If mankind and the Jinns were together to produce the like of this Quran, they could not produce the like thereof, even if they helped one another." 89. "And indeed, We have fully explained to mankind, in this Quran, every kind of similitude, but most of the mankind refuse (the truth and accept nothing) but disbelief."

The content of leadership from an Islamic perspective contain is and should be the Quran and the Sunnah of the prophet (PBUH). The Quran talks about faith, struggle, knowledge, piety, charity, prayers, and many things that guide us on how to deal with daily life activities. Through the Quran, we can understand and apply certain leadership principles that can enhance our selfless servitude toward the betterment of humanity.

Allah/God explained in the Quran why He choose humankind to be his representative on earth and how Allah tested Prophet Ibrahim See Surah (2:124). Many stories in the Quran remind us of leadership responsibilities so that we should not transgress as leaders as followers.

In the Quran the stories of the prophets are there to show us as human that the Prophets were sent to mankind proclaim the message of Allah/God. Seen Surah 11 Hud (11:50), as translated into English by Al-Hilali and Khan (1996, p.285), 50. "And to the Ad (people We sent) their brother Hud. He said, "O my people! Worship Allah! You have no other Ilah (god) but Him." The story of Musa (Mosses) called the children of Israel to worship Allah alone and laid down the laws prescribed in the Torah. This story is affirmed in Surah 5Al Maidah (5:44), as translated into English by Al-Hilali and Khan (1996, p.152), 44. "Verily, We did send down the Taurat (Torah) [to Musa (Moses)], therein was guidance and light, by which the Prophets, who submitted themselves to Allah's Will, judged for the Jews. And the rabbis and the priests [too judged for the Jews by the Taurat (Torah) after those Prophets], for to them was entrusted the protection of Allah's Book, and they were witness thereto.

Therefore, fear not men but fear Me (O Jews) and sell not My Verses for a miserable price. And whoever does not judge by what Allah has revealed, such are Kafirun (i.e., disbelievers-of a lesser degree as they do not act on Allah's Laws." "Thus, the Quran is a book of guidance for all humankind and therefore should be the content of leadership from an Islamic perspective. We can also see in the Quran a story Musa (Moses) when he asked Allah/God to allow his brother Harun (Aaron) to go with him to meet pharaoh and liberate the Jews from Egypt and due to the fact that he know that his brother Harun (Aaron) was more eloquent in speech than him. See Surah 28 Al-Qasas (28:43), as translated into English by Al-Hilali and Khan (1996, p.490), 43. "And indeed We gave Musa (Moses) - after We had destroyed the generation of old- the Scripture [the Taurat (Torah)] as an enlightenment for mankind, and a guidance and a mercy, that they might remember (or receive admonition)."

All the above lessons from the Quran are show that the Quran and the Sunnah should be the content of leadership from the Islamic perspective. The Sunnah of the prophet is going to be examine in the next chapter.

The Holy Prophet (609-632 C.E) 15

Prophet Muhammad (PBUH) was born around the year 570 CE to the Banu Hashim clan of the Quraysh tribe, one of Mecca's prominent families. His father, Abdullah, died almost six months before Muhammad (PBUH) was born. According to Islamic tradition, Muhammad (PBUH) was sent to live with a Bedouin family in the desert, as desert life was considered healthier for infants. Muhammad (PBUH) stayed with his foster mother, Halimah bint Abi Dhuayb, and her husband until he was two years old. At the age of six, Muhammad lost his biological mother,

Amina, to illness. In other words, at the age of five, Muhammad returned to the care of his mother, Aminah bint Wahb, but she died a year later, and was raised by his paternal grandfather, Abd al-Muttalib, until he died when Muhammad (PBUH) was eight. He then came under the care of his uncle Abu Talib, the new leader of Banu Hashim. According to the World Civilisation Chapter 7, The Rise and Spread of Islam, the Prophet (PBUH) at the early ten used accompanied his uncle on trading journeys to Syria, gaining experience in commercial trade, which was the only career open to him as an orphan and that due to his upright character during this time, he acquired the nickname "al-Amin," meaning "faithful, trustworthy," and "al-Sadiq," meaning "truthful." Thus, at the age of twelve, he accompanied his uncle in a merchant's caravan to Syria as noted above which gave him the nickname of Al-Amin and truthful due to his dealings during their trade mission with uncle. Muhammad at early stage was content to work as a shepherd, but his Uncle Abu Talib desired something better for him and obtained him employment with a rich widow, Khadijah bint Khuwaylid ibn Asad. Mohammad continued to work for Khadijah taking charge of her caravan conveying merchandise to Syria and on his return, Khadijah was so pleased with his successful management of her business and was so attracted by his noble character that she sent her sister to offer the young man Khadijah's hand. Muhammad had felt drawn to Khadijah, and so matters were soon arranged. Their 26 years of married life were singularly happy. Muhammad continued to work as a merchant. His fairness further enhanced his reputation as "Al-Amin" (The Trustworthy).

The marriage lasted for 25 years and was reported to be a happy married until the death of Khadija. History tells us of one of the great even in the history of the prophet (PBUH) when he helped set the Black Stone in place in the wall of the Kaaba in 605CE Ibn Ishaq. The black stone was removed to facelifted the renovation of the Kaaba and the leaders of the

Makkah/Mecca could not agree on which clan should have the honor of setting the Black Stone in its place. However, they all agreed to wait for the next man to come through the gate and ask him to choose. The man or the person who came through was Prophet Mohammad (PBUH) five years before revelation. He asked for a cloth and each leader of the clan held the cloth he put the Black Stone on the centre of the cloth and Muhammad (PBUH) set the Black Stone in its place as today in the Kaaba and the leaders where satisfied and all present.

Mohammad (PBUH) at the age of 40 received the revelation in a cave in Mount Hira' outside Makkah during the Month of Ramadan were he use to retire to for silence. One night, while lying absorbed in his thoughts in the solitude of the cave, Muhammad was commanded by a mighty voice to go forth and preach. Muhammad rose trembling and hastened home to seek rest and solace in Khadijah's tender care, and she calmed and comforted him. She later consulted her kinsman, Waraqah ibn Nawfal. He declared that the heavenly message that had come to Moses had now come to Muhammad, and that he was chosen as a prophet of Allah.

Khadijah was the first to accept the truth of Islam. Muhammad then communicated his experience to his cousin `Ali, his adopted son Zayd, and his intimate friend Abu Bakr. The Prophet began by preaching his mission secretly first among his intimate friends, then among the members of his own tribe, and thereafter publicly in the city and suburbs. The Quraysh tribe were the guardians of the Ka`bah, which was a source of great prestige and profit to their city, Makkah. They were, therefore, seriously alarmed and became actively hostile towards Muhammad and for him to avoid their hostility he had to immigrate with his followers. The first migration of the Muslim was to Abyssinia and later to Madinah. The Prophet (PBUH) and his Companions, who were mostly weak people and slaves, received all kinds of torture at the hands of the chiefs of the Quraysh. Thirteen years of calling to Islam yielded only little success. Therefore, the Prophet had to find a shelter for his Companions against the tyranny of the Quraysh. He thought that they would be save in Abyssinia. There in Abyssinia was Christian Emperor who was just and the prophet know that and he send his follower there.

The Prophet Muhammad (PBUH) continued his struggle to spread the call of Islam among his tribesmen and the towns near Makkah but he faced huge oppression and resistance. As Abyssinia was considered a temporary shelter for Muslims, the Prophet (PBUH) did not leave Makkah to Abyssinia with his followers. He began calling Arabs who were visiting Makkah during seasons. A group of men from Yathrib (Madinah), a town about four hundred kilometres away visited Makkah.

The Prophet (PBUH) met them and explained the principles of Islam to them. They consulted among each other whether to accept the call or not. They became sure that the Prophet M was truthful. They all believed in him. The Prophet (PBUH) told them that he needed protection in their city to be able to proclaim Islam. They promised to provide every means of protection needed for the call to continue as destined by Allah/God. They also told him that they would come back the next year with their chiefs to make the final agreement with the Prophet (PBUH). The next year seventy men and women from Yathrib visited Makkah and agreed with the Prophet to provide all means they had to protect him and his followers. Hence, the Prophet M asked his followers to leave to Yathrib. All the Companions of the Prophet M migrated to Yathrib secretly.

The Prophet (PBUH), Abu Bakr (RA) and 'Ali(RA) did not leave with the other migrants. They stayed with the prophet in Makkah until orders came down from heaven to the Prophet (PBUH) to leave to Yathrib. Once Allah orders came down to leave for Madina the prophet of Allah instructed Ali (RA) to stay in Makkah. The prophet told Ali (RA) that some people had entrusted him with some of their precious belongings because they, in spite of their rejection of his call to Islam, believed that he was the most trustworthy man in the tribe. He also asked 'Ali to sleep in his bed and cover his body with his blanket during the night when he and his Companion, Abu Bakr, would leave Makkah.

Ali (RA) accepted the mission and slept in the Prophet's bed. At midnight the prophet left the house and the young people from the clan that were chose to kill the prophet(PBUH) when they entered the house and removed the bed cover to surprisingly find 'Ali (RA) and not Muhammad(PBUH) was sleeping in the bed of the prophet(PBUH). The prophet and his followers left for Madinah gradually and unobtrusively, and the Muhammad (PBUH) remaining to the last. Their departure was soon discovered by the Quraysh, who decided to slay Muhammad (PBUH) before the prophet, too, escaped for Madinah and order Ali (RA) to sleep in his bed as a disguise. The forty young men chosen one from each clan, who took a solemn vow to kill Muhammad (PBUH) were surprised to see that Ali (RA) was the one sleeping in the prophet bed. They were to strike simultaneously so that the murder could not be avenged on any one clan. But on the night they were to kill him, Muhammad (PBUH) left for Makkah with Abu Bakr, IslamiaOnline (2023).

The above is a great and noble brief beginning of Mohammad (PBUH) who is the excellent example and model of leadership from Islamic perspective of all time. His noble and simple beginning is a lesson for us all as leaders and followers of the one Ummah wherever we may be. To be a great leader or follower does not means that we must amass great fortune or wealth to be a leader or follower but to be trustworthy and faithful. We can see from the example of the prophet at his early age that the Prophet of Allah/God, Mohammad (PBUH) was always merciful to all and it is affirmed in Surah Al-Anbiya (21:107) as translated into English by Khan and Al Hilali (1996, p.419) 107- "And We have not sent you, (O Muhammad) not but as a mercy for the Alamin (humankind, jinn and all that exists). The Prophet was kind to everyone, just, and trustworthy. He made people's lives easier and assisted them when necessary before and during his prophethood which lasted for twenty-three years. He created a system and a legacy for his followers and people all over the world. He led his people and transformed them. He created a model for humankind to follow which is to worship Allah/God alone and follow Allah/God laws (sharia). He also exemplified leadership as selflessness servitude purely for the pleasure of Allah/God. In other words, the leadership of the Prophet (PBUH) was process driven. He never used obscene and abusive language; even his worst enemies never accused him of telling a lie. He always had a charming personality that captivated the heart of those who came into contact with him.

He was always just and fair. That is why he was always called the 'Truthful' and the 'Trustworthy' (Al-Amin). Armstrong (2006) in writing Mohammad. Abiography of our Time argue very strongly that "the life of the Prophet Muhammad (c. 570–632 CE) was as crucial to the unfolding Islamic ideal as it is today. His career revealed the inscrutable God's activity in the world, and illustrated the perfect surrender (in Arabic, the word for "surrender" is Islam) that every human being should make to the Divine. Beginning during the Prophet's lifetime, Muslims had to strive to understand the meaning of his life and apply it to their own. Armstrong attest to the fact that Muslims imitate the way Muhammad spoke, ate, loved, washed, and worshipped, so that in the smallest details of their daily existence, they reproduced his life on earth in the hope that they would acquire his internal disposition of total surrender to God. The same is of Muslims Ummah today, they want to live like the prophet and ate like the prophet and follow the model example of the prophet as leaders and followers of their various communities. We can learn a great deal from the prophet last sermon in Arafat Makkah where he warned Muslims and humankind not to take an interest in any money transactions and be just to one another and informed them that he had left behind two things that, if held fast to, man would never go astray; the Quran and his Sunnah.

Those who did not believe in his message in Makkah would give their belonging for safekeeping. He obeyed all treaties he signed, especially the treaty of 'Hudiabia' and others. He asked his people to stop worshiping Idols and only worship Allah/God, who is the creator, the nourisher, sustainer, and, consequently, the absolute sovereign before whom all should bow down and to whom all should pray and render obedience. He was a mercy to humankind as is affirmed in Surah Anbiya 21(21:107), as translated into English by Al-Hilali and Khan (1996, p.419), 107. "And We sent you (O Muhammad (PBUH) not but as a mercy for all Alamin (mankind, jinns and all that exist)." Furthermore, in Surah 9: Al-Taubah (9:32-33), as translated into English by Al-Hilali and Khan (1996, p.244), 32. "They (the disbelievers, the Jews, and the Christians) want to extinguish Allah's light (with which Muhammad (PBUH) has been Sent-Islamic Monotheism) with their mouths, but Allah will not allow except that His Light should be perfected even though the Kufirun (disbelievers) hate (it)."

The prophet (PBUH) never changed his stand because of the threat and abuses to his life and his companions. He was resolute and firm in his faith. His enemies offered him power, kingship, wealth, and all kinds of riches of the world only if he would stop preaching Islam and spreading the Message of Allah/God, but he refused those offers. Prophet Mohammad's (PBUH) faith in Allah was strong, and he never doubted. He was a leader who sat and talked to his people, shared their joy and sorrow, and mingled with them in the crowd in such a way that a stranger would not know who the leader of the people amongst them was. He never wanted any praise or left any property to his heirs. His leadership is a shining example to emulate for all Muslims all over the world.

The Quran bears divine testimony to the fact that he was a great leader who had come to lead humankind from darkness to light. See Surah 33: Al Ahzab (33:21), as translated into English by Al-Hilali and Khan (1996, p. 528), 21. "Indeed, in the Messenger of Allah (Muhammad (PBUH), you have a good example to follow for him who hopes for (the meeting with) Allah and the Last Day and remembers Allah much." Yusuf Ali's complementary comments attest to the fact that the Prophet was a model to follow, "We now have the psychology of the Believers - God-fearing men, led by that pattern of men and leaders, Muhammad." Again, Aisha, the wife of the Prophet (May Allah be Pleased with her), described the Prophet (PBUH) as the embodiment of the Quran. Many Western scholars have attested that our Prophet Muhammad (PBUH) was one of the most outstanding leaders who ever lived; for example, scholars like Shaw, Carlyle, and Larmente, the French philosopher. Larmente observed and ask quote "Is there any man greater than he or who would dare to compare any great man in history with Mohammad (PBUH)? The simple answer is no one." He was just a legislator, a leader, and a father who loved his family. His excellent quality was his faith (Islam). LaMartaine, further assert that "If greatness of purpose, smallness of means, and astonishing result are the three criteria of a human genius, who could dare compare any great man in history with Muhammad? The most famous men created arms, laws, and empires only. They founded, if anything at all, no more than material powers which often crumbled away before their eyes. This man moved not only armies, legislations, empires, peoples, dynasties, but millions of men in one-third of the then inhabited world: and more than that he move the altars, the gods, the religions, the ideas, the beliefs and the souls. Shaw (1936) on Prophet Muhammad (PBUH) quote "I have always held the religion of Mohammad in high estimation because of its wonderful vitality. It is the only religion which appears to me to possess that assimilating capability of the changing phase of existence which can make itself appeal to every age. But the Europe of the present century is far advanced. It is beginning to be enamoured of the creed of Mohammed.

"The Medieval ecclesiastics either through ignorance or bigotry painted Mohammad in the darkest colours. They were in fact trained both to hate the man Mohammad and his religion. To them Mohammad was Anti-Christ. I have studied him—the wonderful man in my opinion far froth being an 'Anti-Christ must be called the Saviour of Humanity." Furthermore "He must be called the Saviour of Humanity. I believe that if a man like him were to assume the dictatorship of the modern world, he would succeed in solving its problems in a way that would bring it much-needed peace and happiness". Hart (1978,p.33) in his book argue that quote "My choice of Muhammad (PBUH) to lead the list of the world's most influential persons may surprise some readers and may be questioned by others, but he was the only man in history who was supremely successful on both the religious and secular level." Gandhi (1924) statement in the young India of Prophet Muhammad (PBUH), "I become more than ever convinced that it was not the sword that won a place for Islam in those days in the scheme of life. It was the rigid simplicity, the utter self-effacement of the prophet the scrupulous regard for pledge, his intense devotion to his friends and followers, his intrepidity, his fearlessness, his absolute trust in God and his own mission. These and not the sword carried everything before them and surmounted every obstacle. When I closed the second volume (of the

Prophet's biography), I was sorry there was not more for me to read of that great life. Leo Tolstoy on Prophet Muhammad (PBUH), "Muhammad has always been standing higher than Christianity. He does not consider God as a human being and never makes himself equal to God. Muslims worship nothing except God and Muhammad is his Messenger. There is not any Mystery and secret in it."

William Draper on Prophet Muhammad (PBUH), "Four years the death of Justinian, A.D. 569, was born in Mecca, in Arabia, the man who, of all men, has exercised the greatest influence upon the human race…To be' the religious head of so many empires, to guide the daily life of one-third of the human race, many perhaps justify the title of a Messenger of God." Rao on Prophet Muhammad (PBUH)," The personality of Muhammad, it is most difficult to get into the whole truth of it. Only a glimpse of it I can catch. What a dramatic succession of picturesque scenes! There is Muhammad, the Prophet. There is Muhammad, the Warrior; Muhammad, the Businessman; Muhammad, the Statesman; There is Muhammad, the Orator; Muhammad, the Reformer; Muhammad, the Refuge of Orphans; There is Muhammad, the Protector of Slaves; Muhammad, the Emancipator of Women; There is Muhammad, the Judge; Muhammad, the Saint. All in all these magnificent roles, in all these departments of human activities, he is alike a hero."

Annie Besant also said this in the life and teaching of Prophet Muhammad (PBUH), "It is impossible for anyone who studies the life and character of the great Prophet of Arabia… To feel anything but reverence for that mighty Prophet, one of the great messenger of the Supreme. And although in what I put to you I shall say many things which may be familiar to many, yet I myself feel whenever I re-read them, a new way of admiration, a new sense of reverence for that mighty Arabian teacher." Montgomery Watt on the other hand have this to say about Prophet Muhammad (PBUH), "His readiness to undergo persecution for his beliefs, the high moral character of the men who believed in him and looked up to him as a leader, and the greatness of his ultimate achievement. All argue his fundamental integrity. To suppose Muhammad an impostor raises more problems that it solves. Moreover, none of the great figures of history is so poorly appreciated in the west as Muhammad... Thus, not merely must we credit Muhammad with essential honesty and integrity of purpose, if we are to understand him at all; if we are to correct the errors we have inherited from the past, we must not forget the conclusive proof is a much sticker requirement than a show of plausibility, and in a matter such as this only to be attained with difficulty."

Prophet Muhammad (PBUH) Way of Life

Prophet Muhammad's (PBUH) life was always an embodiment of leadership, meaning selflessness and servitude purely for the pleasure of Allah/God. He made it clear to his people without hesitation that they should leave the worship of idols and worship Allah/God alone without partnering Him with others. Armstrong (2006) in the prophet (PBUH) biography when dealing with the prophet era during Jahiliyah time acknowledged and argue that "The Quraysh had watched him growing up; they saw him going about his business in the market, eating and drinking like everybody else. They had jettisoned many muruwah values, but had retained its elitist, aristocratic outlook and would expect God to choose a well-born karim from one of the more distinguished clans, rather than a minor member of Hashim. How would they react when Muhammad told them to abandon their lofty independence ina way that violated the Sunnah of their fore fathers? For these reason as acknowledge by Armstrong (2006) the Prophet (PBUH), encountered opposition from his tribe's men in Makkah. The abuses, hostility and insult, to personal violence, and to the bitterest persecution, and his converts were most relentlessly oppressed, persecuted, and tortured.

Therefore, in the fifth year of his mission, Muhammad advised them to leave the country and seek refuge from the persecution of the idolaters among the Christian people of Abyssinia. Muhammad and a few stalwart followers remained in Makkah and suffered untold misery and oppression, but still their number continued to increase. Nonetheless his wife Khadijah, their daughters, 'Ali, and Zayd accepted his new status unconditionally, but though his uncle Abu Talib would continue to love and support him, he was deeply pained that Muhammad (PBUH) had the temerity to depart from the absolute authority of their ancestors. He was splitting up the family. Muhammad's cousins—Ja'far ibn Abi Talib, 'Abdullah and'Ubaydallah ibn Jahsh, and their sister Zaynab—all accepted the revelations, but his uncles 'Abbas and Hamzah did not, though their wives did. Muhammad's son-in-law, Abu l-'As, who had married his daughter Zaynab, refused even to consider the new religion.

Prophethood of Mohammad (PBUH) was not easy for he wanted every man, woman, and child in Mecca to develop within themselves the humble thankfulness that should characterize the human condition which others did not ascribed to. Armstrong (2006) argue that the best way the prophet could affect the attitude of his people at the time was to teach his little group the ritual actions that would enable them to cultivate this new attitude. First, they would meet for prayer (salat): their devout prostration would be a daily reminder of their true condition. Salat interrupted their ordinary business and helped them to remember that Allah was their first priority. It was very difficult for men and women schooled in the muruwah ethos to grovel like slaves, and many of the

Quraysh were offended by this abject posture. But the physical routine of salat symbolized the surrender (Islam) of their entire being to Allah. It taught their bodies at a level deeper than the rational to lay aside the self-regarding impulse to prance and preen arrogantly. A Muslim was a man or a woman who had made this act of submission and was proud to be God's slave.

Second, members of the Muslim community (ummah) were required to give a proportion of their income in alms to the poor. This "pure offering" (zakat) took the egotism out of the traditional Bedouin generosity; instead of exhibiting their reckless, excessive liberality, they made a regular, undramatic contribution to the weaker members of the tribe Armstrong (2006). Armstrong (2006) further ascertain that after the prophet (MPBUH) keeping of low profile and preaching only to carefully selected people, but somewhat to his dismay, in 615 Allah instructed him to deliver his message to the whole clan of Hashim. And acknowledged to Ali that the task was beyond himself, but he went ahead and invited forty elders to a frugal meal. The meagre fare was a message in itself; there was to be no more excessive hospitality. Luxury was not simply a waste of money but Ingratitude, a thankless squandering of Allah's precious bounty. When the elders arrived, they were nonplussed when 'Ali served them a simple leg of mutton and a cup of milk. When he told the story later, Ali(RA) made it sound like Jesus' miracle of the loaves and fishes: even though there was scarcely enough for one person, everybody ate his fill. After the meal, Muhammad rose to address the gathering, told them about his revelations, and started to expound the principles of his religion of Islam, but Abu Lahab, Abu Talib'shalf- brother, rudely interrupted him: "He's put a spell on you!" he cried, and the meeting broke up in disorder.

Muhammad had to invite them back the following day and this time he managed to finish his presentation: "O sons of 'Abd al-Muttalib, I know of no Arab who has come to his people with a nobler message than mine." He concluded, "God has ordered me to call you to Him. So which of you will cooperate with me in this venture, as my brother, my executor, and my successor?

There was an awkward silence, and the elders looked at one another in embarrassment. They could all remember Muhammad as a little boy, living on the charity of his relatives. How dared he claim to be the prophet of Allah? Even Muhammad's cousin Ja'far and his adopted son Zayd were reluctant to speak, but finally 'Ali, a gawky thirteen year old, could bear it no longer: "O prophet of God," he cried, "I will be your helper in this matter! "Muhammad laid his hand tenderly on the boy's neck: "This is my brother, my executor, and my successor among you," he said. "Hearken to him and obey him." This was too much.

The spell was broken and the elders burst out laughing. "He's ordered you to listen to your son and obey him!" they cried derisively to Abu Talib as they stormed out of the house. Undeterred by this humiliating failure, Muhammad continued to preach more widely in the city, but with very little success. Nobody criticized his social message. They knew that muruwah required them to share their wealth with the poorer members of the tribe; it was one thing to be selfish and greedy, but quite another to defend these attitudes. Most people objected to the day of reckoning. This, they argued, was simply an old wives' tale. How could bodies that had rotted away in the earth come to life again? Was Muhammad seriously suggesting that their venerable ancestors would rise from their graves to "stand before the lord of all beings?

The Qur'an replied that nobody could prove that there was no life after death, and that if Allah could create a human being out of a tiny drop of semen, he could easily resurrect a dead body. It also pointed out that the people who poured scorn on the idea of a final reckoning were precisely those who had no intention of changing their oppressive, selfish behavior. See Mohammad the biography by Armstrong (2006). The above are extract from the biography of Mohammad from Armstrong (2006). The Prophet (PBUH) called for accountability of his people to Allah alone and non-other than Him. The Prophet (PBUH) tribe's men were unhappy because his message threatened their beliefs and economic interests of Makkah at the time. However, the Prophet (PBUH) was steadfast in his message because of his faith in Allah/God even when they refused to accept his call when he invited them and only Ali at the age of thirteen years old, who could bear it no longer of the silence of his people and said: "O prophet of God," he cried, "I will be your helper in this matter!" The prophet never give up on Islam even though his people did not support him and Ali in the gathering supported him. Despite of all the objections of his clan of his prophethood he keep on preaching and his message was clear, that was to worship only Allah. The prophet had no political ambition of being a king or anyone above the people of Quraysh but he was simple nadhir a messenger with a warning, and should approach the Quraysh humbly, avoid provocation, and be careful not to attack their gods. This is what the great prophets had done in the past.

The prophet was first and foremost a Muslim, one of "those who have surrendered themselves unto Allah/God alone. He never showed that he was above others. He could live with his companion's despite being a Prophet, a father, and a leader of one nation, the Ummah. He could have chosen to live in a mansion or palace far away from his companions, but he chose to live among them. The Prophet (PBUH) used to say: "Avoid suspicion, for suspicion, is often baseless. Therefore, do not spy on each other. Do not probe into the affairs of others. Nor indulge in worldliness or jealousy, and do not bear grudges against each other. Nor betray anyone. Rather lead lives as servants of God and live as brothers." Narrated by Malik. Accordingly, the Prophet (PBUH) was "Exercising superb statesman. He welded the city's five heterogeneous and conflicting tribes, three Jewish, into an orderly confederation. Thus, we can learn many leadership principles from his saying (Hadith).

Prophet Muhammad (PBUH) Sayings-Hadiths

Hadiths are the sayings and traditions of the Prophet Muhammad (PBUH), which his companions compiled. Prophet Mohammad's (PBUH) sayings reflect profound wisdom and morality, which remain the primary sources of guidance and reflection for all Muslims around the globe today. The Prophet's (PBUH) sayings represent the elaborateness of the truth of the Quran, the word of Allah, revealed to the Prophet (PBUH). Therefore, some of the Quranic precepts are expressed in many ways in the sayings of the Prophet (PBUH). The Prophet (PBUH) is the role model who conveyed the divine message, a social reformer, especially in Madinah, and a spiritual leader guiding the one nation Ummah (Islamic communities). According to Kidwai (2012, p.VII), the Prophet's (PBUH) sayings provide "overflowing love and affection for humanity, especially for the weak, the poor, orphans and women; his commitment to fairness and social justice for all; his modesty and simplicity, reflect in his repeated directives that he not be idolized or extolled, as he took great pride in being only a servant of God; and above all, his ardent desire to promote true faith, high morals and manners and excellent conduct." The speech of Prophet Muhammad (PBUH) during his last sermon during Haj in Arafat 1400 years ago is of great important when he declared: O people! Your Lord is one Lord, and you all share the same father (Adam). Indeed, there is no superiority of an Arab over a non-Arab or of a non-Arab over an Arab; or a white over a black; nor a black over a white, except by taqwa (righteousness) is relevant for all time. You will not enter paradise until you believe, and you will not believe until you love one another. Let me guide you to something in the doing of which you will love one another. Give a greeting to everyone among you. The best of God's servants are those who when seen remind you of God; and the worst of God's servants are those who spread tales to do mischief and separate friends, and look for the faults of the good. God is gentle and loves gentleness. Whoever restrains his anger when he has the power to show it, God will give him a great rewards. Keep yourselves far from envy, because it eats up and takes away good actions as fire consumes and burns the wood. And one of an excellent example of the saying of the Prophet Muhammad (PBUH), which directly and indirectly explains leadership qualities, is: "Each of you is a shepherd, and all of you are responsible for your flocks." Narrated by Bukhari & Muslim.

The second Hadith or saying of the Prophet (PBUH) is: "When three people go on a journey, let them put one of their numbers in command." Abu Da'ud narrated it on the authority of Abu Sa'id. The third saying is: "In your private and public life, you should always fear God. Piety should inform your conduct. Your good deeds will help in getting your sins forgiven. Treat people well." Narrated by Ahmad and Tirmidhi. Tirmidhi narrates the fourth saying of the Prophet. The Prophet said: "God will punish the one who harms others. The one hostile towards others' Allah will afflict him with hardship." The other saying of the Prophet (PBUH) is: "When one dies, one's record of deeds is sealed. However, for the following three deeds, one continues to earn God's reward, even after one's death: (1) an endowment for some charitable work (2) leaving behind such scholarly works that may benefit subsequent generations; and (3) virtuous children who pray for their parents." It is narrated by Kanz al-Ummal of Ali al-Muttaqi. The Prophet (PBUH) said, "A Muslim is the one who avoids harming Muslims with his tongue and hands. And a Muhajir (emigrant) is the one who gives up (abandons) all what Allah has forbidden." Narrated 'Abdullah bin 'Amr. Some people asked Allah's Messenger (PBUH), "Whose Islam is the best? i.e. (Who is a very good Muslim)?" He replied, "One who avoids harming the Muslims with his tongue and hands."

Narrated Abu Musa. A man asked the Prophet (PBUH), "What sort of deeds or (what qualities of) Islam are good?" The Prophet (PBUH) replied, 'To feed (the poor) and greet those whom you know and those whom you do not Know (See Hadith No. 27). Narrated 'Abdullah bin 'Amr.

Allah's Messenger (PBUH) said: Islam is based on (the following) five (principles):1). To testify that none has the right to be worshipped but Allah and Muhammad is Allah's Messenger (PBUH).

2). To offer the (compulsory congregational) prayers dutifully and perfectly.3). To pay Zakat (i.e. obligatory charity).4).

To perform Hajj. (i.e. Pilgrimage to Mecca).5). To observe fast during the month of Ramadan. Narrated Ibn 'Umar. From these Hadith or saying of Prophet Muhammad (PBUH) above it is evident that his sayings, if put into practice by leaders and followers of the Muslims Ummah today, it would constitute an excellent model for leaders and follows. According to the Quran, the Prophet's manner and character are solid examples to follow. Muthi and El-Awaisi (2022) study on Caliph Abu-Baker (RA) argue that after Prophet Muhammad (PBUH) passed away, the situation among Muslims in Arabia changed drastically. Many became apostates (murtad) and followed false prophets. At the same time, others refused to pay Zakat, one of the five pillars of Islam. They cited Ibn Ishaq in Ibn Kathīr (2004) who states that many Muslims in Arabia became apostates after the Prophet had passed away, except for the people of Makkah and Madinah. There are many sayings of the Prophet Muhammad (PBUH) but in this book only a few are narrated. The next chapter focuses on the four Rightly Guided Khalifs/Caliphs/Vicegerent/Successor.

Chapter 15

The Four Rightly Guided Khalifs/ Caliphs/Vicegerent/Successor

The Four Guided Caliphs are the esteemed individuals who assumed leadership of the Muslim Ummah, the unified community of Islamic believers, following the passing of Prophet Muhammad (PBUH). Consequently, the Muslim Ummah faced the challenge of determining who would assume the role of leader after the demise of Prophet Muhammad (PBUH). In essence, since the Muslim Ummah had only recognized Prophet Muhammad (PBUH) as their leader, and he was no longer present, the question arose as to how to proceed in selecting a successor to lead the Ummah in the event of his death. There were four individuals who were particularly close to the Prophet (PBUH) and were considered potential candidates for leadership of the Muslim Ummah or Islamic society.

These four individuals included Abu Bakr al-Siddiq (RA), who had accompanied the Prophet (PBUH) to Medina during his migration to Madinah and had been appointed by the Prophet (PBUH) to lead public prayer during his last illness. Umar ibn al-Khattab (RA), a trusted and capable Companion of the Prophet (PBUH), Uthman ibn 'Affan (RA), an early convert who was highly respected, and 'Ali ibn Abi Talib (RA), the Prophet's cousin and son-in-law. These four individuals were believed to have followed the Qur'an and the Sunnah of the Prophet (PBUH) closely, as they were his close companions and believed in him when he received the revelation in Makkah. As such, they were considered the most suitable candidates to succeed the Prophet (PBUH) after his passing.

Wilferd, (1997) ague that after the passing of the prophet (PBUH) in June 632, a gathering of the Ansar ('Helpers'), the natives of Medina, took place in the Saqifah (courtyard) of the Banu Sa'ida clan. The general belief at the time was that the purpose of the meeting was for the Ansar to decide on a new leader of the Muslim community among themselves, with the intentional exclusion of the Muhajirun (migrants from Mecca/Makkah), though this has later become the subject of debate.

Winfred (1997) further argue that Abu Bakr and Umar, both prominent companions of Muhammad (PBUH), upon learning of the meeting became concerned about a potential coup and hastened to the gathering. Upon arriving, Abu Bakr (RA) addressed the assembled men with a warning that any attempt to elect a leader outside of Muhammad (PBUH) own tribe, the Quraysh, would likely result in dissension as only they can command the necessary respect among the community. He then took Umar (RA) and another companion, Abu Ubaidah ibn al-Jarrah, by the hand and offered them to the Ansar as potential choices. He was countered with the suggestion that the Quraysh and the Ansar choose a leader each from among themselves, who would then rule jointly. The group grew heated upon hearing this proposal and began to argue amongst themselves.

Umar hastily took Abu Bakr's hand and swore his own allegiance to the latter, an example followed by the gathered men. Thus, Abu Bakr was near-universally accepted as head of the Muslim community (under the title of Caliph) as a result of Saqifah, though he did face contention as a result of the rushed nature of the event. The Caliphs were and the pillars and inspiration for leadership from an Islamic perspective after previous Prophets, especially the final prophet of Allah/God Muhammad (PBUH). These Caliphs ruled (Muslims Ummah/Islamic state/ Islamic communities) by obeying Allah/God and the previous prophets, following sharia Divine Laws and also consulting with their followers were required. The rightly guided Caliphs inspired some Muslim thinkers who wrote about Islamic political leadership, such as Al Mawardi and in this chapter discusses all the four of them one by one by starting with the first caliph Abu Bakr (RA).

The First of the Four Rightly Guided Caliph is Abu Bakr (RA) (632-634 A.C)

When Prophet Mohammad (PBUH) died, Abu Bakr (RA) was his Successor and the first Caliph. The word Caliph is the English version of the Arabic word 'Khalifa,' meaning successor to the Prophet (PBUH). Abu Bakr (RA) was the first Caliph as noted above after the passing of the prophet Muhammad (PBUH). Thus after the death of the Messenger of Allah (PBUH), Abu Bakr (R.A.) was unanimously accepted caliph. However, as a first caliph he had faced many crises after becoming the first caliph.

According to the Islamic finder (2023) Abu Bakr Siddiq (R.A.), popularly known as Abu Bakr, is the first Caliph after the Prophet Mohammad (PBUH). His full name is Abdullah bin Abu Quhafah Uthman bin Aamer Al Qurashi Al Taymi. His lineage joins with that of the Prophet (PBUH), six generations before himself, in Murrah Ben Kaab. In his early years, he played with the camel calves and goats, and his love for camels earned him the nickname "Abu Bakr", meaning 'the father of the camel's calf.' When Abu Bakr (R.A.) embraced Islam, the Prophet (S.A.W.) was overjoyed, as Abu Bakr (R.A.) was a source of triumph for Islam, due to his intimacy with Quraish tribe and his noble character that Allah Has exalted him. Islamic finder further attest to the fact that the name As-Siddiq, the most well-known of Abu Bakr's (R.A.) titles, comes from the word 'Sidq' which means truthfulness. Therefore, the word As-Siddiq means a person who is constantly truthful or who constantly believes in the truthfulness of something or someone.

In Abu Bakr's (R.A.) case, in the truthfulness of the Prophet Mohammad (PBUH). The title 'As-Siddiq' was given to Abu Bakr (R.A.) by none other than the Prophet (PBUH). When the Prophet Muhammad (PBUH) died in 11 AH (632 AD), many people, among whom was Umar bin Khattab (R.A.), refused to believe that the prophet (PBUH) had died. But Abu Bakr (R.A.), was steadfast as usual, addressed the bewildered multitude Muslims at the time and convinced them that Mohammad (PBUH) was no more and there was no reason why they should not acknowledge his death.

Ibn Abbas (R.A.) attest to the fact that when the Prophet (PBUH) died, Abu Bakr Siddiq (R.A.) went out while Umar (R.A.) was speaking to the people. Abu Bakr (R.A.) said to Umar, Be seated down O Umar,' twice, but Umar refused to sit. Abu Bakr (R.A.) said: "To proceed, if anyone amongst you used to worship Mohammad (PBUH), then Mohammad (PBUH) is dead, but if you used to worship Allah/God, then Allah/God is Alive and shall never die."

The statement of Abu Bakr (RA) is confirmed in the Quran in Surah 3 Al-Imran(3:144) as translated into English by Al-Hilali and Khan (1996, p.100), "Muhammad (PBUH) is no more than a Messenger, and indeed (many) Messengers have passed away before him. If he dies or is killed, will you turn back on your heels (as disbelievers)? And he who turns back on his heels, not the least harm will he do to Allah; and Allah will reward those who are grateful."

Henceforth, as narrated in Bukhari 9952, 4453 that Umar bin Khatab (RA) said when hearing of the death of the prophet PBUH) "my legs could not support me and I fell down at the very moment of hearing him reciting it, declaring that the Prophet (PBUH) had died." Furthermore according to Ibn Abbas (R.A) said: "By Allah, it was as if the people never knew that Allah Had revealed this verse of the Quran before, till Abu Bakr recited it and all the people took it from him, and I heard everybody reciting it."

This show that when the prophet(PBUH) died there was a big shock to all his companions with the except of Abu Bakr (RA) who took to himself to remind them of the Surah they used to recited which show that the prophet (PBUH) was mortal and Allah/God only is being immortal. Abu Bakr (R.A.) was a very close companion to the prophet (PBUH) and had also liberated many slaves as he felt compassion for them. Abu Bakr (RA) had purchased and freed eight slaves, four men and four women, by paying forty thousand dinars for their freedom. One of the best example of the salves Abu Bakr (RA) free is Bilal bin Ribah (R.A), one of the most loyal and trusted Companion of Prophet Mohammad (PBUH), whom the prophet made him the one who call for prayer in the prophet Masjid a noble job and was given to a salves that Abu Bakr (R.A) freed from slavery.

According to the narration of Tirmidhi (3661) Allah/God Messenger (PBUH) once said about Abu Bakr (R.A): No one has helped me without reciprocating it, except for Abu Bakr, who has given me help, which Allah/God will reciprocate to him on the Day of Resurrection. No one's property has benefited me to the extent of Abu Bakr (RA), and if I were to take a Khalil (friend), then I would have taken Abu Bakr as a Khalil, and indeed your companion is Allah/God Khalil."

Abu Bakr first speech as the caliph of the Muslim Ummah at the time affirmed his love for the Divine and, at the same time, affirmed sovereignty to Allah. In his famous speech, he asked his followers only to obey him so long as he obeyed Allah and the Prophet Mohammad (PBUH) and that if he did not obey them, no one should obey him. He stated clearly, "The weak among you shall be firm with me until their rights have been vindicated, and the strong among will be given their due. The dead of Prophet Mohammad (PBUH) shocked many companions as noted above, especially Umar Ibn Al Khattab (RA). Umar Ibn Al Khattab (RA) threatened with a sword to fight anyone who said the Prophet Mohammad (PBUH) was dead. Even the more robust companion like Umar Ibn Al Khatab (RA) was shaken and confused by the death of Prophet Mohammad (PBUH) and the Muslim Ummah.

It is also known at the time of the death of the Prophet (PBUH), several tribes rebelled and refused to pay Zakat (poor-due), citing that this was only due to Prophet Mohammad (PBUH). Furthermore, some tribes claimed that they had submitted to Muhammad (PBUH) and that with prophet Muhammad (PBUH) death, their allegiance was ended and therefore they don't have to pay anything. Open hearing these from those tribes then Caliph Abu Bakr (RA) insisted that they had not just submitted to a leader but joined an ummah (community) of which he was the new leader as Caliph. Abu Bakr (RA) rejected that notion and explained that the Divine Law cannot be divided, that there is no distinction between the obligation of Zakat and prayer, and that any compromise with the injunction of Allah/God would erode the foundation of Islam.

Thus, the death of the prophet Muhammad PBUH) lead to some tribes trying not to pay zakat citing that the paying of Zakat was only to the prophet Muhammad (PBUH) as narrated by Imam Al-Dhahabi who said: "When the news of the death of the Prophet (PBUH) spread, many groups of people among the Arabs apostatized from Islam. Some of these tribes objected to pay the almsgiving (Zakat) and caliph Abu Bakr Siddiq (R.A.) decided to fight them.

Umar (RA) and others impressed upon Khalifah Abu Baker to refrain from fighting these tribes but Abu Bakr (RA) said: 'By Allah, if they refuse to pay a rope which they used to pay at the time of the Messenger of Allah/God (PBUH), I will fight them for withholding it." Then Umar (RA) insisted: "How can you fight with these people although the Prophet Muhammad (PBUH) said: "I have been ordered by Allah/God to fight the people till they say: None has the right to be worshiped but Allah/God, and whoever said it then he will save his life and property from me except on trespass the law, and his accounts will be with Allah/ God."

Abu Bakr (R.A.), reiterated: "By Allah/God! I will fight those who differentiate between the prayer and almsgiving (Zakat), for almsgiving (Zakat) is a compulsory right to be taken from the property (according to Allah/God orders)." Then Umar (R.A.) said: "By Allah/God, it was nothing, but Allah/God brought relief to Abu Bakr (RA) toward the decision (to fight) and I came to know that this decision was right."

The result of the fight that Abu Bakr undertake against apostasy was known as the Ridda wars. According to Muthi and El-Awaisi (2022) the Apostasy war which means in Arabic (al-Riddah) is one who is leaving Islam after having been a Muslim for some time. At the time of Abu Bakr (RA) reign as a Caliph, there were two forms of people or group who rebel: some individuals claimed prophethood, then became false

Prophets, and those who refused to do one of the pillars of Islam, of not giving Zakat.

The apostasy spread in the Arabian Peninsula, but the main problem was the false prophets within the south of Madinah (Yemen) and the east of Madinah (Yamamah). For those in Yemen, the false Prophet's name was Al-Aswad Al-'Ansī, while in Yamamah, it was Musailamah. Ibn Ishaq also stated that, all Arabs except for the inhabitants of Makkah and Madinah, became apostates after the death of Prophet (PBUH) and also Muhammad Ibn Kathīr, (2004).

The above describes the critical situation faced by Abū Bakr as the first Caliph of the Muslims Ummah/One nation Islam/Muslims community, which caused disputes among the Muslims at the time of the reign of Caliph Abu Bakr (RA). There were some Muslims at the reign of Khalifah Abu Bakr (RA) who were of the onions that those who refused to pay Zakat would in the long run as Muslims would continue to pay Zakat. One of the companion who had this opinion is Umar Ibn Khatab (RA) as noted earlier. Henceforth, Muthi and El-Awaisi (2022) attest to the fact that Umar Ibn al- Khattāb (RA) was one of the companions who believed in this opinion because he assumed their faith would escalate along with time, and then they would pay Zakat.

Umar Ibn al- Khattāb (RA) also believed that fighting them while 'Usamah's army was still gone was not a good idea because the number of the army in Madinah was limited. However, as noted earlier Caliph Abū Bakr (RA) could not accept the arguments of 'Umar Ibn al-Khattāb RA) and hence the Hadith narrated by Abū Hurairah, which affirmed that Abu Bakr (RA) said: By Allah! I will fight whoever differentiates between Salat (prayer) and Zakat, as Zakat is the right to be taken from property [according to Allah's order] see Al Bukhārī, (1997, v. 9:47).

Based on this Hadith, it is clear that Caliph Abū Bakr (RA) had no option to bargain with the apostates. So, when 'Umar Ibn al-Khattāb (RA) observed his unwavering belief, he quickly changed his mind and decided to support him.

Subsequently, encyclopaedia Britannica also affirmed the argument by Muthi and El-Awaisi (2022) in that during the rule or the reign of Abu Bakr (RA) (632–634), he suppressed the tribal political and religious uprisings known as the Riddah ("political rebellion," sometimes translated as "apostasy"), thereby bringing central Arabia under Muslim control.

Under Abu Bakr caliph rule or reign the Muslim conquests of Iraq and Syria. The compilation of the Quran is one of the greatest achievements of Khalifah Abu Bakr Siddiq (R.A.) which he rendered to Islam by compilation of the Holy Quran. The Britannica affirmed that the first written compilation of the Quran is said to have taken place during Abū Bakr caliphate reign after the deaths of several Quran reciters in the Battle of Yamama which raised the possibility that parts of the text could be lost.

Umar ibn al-Khaṭṭab (RA), the second Khaliah after Khalifa Abū Bakr was the eventual successor as caliph who urged Abū Bakr (RA) to have the Quran written down. Hence at that time, there were hundreds of memorizers who had memorized the entire Quran among the Companions during the life time of the Prophet (PBUH), but the Holy Quran had never been complied in a book-form, although its memorization continued after the death of the Prophet (PBUH).

However, numbers of those memorizers had been martyred in the various battles that had ensued after the Prophet Muhammad (PBUH) passing. Consequently, it occurred to Umar (R.A.) that steps should be taken to preserve the Quran intact in its original form, against any kind of risk, and he saw that it was not prudent to depend exclusively upon those who had committed its memory to heart. Therefore, he urged Abu Bakr (R.A) to have it written down in the form of a book.

Abu Bakr (R.A) at first hesitated because this had not been done by the Prophet (PBUH) himself before passing. However, after some debate on the subject, he agreed and appointed Zaid ibn Thabit (R.A) for this work, Zaid (R.A) hesitated at the thought of undertaking such a momentous task, but he later took heart and began the work.

Zaid (R.A) was the most capable person to be charged with this momentous work or task because he had acted as someone who could writer for the Prophet (PBUH), and one of the Companions, who had learnt the Quran directly from the prophet Muhammad (PBUH). When the appointment was given to Zaid as the one task to lead the compilation of the Quran Zaid ibn Thabit (R.A), he had this to say: "By Allah, If Abu Bakr (R.A) had ordered to shift one of the mountains from its place it would not have been harder for me than what he had ordered me concerning the collection of the Quran." He contended that he continued, "I started locating Quranic material and collecting it from parchments, scapula, and leaf-stalks of date palms and from the memories of men." Ali bin Abi Talib (RA) also had this to say: "The one who has the greatest reward amongst the people is Abu Bakr (RA) because he was unique in compiling the Quran."

The above show the leadership qualities of the first Khaliah Abu Bakr (RA), who could not compromise with the principles of Islam despite the difficulties he faced after the death of the Prophet (PBUH) while assuming leadership of the Islamic Ummah. Abu Bakr (RA), under his reign as the first kahlifah of the Muslims Ummah had, ordered the collection and compilation of the verses of the Quran, He fought against apostasy and those challenges that come his way as the first Caliph. Muthi and El-Awaisi (2022) argue very strongly that the first Muslim Caliph, Abū Bakr al-Siddiq, since his appointment as Caliph, Abū Bakr (RA) made crucial contributions not only to strengthen the foundation of the Islamic State in Madinah but also to liberate Islamic Jerusalem.

Muthi and El-Awaisi (2022) attest to the fact that after the passing away of Prophet Muhammad (PBUH), Abū Bakr, as the first Caliph, had to take the reins of the Ummah and continued what the Prophet Muhammad (PBUH), had initiated for Islamic Jerusalem and that during his reign as the first Caliph Abū Bakr (RA) realised that a military operation was needed initially to stabilise the Arabian Peninsula, which became one of his most significant contributions as the leader of Muslims Ummah.

They went on to argue that in the midst of debates among the companions, Caliph Abū Bakr(RA) decided against all odds to dispatch the army of 'Usamah towards the Holy Land. In other words, some of the Caliph Abu-Bakr (RA) significant contributions included sending out 'Usamah's army, securing domestic threats and uniting Muslims during the Apostates War, prioritising and directing armies to al-Sham, and even the selection of his successor, all of which has contributed to the liberation of Bayt alMaqdis.

Al-Suyūtī (1995) also argue that if Abū Bakr (RA) had not been appointed as a Caliph, then Allah/God would not have been worshipped. The context of this statement is that Caliph Abū Bakr (RA) insisted on sending Usamah army despite Madinah being under imminent threat from the apostates in the Arabian Peninsula who rebelled after the death of the Prophet Muhammad (PBUH). If he did not send the army of 'Usamah, those people would think Muslims were weak after Prophet

Muhammad (PBUH) death and could drive them to attack the city state of Madinah. Hence Caliph Abū Bakr (RA) knew the importance of securing Madinah from those who wanted to obliterate Islam, since this city was the capital of the Islamic state and should never collapse in order to keep the power of Muslim leadership.

Muthi and El-Awaisi (2022)) subsequently argue that, Abū Bakr (RA) succeeded in using his leadership as the Caliph; maintaining his trust in the directive of the Prophet Muhammad (PBUH), even though all his companions disagreed with him. He could not have done this unless the Prophet (PBUH) informed him about the importance of sending the 'Usamah's army, which he did even publically. Thus, Caliph Abū Bakr (RA) understood that the army was a stepping stone for keeping the integrity of the state and the liberation of Islamic Jerusalem. As a result, the dispatch of 'Usamah's Army into al-Sham significantly influenced the Arabian Peninsula, particularly in the political aspect. Caliph Abū Bakr (RA), through his action, conveyed an important message to all parties that, Muslims were still in a powerful condition; it made the apostates and the Byzantines in al-Sham think twice about attacking Muslims.

Caliph Abu-Bakr (RA) died on (23 August 634 A.C) at the age of sixty-three and was buried beside the Holy Prophets' (PBUH) grave in the city state of Madinah. Caliph Abu-Bakr (RA) was one of the Islamic Ummah's strong leaders and a model to emulate by those who want to lead or are inspire to be leaders in their various communities. Khalifah Abu Bakr (RA) held the view that a government should be a sacred trust, and he ran the Islamic government as if he were administering the affairs of a trust. Caliph Abu-Bakr (RA) regarded his position as the first Khalifah of the Muslims Ummah as a trust (Amanah). Caliph Abu-Bakr (RA) took his responsibilities very seriously and argued that he would not be the same as the Prophet (PBUH) because the Prophet (PBUH) was immune from all sins and had the assistance of divine revelation while he was just an ordinary man who was fallible. Under the leadership of Caliph Abu-Bakr (RA), all were equal before the law, with no difference between the poor and rich, and he used divine laws to judge.

Caliph Abu-Bakr (RA) when he was ill Caliph Abu-Bakr (RA) instructed that Umar bin Khatab (RA) should be leading prayers. Henceforth his reign as khalifah/Caliph was for two years and three months and died at the age of 63 years and during his short reign as Caliph he accomplished a lot of things as noted above and created unity for the Ummah and in the end decided to confer the caliphate to Umar bin Khatab (RA) and also advise him on how to lead the Ummah by saying this word: "If you follow my advice, nothing unknown will be more acceptable to you than death; but if you reject it, nothing unknown will be more frightening than death."

The final wish of Abu-Bakr (RA) was to be buried beside the final Prophet of Allah/God Muhammad (PBUH). Abu Bakr (R.A) therefore, recommended to Aisha (R.A), his daughter and wife of Prophet Mohammad (PBUH), to bury him beside the Prophet (PBUH). Caliph Abu-Bakr (RA), was buried in Aisha's room, just beside the Prophet Muhammad (PBUH), grave in Prophet (PBUH) Mosque (Masjid-e-Nabawi) in the city state of Madinah, Saudi Arabia.

When he died, the funeral prayer was led by Umar (R.A.) and his grave was placed adjacent to the Prophet Muhammad (PBUH). His grave was dug in such a way that his head was parallel to the shoulder of the Prophet Muhammad (PBUH).

The Islamic Finder (2023) had this to attest and affirmed as the words of Ali bin Talib (RA) upon hearing of the death of Caliph Abu-Bakr (RA), Ali (RA) rushed to his house and made a long speech which he addressed to Abu Bakr (R.A.) and said: "O Abu Bakr (R.A.), you were the closest companion and friend of the Messenger of Allah (PBUH), you were a comfort to him; you were the one he trusted most. If he had a secret, he would tell it to you and if he needed to consult someone regarding a matter, he would consult you. You were the first of your people to embrace Islam and you were the sincerest of them in your faith. Your faith was stronger than any other person's as was the degree to which you feared Allah/God and you were wealthier than anyone else in terms of what you acquired from the religion of Allah/God. You cared most for both the Messenger of Allah (PBUH) and Islam. Of all people, you were the best Companion to the Messenger of Allah (PBUH). You possessed the best qualities, you had the best past, you ranked highest and you were closest to him. And of all people, you resembled the Messenger of Allah (PBUH) the most in terms of his guidance and demeanour. Your ranking was higher than anyone else's and the Prophet Muhammad (PBUH) honoured you and held you in higher esteem than anyone else. On behalf of the Messenger of Allah (PBUH) and Islam, may Allah/God reward you with the best of rewards. When the people disbelieved in the Messenger of Allah (PBUH), you believed in him.

Throughout Prophet Muhammad (PBUH) life, you were both his eyes with which he saw, and his ears with which he heard. Allah/God has named you truthful in His book when He said:" and this is affirmed in Surah 39 Az-Zamar (39:33) as translated into English by Al-Hilali and Khan (1996, p.582), "33, And he (Muhammad (PBUH) who has brought the truth (this Quran and Islamic Monotheism) and those who) believed therein (i.e. the true believers of Islamic Monotheism) those are the Al-Multtaqun (the pious and righteous persons.

Abu-Bakr was those who believe in Allah/God as preach by our beloved prophet and his leadership is to be followed by leaders and followers of the Muslims Ummah today. Also see Surah 2 Al-Baqarah (2:2) as translated into English By Al-Hilali and Khan (1996, p.12), 2, This is the Book (the Quran), whereof there is no doubt, a guidance to those who are Al-Muttaqun [the pious and righteous persons who fear Allah much (abstain from all kinds of sins and evil deeds which He has forbidden) and love Allah much (perform all kinds of good deeds which He has ordained)].

As well said by Ali (RA) above, Abu Bakr (R.A) was a source of comfort and constant help for the Prophet (PBUH), Abu-Bakr was always willing to sacrifice his wealth and his very life for the cause of Islam by fighting for the unity of the Ummah after the death of the prophet and the challenges he faced and when he Prophet Muhammad (PBUH) died, Abu Bakr (R.A) continued where the Prophet Muhammad (PBUH.) had left off without any hesitation. Caliph Abu-Bakr (RA) further strengthened the foundations of the Muslim nation/Islamic Ummah, first by fighting against and defeating the apostates and then by spreading Islam in some of the major conquests that took place during his caliphate both in Iraq and Syria. His leadership is an inspiration for all us irrespective of faith and background as one of the great companions of prophet Muhammad (PBUH).

The Second Caliph, Umar (RA) (634-644 A.C)

The second Caliph after Abu Bakr (RA) was Umar Ibn Al-Khattab (RA). Umar Ibn Al-Khattab (RA), had been assigned the duty of leading the prayers when Caliph Abu-Bakr (RA) was very ill. Henceforth before Abu-Bakr (RA) death he ordered that his garment should be delivered to his successor Umar Ibn Al-Khattab (RA). On seeing the garment, Umar (RA) wept and said: "Abu Bakr (R.A.) has made the task of his successor very difficult.". Here we also know that Abu-Bakr (RA) advised Umar bin Khatab (RA) and said: "If you follow my advice, nothing unknown will be more acceptable to you than death; but if you reject it, nothing unknown will be more frightening than death."

In the history of Islam at the early stage or before Islam, Umar (RA) was originally one of the bitterest opponents of Prophet Muhammad (PBUH) and Islam, but then later suddenly accepted Islam and became one of the strongest supporters of Islam. When he accepted Islam, it was an excellent success for Muslims because of his strength. After the death of the Prophet (PBUH), he was instrumental in Abu Bakr's (RA) leadership of the Muslim community and stayed loyal.

During the leadership of Umar Ibn Al-Khattab (RA), Muslim forces captured Syria, Jerusalem, Egypt, Iraq, and Persia. Under Umar Ibn Al-Khatab (RA), Islam expanded widely in Syria, Egypt, and Persia. Umar Al-Khattab (RA) was one of the principal figures in the spread of Islam in those countries named above and beyond, for the Islamic openness to those countries helped spread Islam. Umar Al-Khattab (RA) was just, and he believed that all humans are born free, and no one should subjugate one another.

One of the important stories was when a son of Amr Ibn As abused someone less in status in the community, Umar (RA) heard of the abuse that the young man was subjected to by the son of somebody in authority and said, to the boy who abused, "Since when have you turned men into slaves, whereas they are born free of their mothers."

Another story of Umar Al-Khattab (RA) of great significance is the story when on one of his outings heard a woman asking a daughter to add water to milk to make more money. Thus, Umar Al-Khattab (RA) used to go out at night to see the condition of the people with Ibn Abbas accompanying him.

They strolled from one area to another; while passing by a small hut, Umar Al-Khattab (RA) heard a whispering talk in which the mother was telling her daughter that they should add water with the milk so that they could make more profit because she used to do that when she was young. The daughter told her mother, you used to add water to milk when you were in Jahilia, but now that we are Muslim, we cannot add water into milk to make more money. Her mother said we are poor, and Islam does not allow us to add water into milk to increase our profit. The daughter said, "Have you forgotten the Caliph's order? Adding water to the milk would not be lawful, and as a Muslim, she would not do anything against the order of the Caliph. But, the mother said, neither the Caliph nor any of his officers are here to see what we do. So the girl refused to obey her mother's orders. Instead, she said, "Caliph may or not be here, but his orders are orders and must obey.

The girl said we might escape the notice of the Caliph and his officers, but how can we escape the notice of Allah? The mother remained quiet, and both mother and daughter went to bed. Umar Al-Khattab (RA) turned to his companion and said, "The girl has kept her resolve in the inspiration of the exhortation of her mother. She deserves a reward. What reward should I give her?" Ibn Abbas said, "She should be paid some money." Umar Al-Khattab (RA) said such a girl would become a great mother. Her integrity is not to be weighed with a few coins; it is to be measured on the scale of national values.

The Caliph Umar Al-Khattab (RA) summoned the daughter and the mother to his court. The mother trembled as she stood before the great ruler. However, the girl faced the Caliph Umar Al-Khattab (RA) boldly and with great composure. She was beautiful and, above all, dignified in her personality. Umar Al-Khattab (RA) related how he overheard their conversation and how she kept her resolve. Umar (RA) forgave the mother for the sake of the daughter. He turned to the girl and said, "Islam needs a daughter like you, and as a Caliph of Islam, it devolves on me to reward you by owning you as a daughter." Then Caliph Umar Al-Khattab (RA) called his sons and, addressing them, said, "Here is a gem of a girl who would make a great mother. He desires that one of his children marries this girl as a wife. Asim, the third son, Caliph, Umar Al-Khattab (RA) was yet unmarried, and he offered to marry the girl. From this union was born a daughter Umm Asim, who became, in due course, the mother of Umar bin Abdul Aziz (RA).

Umar bin Abdul Aziz became a Caliph. When he was Caliph, Umar bin Abdul Aziz (RA) set up some austerity measures to stabilize the Ummah finances, and the poor did not even need any financial help or support.

During Umar Al- Khattab's (RA) reign as Caliph, he achieved many things, including the openness of Islam to different parts of the world. See Surah4: Al Nisa (4:135), as translated into English by Al-Hilali and Khan (1996, p.135), 135. "O you who believe! Stand out firmly for justice as a witness to Allah, even though it be against yourselves, or your parents, or your kin, be he rich or poor, Allah is a Better Protector to both (than you). So follow not the lusts (of your hearts), lest you avoid justice; and if you distort your witness or refuse to give it, verily Allah is Ever Well-Acquainted with what you do." Umar (RA) was a simple man with great principles and no bodyguards to guard him, as is the case of our leaders today. There are many stories of envoys and foreign messengers sent to him, and they would find him resting under a palm tree or praying in the mosque among the people and would not distinguish him as the

Caliph. He spent nights walking the streets of the community to know their problems so he could solve them.

According Muthi and El-Awaisi (2022) the reasons for Caliph Abu-Bakr (RA) choosing Umar (RA) as his successor was his potential to become a vital factor in maintaining the unity and order of the growing Muslim state. ʿUmar (RA) was Abū-Bakr(RA) solution for this nation because he saw that the world was coming to the Muslims with its riches and temptations, and he feared that if they embraced those temptations with open arms, then they would be heading down the path of destruction. They assume that since Caliph Abū Bakr (RA) priority was to maintain the unity of Muslims, he would like to make sure the process of electing the next leader went smoothly and without any disputes that might harm the solidarity of Muslims. Caliph Abū Bakr (RA)'s expectations and hope for ʿUmar (RA) were later fulfilled.

Umar (RA) prioritised the liberation of Islamic Jerusalem and continued on the strategic plan of Prophet Muhammad and its implementation commenced by Abū Bakr (RA). For them Umar (RA) as a caliph was able to reap the fruit planted by Prophet Muhammad, nurtured by Abū Bakr (RA). Thus, the prophet Muhammad (PBUH), established a solid foundation for Muslims to follow in his footsteps in the spiritual, religious, political, and military scopes for the Ummah and today's leaders and followers should emulate in order to keep the Ummah in a sound footing.

Abu-Bakr on his deathbed Abu Bakr nominated Umar Al Khattab (RA) as his successor as noted earlier in the chapter. Umar Al-Khattab (RA) was a good administrator and, astute political leader and military general. Umar (RA) Caliphate was spent in warfare, with Jerusalem falling in 638. Umar Al-Khattab (RA) and the Muslim army conquered

Syria and part of Egypt and Mesopotamia. No one was forced to convert to Islam, though those who did convert lived tax free. Today Muslims leaders and followers should remember that the same Majid Aqsa that the prophet and his companions fought to keep in the realm of Islam is under occupation.

Their long term strategy had been achieved during their time but today we should not forget that we should all remember as leaders and followers the strategy put forward by Prophet Muhammad (PBUH) with the participation of Umar (RA) with thousands of the Prophet (PBUH) companions and praying for the first time inside their first Qiblah, al-Aqsa Mosque and brining the holy city under the realm of Islam.

Furthermore, here is a brief of Umar Ibn al-Khattab (RA) many achievements and accomplishments, as cited here: 1)Umar (RA) supported the Messenger(PBUH) call to go public in Mecca after he embraced Islam, something the Muslims had been unable to do prior to that; 2) Umar (RA) was one of the ten companions to be guaranteed paradise; 3) He was the second caliph in Islam; 4)He entrusted Shifa Abdullah, one of Prophet's (PBUH) female companions, with a public role in monitoring and supervising commercial transactions in the entire marketplace of Medinah; 5) He expanded the caliphate at an unprecedented rate, ruling the Sasanian Empire and more than two-thirds of the Byzantine Empire. His attacks against the Sasanian Empire resulted in the conquest of Persia in under two years (642–644); 6) He established the garrison cities of al-Fustat in Egypt and Basra and Kufah in Iraq; 7) Umar (RA) legendary administration is quoted by scholars throughout Islamic history, as he systematized the rule of vast territories, established the Islamic calendar, organized state pensions and upheld justice and security.

Islamic finders (2023) also highlighted some of the achievements of Khalifah Umar Ibn Al-Khatab (RA) as: 1.He is the one who founded the Lunar Calendar (Hijri Year i-e according to the date of Prophet Mohammad's (PBUH) migration to Madinah). 2. In his era Islam gained a great position, as the Islamic Empire expanded at an unprecedented rate ruling the whole Iraq, Egypt, Libya, Tripoli, Persia, Khurassan, Eastern Anatolia, South Armenian and Sajistan. Jerusalem (first Qiblah) was conquered during his reign alongwith the whole Sassanid Persian Empire and two thirds of the Eastern Roman Empire. 3. Introduction and implementation of different Political and civil administration jobs such as Chief Secretary (Khatib), Military Secretary (Khatib ud Diwan), Revenue Collector (Sahib ul Kharaj), Police Chief (Sahib ul Ahdath), Treasury Officer (Sahib Bait-ul-Maal) and many other official posts.

4. Umar (R.A.) was the first to establish a special department for the investigation of complaints against the officers of the State. 5. Umar (R.A.) was the first to introduce the public ministry system, where the records of officials and soldiers were kept. He was also the first person ever to appoint police forces to keep civil order.

Another important aspect of Umar Al-Khattab (RA) rule was that he banned any of his governors/officials from engaging in trade or any sort of business dealings whilst being in a position of power. Thus, the above are some of the brief of many achievements and contributions of Khalifah Umar (RA) during his reign.

The Third Caliph, Uthman (RA) (644-656 A.C)

The third Caliph was Uthman (R.A). When Umar (R.A) fell under the assassin's dagger before his death, people asked him to nominate his successor. Umar Al-Khattab (R.A.) appointed a committee consisting of six of the ten companions of the Prophet (PBUH) to select the next Caliph from among themselves. He outlined the procedures to follow if differences of opinion were to arise. After deliberations for days, the next Caliph was chosen to be Uthman (R.A).

Uthman (R.A) became the third Caliph of Islam in the month of Muharram, 24 A.H. He was married to Ruqayyah, the second daughter of Prophet Mohammad (PBUH), and he was a generous person. He spent much of his wealth on the welfare of Muslims, charity, and equipping the Muslim armies. He memorized the Quran and participated in many battles. He was fair and just to all, irrespective of creed or colour. Islamic openness continued during his leadership as the Caliph of the Muslim Nation started and expanded West to Morocco, East to Afghanistan, and in the North to Armenia and Azerbaijan. However, Uthman (R.A.) most notable contribution to Islam was the compilation of a complete and authoritative text of the Quran. Many copies were made and distributed to the Ummah (Islamic communities).

The life of Uthman (RA) bin Affan is that he was born seven years after the Holy Prophet (PBUH). He belonged to the Omayyad branch of the Quraish tribe. He learned to read and write at an early age, and as a young man became a successful merchant. Even before Islam Uthman (RA) had been noted for his truthfulness and integrity. He and Abu Bakr were close friends, and it was Abu Bakr who brought him to Islam when he was thirty-four years of age. Some years later he married the Prophet Muhammad (PBUH) second daughter, Ruqayya.

In spite of his wealth and position, his relatives subjected him to torture because he had embraced Islam, and he was forced to immigrate to Abyssinia. Sometime later he returned to Mecca but soon migrated to

Medina with the other Muslims companions of the prophet (PBUH). While in Medina his business again began to flourish and he regained his former prosperity. Uthman (RA) generosity had no limits, he was very generous and helpful to the case of Islam. On various occasions he spent a great portion of his wealth for the welfare of the Muslims, for charity and for equipping the Muslim armies. That is why he came to be known as 'Ghani' meaning 'Generous.

During Uthmanruleascaliphofthe Muslim Ummah, Islamextendedwest to Morocco, east to Afghanistan, and north to Armenia and Azerbaijan. During his caliphate a navy was organized, administrative divisions of the state were revised, and many public projects were expanded and completed. Uthman sent prominent Companions of the Prophet (PBUH) as his personal deputies to various provinces to scrutinize the conduct of officials and the condition of the people.

One of Caliph Uthman (RA) contribution to the religion of God was the compilation of a complete and authoritative text of the Qur'an. A large number of copies of this text were made and distributed all over the Muslim world. In other words, Uthman (RA) is credited with establishing the canonical version of the Qur'an during his caliphate. Thus, Uthman (RA) the greatest legacy is the way the Quran, the Holy Scripture of Islam, is read today. The first Caliph, Abu Bakr (RA) took a momentous step in compiling the Quran, while ensuring that the text was not tampered.

Uthman (RA) ruled the Islamic Ummah for twelve years with the first six years as being peaceful and the other six saw some dissatisfaction among the people and some of the dissatisfaction with Uthman (RA) are that he was appointing his relatives as governors of Kufa, Basra, and Egypt. The allegations against Uthman (RA) were that of nepotism against him during his rule as Caliph.

Some of the complaint by the leaders of the rebels were financial only. Some of these rebel leaders ask Uthman (RA) to step down from the caliphal seat, he said that he would not let go of what Allah/God had given him, and having said that he went inside his house. He did not want to fight the rebellion that brock up but preferred to reason with them, to persuade them with kindness and generosity.

However after a long siege by the rebels they brock into Uthman (RA) house and murdered him. He was reciting Surah 2 Al Baqarah (2:137) as translated into English by Al-Hilali and Khan (1996, p.35), So if they believe in the like of that which you believe then they are rightly guided; but if they turn away, then they are only in opposition. So Allah will suffice for you against them. And He is the All-Hearer, the All-Knower. Uthman died on the afternoon of Friday, 17 Dhul Hijja, 35 A.H. (June. (656 A.C.) and was not buried until Saturday night when he was buried in his blood-stained clothes, the shroud which befits all martyrs in the cause of God.

According to Khan (2020) the rebels had resolved on killing him and upon finding the front entrance to his house guarded, they climbed in from the back wall. They found the old caliph reading the Quran and struck him down. Uthman (RA) wife Naila valiantly rushed to protect her husband and shielded him with her bare hands, only to have many of her fingers cut. As Uthman (RA) blood flowed over the Holy Scripture and his body lay lifeless upon the floor, one of the assailants raised his sword to decapitate his body, at the sight of which his wives (two of whom were with him at that time) threw themselves on their dead husband and wailed. Unable to do anything else, the rebels looted his house and even snatched the women's veils on their way out. Uthman (RA) body lay on the floor of his house before he was buried in the dark of the night. His death created deep fissures within the Islamic society and pushed it to its first civil war: the First Fitna (661-656 CE) Khan (2020).

Uthman (RA) died at the age of eighty four years old. Uthman (RA) had the high privilege of having two daughters of the Prophet as wives Uthman was known as 'The Possessor of the Two Lights. Uthman (RA) was known for honesty, mild, generous and very kindly man, noted especially for his modesty and his piety. He often spent part of the night in prayer, fasted every second or third day, performed hajj every year, and looked after the needy of the whole community. In spite of his wealth, he lived very simply and slept on bare sand in the courtyard of the Prophet's mosque.

This is a life of a caliph who was modest and spend in the way of Islam and had great faith on Islam and died as a martyrs in the cause of Allah/ God. Finally the greatest achievement of Uthman (RA) his decision to standardize the text of the Quran is well appreciated in the present time, as people from all around the world recite it similarly, and the text has been flawlessly preserved. He died and the Ummah was quite divided before Ali (RA) to over as the fourth Caliph.

The Fourth Caliph, Ali (RA) (656-661 A.C)

After the death of Umar (R.A.), there was a power vacuum in the office of the Caliphate for three days as these who rebelled against Uthman (RA) killed in his house and he was buried at night and many Muslims at the time urged Ali (R.A) to be the next Caliph of the Muslim Ummah and he finally agreed to be the next Caliph.

Ali (RA) was known for his bravery and humility, especially when disbelievers of Makkah plotted to kill the Prophet Muhammad (PBUH), the Angle Gabriel (A.S.) revealed to him the details of that evil conspiracy and asked him (PBUH) not to sleep in his bed that night. So, the Prophet (PBUH) asked Ali (R.A.) to sleep in his bed to impersonate him, while the Prophet (PBUH) left his house safely at night and migrated to Madinah. This show the bravery of Ali (RA) and his support for the prophet of Allah/God Mohammad (PBUH). Ali (RA) participated in almost all the battles against the unbelievers during the time of the Prophet Muhammad (PBUH), except for the Battle of Tabuk in the year 9th Hijri, as the Prophet (PBUH) had placed Ali (R.A.) in charge of the city.

Ali (R.A) was the first cousin of Prophet Muhammad (PBUH) and grew up in Prophet's household, and he later married Fatima. He was ten years old when the Prophet Muhammad (PBUH) received the revelation and accepted Islam. Ali (R.A.) was extremely active in serving the Prophet (PBUH), being so close to him, following his orders and learning from his guidance. According to Islamic Finder, Ali (R.A) married the Prophet's (PBUH) most beloved daughter Fatimah (R.A), one of the best women all over, her mother was Khadijah Bint Kuwailid (R.A).

The blessed marriage took place in Madinah after the Battle of Ohud, as Fatimah (R.A) was fifteen years old. Thus, Ali (R.A) had the additional honor of being the father of the Prophet's (PBUH) progeny through his sons from Fatimah (R.A), Al-Hasan (R.A.), Al-Husayn (R.A), Zainab (R.A), and Umm Kulthoom (R.A).

There is a great story: the Prophet (PBUH) received revelation and invited relatives for a meal. After they had finished, the Prophet (PBUH) addressed them and asked who would join him in the cause of Allah/God. There was silence, and then Ali stood up and said, "I am the youngest of all present here, my eyes trouble me because they are sore, and my legs are thin and weak, but I shall join you and help you in whatever way I can." Ali (R.A) and how he supported the Prophet (PBUH). He slept in the Prophet Mohammad's (PBUH) bed when the Quraish planned to murder him. Ali (R.A) fought in all the early battles of Islam with great courage and distinction, for example, in the battle of Uhud. The Prophet (PBUH) used to call him the 'Lion of God. Other Caliphs always consulted Ali (R.A) before him. He was a great Caliph, like others, who preserved Islamic principles. During the leadership of Ali (R.A) as Caliph, there was pressure on him to identify the murderer of Uthman (R.A).

The greatest pleasure for Ali (R.A) was from Muawiya, who was the governor of Sham (great Syria), and also the cuisine of Uthman (R.A.). Muawiya urged Ali (R.A.) to enforce the rule of Allah and find out who was behind the murder of Uthman R.A). Ali (R.A) wanted to identify the person before justice could be done or seen to be done.

During Ali (R.A) reign, there was civil strife, but he introduced some reforms to the levying and collection of revenues. Ali (RA) rule as the fourth caliph had some problems. He had to establish peace in the state and to ameliorate the deteriorating political situation. Secondly, he needed to take action against the assassins of Uthman (R.A), which consumed much of his time. His main achievement were the civil and cultural accomplishments such as; police organization, constructing the court of arbitration and building jails. Besides, Ali (R.A) transferred the capital of Caliphate from Madinah to Kufah in Iraq, due to its strategic position in the mid of the Islamic country at that time. Kufah thrived as the schools of jurisprudence and grammar were established. In addition, Ali (RA) gave his orders to furnish the letters of the Holy Quran with vowel signs for the first time.

However, unfortunately, Ali's (R.A) reign as Caliph also came to an end when one morning, he was absorbed in prayers in a mosque, Ibn-Muljim stabbed him with a poisoned sword, and on the 20th of Ramadan, 40 A.H., he died and (May Allah be Pleased with him) and all the Caliphs before him. Ali (RA) was really a man of honor like other Caliphs who came before him namely Abu-Bakr (RA), Umar (RA) and Uthman (RA) they were truly men of honour and faithful to the Allah/God and prophet Muhammad (PBUH). The above periods of these four guided caliphates are seen to be where the Quran and the Sunnah of the Prophet (PBUH) were rightly practiced. Let us hope that we learn from these periods which are remarkable and a blueprint for leadership from an Islamic perspective.

Chapter 16

Cardinal Principles of Leadership in Islam and Values

In this chapter, the author will examine the cardinal leadership principles from Islamic perspectives, focusing on faith and belief, knowledge and wisdom, courage and determination, mutual consultation, unity, morality and piety, communication, justice and compassion, and finally, gratitude and prayers.

Faith and Belief

Faith is fundamental in Islam because it lays the foundation for the belief. According to Baig (2012, p.19), faith is a dynamic process that is based on the intention of three factors, (1) Patience in the face of hardship and thankfulness to Allah/God bounties; (2) repentance for our transgressions and mistakes and (3) seeking Allah's pleasure and closeness to Him by worship because we love Him. He went on to assert that faith is not blind as the materialistic world likes to believe and that faith is to be able to see beyond the material to that which cannot be described or seen with the eye of the head but which is perceptible to the eyes of the heart. Baig (2012) cited Barbara Winter, who acknowledged that faith is to know.

The notion of faith in Islam is affirmed in Surah 2: Al Baqarah (2:257), Yusuf Ali (1989, p.107), "Allah/God is the protector of those who have faith: from depths of darkness He leads them forth into the light, of those who reject faith the patrons are the evil Ones: from light they will lead them forth into the depths of darkness. They will be companions of the fire, to dwell therein (forever)." Faith and belief played an essential factor in the leadership qualities of Muslims.

This notion of faith and belief having an essential impact on leadership and followers in Muslim communities started with the previous prophets right to the final prophets of Allah/God Prophet Muhammad (PBUH), the guided Caliphs, and other Muslim leaders and followers who came after them. Faith and belief played a significant part in their lives and the communities they led. As Abu Bakr said in his first speech as Caliph of the one Nation Islam/Islamic Ummah/Muslims Communities and societies you can only: "obey me only if I obey Allah/God and Prophet Muhammad (PBUH)."

Thus, Islam puts a significant emphasis on faith and belief as the guiding principles of leadership from an Islamic perspective. Without faith and belief, leadership becomes what it is today, weak, easily manipulated by the big powers just for the sake of power or for leadership or personal acceptance. Prophet Mohammad (PBUH) said, "God will harshly punish those rulers who cause hardship to the public. On the other hand, the ruler who is kind and affectionate to his subjects will be blessed with God's mercy in the Hereafter." It was narrated by Muslim.

The Prophet (PBUH) also said: "Do not run after a good position: if you do so, you will fail to discharge your duty. However, if a position of responsibility is assigned to you, God will help and support you." It is narrated by Bukhari and Muslims as cited in Kidwai (2012, p.292). Faith and belief are the righteous pillars, not evil, for the Prophet (PBUH) said: "The best among people is he who is the most pious, God-fearing and truthful. His conduct is not tainted by any sin, injustice, jealousy, or rancour." Narrated by Ibn Majah & Bayhaqi. The prophet (PBUH) upon appointing Mu'adh as governor of Yemen, the Prophet (PBUH) advised him, "Keep away from a life of luxury. God's chosen servants do not lead a life of ease and comfort." Narrated by Ahmad.

Knowledge and Wisdom

Knowledge and wisdom are fundamental in Islam. The first encounter the Prophet (PBUH) had with Angel Gabriel during revelation was about seeking knowledge. Unfortunately, many Muslims countries and societies today do not take seeking knowledge very seriously. Therefore, it is of fundamental importance that leaders and followers in Islamic communities acquire not only knowledge but to promote and inspire Muslims all over the Ummah to acquire knowledge and wisdom as a form of worship. See Surah 96: Al-Alaq (96:1-5), Al-Hilali and Khan (1996, p.779), 1. "Read! In the name o your Lord Who has created (All that exist)… 5. He has taught man that which he knew not." This is the beauty of Islam toward knowledge seeking. Furthermore, the Prophet (PBUH) said, "Seek knowledge from the Cradle to the Grave." In Surah 39: Al Zumar (39:9), as translated into English by Al-Hilali and Khan (1996, p.579), 9. "Is one who is obedient to Allah prostrating himself or standing (in prayer) during the hours of the night, fearing the Hereafter and hoping for the Mercy of his Lord (like one who disbelieves)? Say: "Are those who know equal to those who know not?" Only men of understanding will remember (i.e., get a lesson from Allah's Signs and Verses).

The Prophet (PBUH) also said: "Seek knowledge even if it is in China. So "Seeking knowledge is obligatory for every Muslim man and woman."

The reason that many Muslims countries and communities are not seeking knowledge is not with Islam but rather with the leaders and follower of Muslim Ummah. During the era of the four rightly guided Caliphs, Muslims were very knowledgeable and sophisticated in their dealing with other empires at the time. As a result, the Muslim communities expanded from East to West and South to North. As a result, Muslims created communities at ease with themselves, a civilization that balanced spiritual and worldly development. Many in Muslims countries and societies today may blame colonization for some of their misfortune, but the reality is that when Muslims stop seeking knowledge, as was in the case of the prophet's time and the guided Caliphs period they become weak and powerless.

Many Muslim elite are being educated in the West and that affect their thinking positively and also might be negative if they use their knowledge to look down on their brothers and sister who studies in traditional madrasas. There should be coexistence between Muslims who studied in the Western universities and those who studied in local Madrasa to forge away forward for the benefit of the Ummah. There should not be any conflict between western educated Muslims elite with their traditional Islamic leaders/and follower and those who studied in local Madrasas or local institutions.

The father of the author, who was a respected Islamic scholar, was compelled to relinquish his role as a manager and leader of Anglo-Arabic schools that he played a significant role in establishing and founding alongside the communities where these schools were constructed. This occurrence is not uncommon in numerous Muslim communities across the globe. One notable achievement of my father, Mallam Inua Wirba, was his decision to involve Parent Teachers Associations (PTA) in the administration and operation of these Anglo-Arabic schools in different communities within the North West province of Cameroon.

This collaboration between the teachers, the entire community, and the parents ensured that the parents became the guardians of their respective schools in their communities or localities. This approach was implemented to prevent any conflicts of interest, as these schools were established for the benefit of the community as a whole, rather than for the benefit of any individual within these communities or localities. This practice continues to be upheld until the present day. Consequently, it is imperative that we avoid a scenario where only Western-educated Muslim elites assume leadership positions in our community schools or marginalize those who have received traditional education in Madrasas.

It is obvious that most Muslim elite educated in the western universities in various Muslim occupy leadership or important positions within their communities, and the traditionally educated Muslims are side-lined. There is a need for coexistence for each need one another which is to serve the Ummah. Thus, a clashes between these two forces are a concern. However, on a serious note, the Western-educated Muslim elite is strongly supported by the Western powers, even when they are corrupt; or subjugate their people. We need to solve these problem because some of the traditionally educated leaders in many Muslims countries or communities are called names and at time are thrown in jail or left in exile.

Therefore, leadership in the Muslims Ummah should be purely for the pleasure of Allah/God. We as leaders and followers in the Muslim Ummah should remember that weather educated in western university or traditional madrasa our first duty is to worship Allah/God only and also remember that your religion is one religion. Our focus should not be were one was educated but that we are all brothers and sisters who have only one religion but educated in difference settings. See Surah 23: (52-53), "And surely this your religion is one religion, and I am your Lord, therefore be careful (of your duty) to me. But they cut off their religion among themselves into sects, each part rejoicing in that which is with them." From the above verse, Prophet Mohammad (PBUH) told his companions about the end of time.

The Hadith narrated by Abu Dawood said: "Verily the people before you from the People of the Book split into seventy-two religions, and this religion will split into seventy-three; seventy-two are in Hell and one is in Heaven, and it's the group" And who shall it be o' Messenger of God? He said: what I'm upon and my companions, the Hadith of the Prophet (PBUH) said, "There are two classes in my Ummah (Muslims communities)-If they are right, the Ummah (Muslims communities) is set right; if they go wrong, the Ummah goes wrong."

Today, knowledge is power, and security is the strength of all those who reside within Muslim communities. Why has the leadership within the Muslim communities not done enough to create opportunities so that Muslim youths can seek knowledge as was in the Prophet's (PBUH) time and the four guided Caliphs?

Every great civilization is built around knowledge. Unless leaders and followers in Muslim communities start valuing the importance of seeking knowledge in developing themselves and the Ummah, they will be left behind in development and advanced technology. Leaders and followers of Muslim Ummah should know that seeking knowledge is as important as worship. The importance that we all take to build Masajid for prayers we should also do the same for the education of our next generation.

We can now start to use the Masajid that we have already build to start at least kindergarten education of our kids and let them start studying there and they will have a good grasp of our religion and education as well. See Surah 96, Al Alaq (96:1), Yusuf Ali (1992, p.1672), "Proclaim! (Or Read!), In the name of thy Lord and cherisher who created". This proclamation was seen as a divine commission to preach and proclaim Allah's message. From this proclamation, the Prophet (PBUH) was able to build the Islamic city of Madinah with a great constitution.

The guided Caliphs learned from Prophet Mohammad (PBUH) the importance of seeking knowledge and maintained their desire for the Ummah to stay knowledgeable. Knowledge is a cornerstone of any great civilization. The primary reason for the rise and fall of many civilizations is knowledge. History is there as evidence. The rise and fall of all civilizations are built by knowledge and faith. The fall of every civilization is when its citizens forget the past and indulge in seeking pleasure and lust and charm in the place of education and faith.

The Prophet (PBUH), in his last sermon in Arafat during the pilgrimage, said to all of us, "I have left behind with you two things that if you hold to, you will not despair, Quran and the Sunnah of the Prophet (PBUH). See Surah 2: Al Baqarah (2:269), Al-Hilali and Khan (1996, p.68), 269. "He grants Hikmah to whom He wills, and he, to whom Hikmah is granted, is indeed granted abundant good. But none remember (will receive admonition) except men of understanding."

All the above are some evidence of the importance of knowledge in Islam. Why are we Muslim leaders and followers not following the example of the Prophet Muhammad (PBUH) and the guided Caliph?

Courage and Determination

These principles of courage and determination are the qualities that all leaders and followers must have or aspire to have irrespective of their faith. The history of Islam is built around courage and determination from when Prophet Mohammad (PBUH) received revelation. Remember, prophet Mohammad (PBUH) was not literate when he received revelation. See surah 96 Al-Alaq (96:1-6) as translated into English by Al-Hilali and Khan (1996, p.779). 1, Read in the Name of your Lord Who has created (all that exists). 2, He has created man from a clot (a piece of thick coagulated blood). 3, Read! And your Lord is Most Gracious. 4, Who has taught (the writing) by the pen. 5, He has taught man that which he know not. 6, Nay! Verily, man does not transgress (in disbelief and evil deed). The prophet (PBUH) took his prophethood with great courage because he know that his tribesmen were not interested in hearing about Islam which was about worshiping Allah/God alone and some of the were Idol worshipers. Therefore he was besieged by tribes who wanted to eliminate him and his followers on any occasion, but courage and determination helped them through.

The Prophet (PBUH) had to endure hardship with his followers and they treated to kill him with his followers and he has to ask some of companions to migrate to Abyssinia where there was a king there who was just to his people even he was not a Muslim. He had to wait in Makkah and when the prophet(PBUH) receive the revelation to immigrate to Madinah with his followers he left with Abu-Bakr one of his companion and left Ali(RA) to give back some of the belongings that were given to him for safe keeping since he was known to be trustworthy. All these requires courage and it was the same courage the four guided Caliphs went through to continue on the footsteps of the prophet and many of them were killed by the enemies of Islam. Without the courage and a strong faith and belief in Islam the companions and Prophet Mohammad (PBUH) we would not have Islam that we have today and this is due to them and those who believe in Islam. The Islam we have today is because the courage of all the prophets starting with prophet Adam (PBUH) to the final prophet of Allah/God Mohammad (PBUH) and the guided caliphs and pious Muslims.

Communication

Muslim leaders must learn how to communicate with their subordinates or followers. Muslim leaders and follower should learn to be eloquent and articulate their ideas and policies with vigour. The Prophet Muhammad (PBUH) was a good communicator, especially when he received the revelation that he had to communicate clearly to the non- believers about Islam. To be able to preach about Islam he had to know how to communicate and spread the message. Prophet Mohammad (PBUH) articulated the message of Islam in a way that was immediately accepted by those who were against Islam at the beginning.

We can also see the good example of communication from Musa (Moses when he was ordered by Allah/God to go to Firaun (Pharaoh) of Egypt and asked Allah/God to make his communication easy by asking Allah/God to open and grand him confidence. See Surah 20 Taha (20:25-36), as translated into English by Al-Hilali and Khan (1996, p.396-397). 25, [Musa (Muses)] said: O my Lord! Open for me my chest (grant me self-confidence, contentment, and boldness).26. "And ease my task for me.27. And loose the knot (the defect) from my tongue, (i.e. remove the incorrectness from my speech) [That occurred as a result of a brand of fire which Musa (Moses) put in his mouth when he was an infant]. 28." That they understand my speech.29. And appoint for me a helper from my family, 30. "Harun (Aaron), my brother.31. "Increase my strength with him, 32. "And let him share my task (of conveying Allah's Message and prophethood). 33. "That we may glorify you much.34. And remember you much, 35. Verily, you are Ever a Well-Seer of us."36. (Allah) said: "you are granted your request, O Musa (Moses)!

Allah/God grated Musa (Moses) his request of opening his chest to be able to speak with clarity and also his brother Harun (Aaron) to accompany him to the pharaoh in sharing his task of conveying Allah/ God Message and Prophedhood.

Justice and Compassion

Justice and Compassion are essential for every Islamic leaders and followers alike. These two were the cornerstones of Islamic leadership that started from Prophet Adam (PBUH) till the final prophet of Allah/ God Prophet Muhammad (PBUH) and the four guided Caliphs. Without justice and Compassion, there would be tyranny. See Surah 5: Al Maidah (5:8), as translated into English by Al-Hilali and Khan (1996, p.779), 8. "O you who believe! Stand out firmly for Allah as just witnesses, and let not the enmity and hatred of others make you avoid justice. Be just: that is nearer to piety, and fear Allah. Verily, Allah is Well-Acquainted with what you do." Justice and companionship are fundamental principles of Islamic leadership as it was practice during the Prophets time and more importantly during prophet Mohammad's (PBUH) time and followed by the guided Caliphs.

Gratitude and Prayers

Gratitude and prayers are essential for leadership from an Islamic perspective. Our beloved Prophet Muhammad (PBUH) always advised his follower to always have gratitude. Human beings owe much gratitude to their Creator, as nothing can happen without His blessings and power. Prophet Muhammad (PBUH) has said that "Gratitude (shukr) for the abundance (ni'math) you have received is the best insurance that the abundance will continue." Gratitude is a morally beneficial, emotional state that encourages reciprocal kindness and receipt of other gifts from God. Related to gratitude is the importance of prayers and supplications. It is reported that the Messenger of Allah said, "Supplication is the weapon of the believer, the pillar of the religion, and the light of the Heaven and earth" (Al-Hakim). Prayers and supplications bring us nearer to Allah/God and protect us from calamities and destruction.

On the positive note, prayers and supplications are good for us as leaders and followers. See Surah 40 Mu'min (40:60) Al-Hilali and Khan (1996, p.595), God commands us, "And your Lord said: Invoke Me, [i.e., believe in My Oneness (Islamic Monotheism) and ask Me for anything] I will respond to your (invocation). Verily, those who scorn My worship [i.e., do not invoke Me, and do not believe in My Oneness (Islamic Monotheism)] they will surely, enter Hell in humiliation!" The Quran contains stories of God's Prophets such as Moses, Jesus, Muhammad and Elijah, Job, and many others who received freedom from troubles and persecution through prayers.

All great Muslim leaders showed good gratitude, offered keen prayers, and were thus successful in their endeavours and struggles. Ismail (2007) noted two fundamental principles practiced by the Prophet

(PBUH), namely, (1) receiving the message (i.e., seeking guidance and knowledge in order to direct the affairs to the followers) and (2) spreading the message (i.e., delegating tasks and ensuring that they are well accomplished). Abed (2006) identified ten personal qualities of a Muslim leader, namely, conviction (yaqīn), mutual consultation (shūrā), knowledge (ILM), justice (adl), self-sacrifice (taĪyah), humility (tawāĪluc), eloquence (faĪah), patience (Īabr), leniency (līn) and enterprise (iqdām).

Lukman (1995) identified six general principles: sovereignty (siyādah), mutual consultation (shūrā), justice (cadālah), equality (musāwah), freedom (Īurriyyah) and enjoining the right and forbidding the evil ('amr bi al-macrūf was nahī Munkar). Ali (2009) concluded that there are two types of Islamic leadership model, (1) the Prophetic and (2) the Caliphate model.

A good example of gratitude from the Quran can be seen in Surah 31 Luqman(31:12), as translated into English by) Al-Hilali and Khan (1996, p.518), 12, And indeed We bestowed Luqman Al-Hikmah (wisdom and religious understanding) saying: "Give thanks for (the good of) his own self. And whoever is unthankful, then verily, Allah is All-Rich (free of all needs) Worthy of all praise. In this example above Luqman is recognized with the title of "The wise" just because he is thankful to God. Luqman recognizes that God is the one who grants everything so therefore He is the One who deserves thankfulness.

May Allah/God give us wisdom to give thanks for all blessings by which we survive and thrive day after day. We as leaders and followers should be thankful to Allah/God for all that Allah/God have given to us and made us His vicegerent on earth. See Surah 27 An-Naml (27:19) as translated into English by Al-Hilali and Khan (1996, p.477), So he [Sulaimon (Solomon)] smiled, amused at her speech and said: My Lord! Inspired me and bestowed upon me the power and ability that I may be grateful for Your Favours which you have bestowed on me and on my parents, and that I may do righteous deeds that will please You and admit me by Your Mercy among Your righteous slaves."

Finally, gratitude as shown in the Surah's of the Quran above invites us all towards belief in the One God. Therefore, gratefulness leads to the path of faith.

Conclusion

The author of this book presents a compelling argument for the Quran to remain the primary source of leadership in Islam, drawing from the Sunnah of the Prophets, particularly the final prophet of Allah/ God prophet Mohammad (PBUH), as well as the four Rightly Guided Caliphs. Additionally, the author advocates for a shift in the Western understanding of leadership, emphasizing the importance of biblical teachings, the Ten Commandments, and moral and ethical principles as guiding principles to prevent scandals in political, social, cultural, and developmental contexts.

The current state of Western civilization is characterized by lack of effective leadership and a decline, primarily attributed to the abandonment of fundamental principles that define humanity, which is to sick Allah/God in all our undertaking by knowing that is Allah/ God is our creator and that we all are merely His servants who in their endervouse pursuit the truth, justice, and fairness in times of adversity.

There is a prevailing inclination towards destructive behaviour and an unwavering focus on achieving victory at any cost or at all cost. This has resulted in the proliferation of decay and turmoil worldwide, while simultaneously eroding ethical and moral values due to the pervasive influence of power politics and electioneering, rather than the per suite of truth.

Egan (2019) argue that one only need consider the crusades or the slave trade to see that Western civilization has taken its wrong turns along the way. There are many examples that reflect Egan argument. For example the colonisation of others nations by the western imperial powers, the drop of atomic bomb in Hiroshima and Nagasaki, the continuous exploitation of resources from Africa and other parts of the world, the war in Iraq and Afghanistan and many others and all these reflects the failure of effective leadership in the west that Allah/God fearing or is rooted in the teaching of the Bible, the Ten commandments and some religious principles.

Leadership is trust and when it is incline toward power politics and electioneering calculus it is very dangerous. Despite all these assertions there are some genuine value in learning the deep structures of Western culture despite being flawed. Hence, "Those who fail to learn from history are condemned to repeat it." Therefore the west need to go back or re-examine it Judeo-Christian ideas: the lineage of theological thought centred around monotheism, divine revelation and the covenantal relationship between God and man, the west should be committed to committed to democracy and human rights as fundamental values, the west should be committed to the flowering of rationality, including modern invention, science, humanities and the creative arts. This is the only way leaders and followers in the west can regain it past and failure to do that it decline is eminent and would be disastrous in the eyes of others.

The west does not have the monopoly of ideas and the full control of the media as it used to do with the big medias in the world, therefor the advent of social media has further exposed the fallacy of the Western project, and unless substantial reforms are implemented within the westerns civilization, its downfall appears to be inevitable and this requires effective leadership and leaders and followers who are just and fair in their world view and at the same time goes back to the creator Allah/God.

Subsequently, the author maintained in this book that the definition of leadership is selfless servitude are purely for the pleasure of Allah/ God, and the leaders and followers have a mutual interest and most be just. The author also strongly argues in this book that Muslims elites who have Western education should cooperate with those who have traditional Madrasah education as a complementary measures and not rivals. Thus the legitimacy of leaders who are educated in the west should be from the Muslims communities and not outside powers wherever they may be.

The challenge for the leaders and followers of the Muslims Ummah is on how to build a strong brotherhood as was established between the Helper (Ansar) and the Immigrant (the Muhajirun), which laid to a solid foundation for the first Islamic State in Madinah during prophet Muhammad(PBUH) and the four guided Caliphs even though they had their own challenges. How can Muslim leaders and followers become brothers and sisters irrespective of different nationalities and nations for the pleasure of Allah/God and for unity of Islam as one Ummah, whether educated in the West, from Africa, Europe, Asia, America, or anywhere in the world.

Today the Islamic Ummah/Muslims communities are divided into factions, Arab Muslims, African Muslims, European Muslims, and

Asian Muslims. In these book the author argue that these differences should be our strength, as affirmed in Surah 49 Al Hujurat(49:13) as translated into English by Al-Hilali and Khan (1996, p.651), O mankind! We have created you from a male and female, and made you into nations and tribes, that you may know one another. Verily, the most honourable of you with Allah is that (believer) who has Al-Taqwa [he is one of the Muttaqun (the pous) Veriley, Allah is All-Knowing, All-A wear. See Surah 2 Al-Baqarah (2:2) as translated into English by Al-Hilali and Khan (1996, p.12), 2. This is the Book (the Quran), whereof there is no doubt, a guidance to those who are Al-Muttaqun [the pious and righteous persons who fear Allah much (obstain from all kinds of sins and evil deeds which He has forbidden) and love Allah much (perform all kinds of good deeds which He has ordained.

The Quran to us the kind of leaders and the followers that the Muslims most be as decree by Allah/God for the Ummah. Thus, any deviation from Allah/God decree is not accepted and it is alien in Islam and therefore leaders and followers in the Islamic Ummah should take note.

Leaders and followers should learn from the kind of brotherhood in Islam that was practice in Madinah were the Ansar (Helper) gave the Muhajirun (Immigrant) sanctuary and protection.

The critic of Muslims in the Western media are asking questions that why is it that when there is conflict in Muslims countries or where there is economic migration Muslims are migrating to the west instead of migrating Muslims countries or communities which is a valid question and a concern. The answer to this question is very simple as seen is Surah 49 Al Hujurat (49:13) that is we Muslims must follow Allah/God decree pure and simple. We should not be attracted to material wealth only but to our brotherhood in Islam and the victory will come our way.

We should not be afraid of the big powers pressurizing some Muslims leaders to be doing their biddings around the world, we should not forget our history and remember that during the prophet (PBUH) time there were great powers and what happen to them all, truth will always defeat falsehood. See Surah 17 Al-Isra (17:81-2), 81, And say: Truth (i.e. Islamic Monotheism or this (Quran or Jihad against polytheists) has come and Batil (falsehood, i.e. Satan or polytheism) has vanished. Batil is ever bound to vanish." 82, And we send down of the Quran that which is healing and a mercy to those who believe (in Islamic Monotheism and act on it), and it increase the Zalimun (polytheism and wrongdoers) nothing but loss. The above surah's are very important for all Muslims leaders and followers and they are decree from Allah/God.

There is a critical need for Muslims Ummah to have a solidarity fund to help some Muslim nations who are in distress or facing natural calamity or wars. These money could come from Byt al-mal set by government within the Islamic Ummah. We all know that some Muslims countries have been pumping a lot of money to global organisations, however, beside that the Ummah could create its own body to funds similar crisis around the world and in particular around the Muslim Ummah. In other words, why can the Muslim Ummah not create its own international organisation to support brothers and sisters in distress and that fund can come straight away from Bit-tul Mal (Zakat house money).

Muslims leaders and followers should follow Allah/God decree and should be a keeper of one another and hold fast, all together, by the rope which Allah (stretches out for you), and be not divided among yourselves; and remember with gratitude Allah's favour on you; for ye were enemies and He joined your hearts in love, so that by His Grace, ye became brethren; and ye were on the brink of the pit of Fire, and He saved. See Surah3 Al-Imran (3:103-) as translated by into English by Al-

Hilali and Khan (1996, p.93), 103, "And hold fast, all of you together, to the Rope of Allah (i.e. this Quran), and be not divided amongst yourselves, and remember Allah's Favour on you, for you were enemies one to another but He joined your hearts together, so that, by his Grace, you become brethren(in Islamic faith), and you were on the brink of a pit of Fire, and He saved you from it.

Thus Allah makes His Ayat (proofs, evidence, verses, lessons, signs, revelation, etc.,) clear to you, that you may be guided. 104, Let there arise out of you a group of people inviting to all that is good (Islam), enjoying Al-Maruf (i.e. Islamic Monotheism and all that Islam orders one to do) and forbidding Al-Munkar (Polytheism and disbelief and all that Islam has forbidden). And it is they who are the successful. 105, And be not as those that divided and differed among themselves after the clear proofs had come to them. It is they for whom there is an awful torment.106, On the Day (i.e. the Day of Resurrections) when some faces will become white and some faces become black; as for those faces will become black(to them will be said): "Did you reject Faith after accepting it? Then taste the torment (in Hell) for rejecting Faith." 107, And for those whose faces will become white, they will be in Allah's Mercy (Paradise), therein they shall dwell forever. 108, these are the Verses of Allah: We recite them to you (O Muhammad (PBUH) in truth, and Allah wills no injustice to the Alamin (mankind, inns, and all that exists). 109, You [true believers in Islamic Monotheism and real followers of Prophet Muhammad (PBUH) and his Sunnah are the best of people ever raised up for mankind; you enjoin Al Maruf (i.e. Islamic Monotheism and all that Islam has ordained) and forbid Al- Munkar (polytheism, disbelief and all that Islam has forbidden), and you believe in Allah. And had the people of the Scripture (Jews and Christians) believed it would have been better for them; among them are some who have Faith, but most of them are Al-Fasiqun (disobedient to Allah and rebellious against Allah's

Command) The surah above remind us all the need of being together and holding unto the Rope of Allah/ God as decree to us.

Thus, the model of leadership from an Islamic perspective is the previous prophets and more importantly our beloved Prophet Muhammad (PBUH) and the previous Prophets of Allah/God, starting with Adam (PBUH), Dawud (David), and Yusuf, who asked Allah/God to make him a leader for his people. Allah/God warns us to be careful when we are leaders.

We as leaders and followers should be just and fair to one another because Muslims are brothers to one another, and there is no compulsion in religion. See Surah Al-Imrana (2:256) as translated in English by Khan and Al Hilali (1996, p.65), 256- "There is no compulsion in religion. Verily, the Right Path has become a district from the wrong path. Whoever disbelieves in Taghut and believes in Allah, then he has grasped the most trustworthy handhold that will never break. And Allah is All-Hearer, All-Knower. Khan and Al-Hilali (1996, p.65) went on to comment that the meaning of Target is anything worshiped other than the Real Allah/God, i.e., all the false deities. It may be satan, devils, idols, stones, sun, stars, angels, human beings for example.

Messengers of Allah/God who were falsely worship. Saints, graves, rulers, and leaders who are falsely worshiped and wrongly followed. To them Tagut means a false Jude who gives a false judgment. Also, see Surah An-Nisa (4:60 and 4:51). We need leaders in Muslim communities to feel for their brothers and Sisters Muslims all over the Ummah, even though they may not be their countries. Why is the saying that a Muslim is a brother of another brother becoming less practical by those who are supposed to uphold it, especially our leaders and even follower?

How many Muslim countries accept children of other Muslims born in their countries, like the case of the United States of America, the UK, and some Western countries? None, to my knowledge and it is a challenge and a concern. We should not be adopted nationalism and used the concept of the nation-state to create the concept of us and them as a way of life, the Ummah should be a keeper of one another, not only in crisis. If the other Muslim brother or sister is not a citizen of a given Muslim society, he or she should be treated fairly to avoid this constant question of why are Muslims not staying in their brother's nation but migrating to the west. We owe our brothers and sister a duty of care if possible.

The creation of nation state does not means that Muslim communities be building walls like in some western countries preventing others to enter their countries. Leaders of the free world are building high fence to retire others from coming to their countries which is a concern and should not be copy by those in the affairs of leadership in the Muslim Ummah.

Furthermore, the author postulates that there should be no compulsion in religion. See Surah (3:20). Therefore, Muslim leaders and followers should not commit atrocities in the name of Islam, they should preach Islam and let their deed embodied Islam. Allah protects Islam, and we should not fear any forces that aim to destroy it. The life of Prophet Mohammad (PBUH) is our leadership model, and therefore we should follow him as he said in his farewell speech to the Ummah (Muslim communities), "I have left behind two things if you hold fast to it you will not go astray Quran and his Sunnah."

Today the most significant challenge facing the Muslim communities and their leaders is not the Sunni and Shia divide, as noted above, or the West against Islam but rather the lack of brotherhood between Muslims.

We must try to win the heart and minds of those who oppose us or are misguided. We can learn from Prophet Mohammad's (PBUH) life. He tried to make some of tribe's men Muslims but Allah/God replied to him in Surah. See Surah 28 Al Qasas (28:56), as translated into English by Khan and Al Hilali (1996, p.493), 56."So verily, you (O Mohammad (PBUH) guide not whom you like, but Allah guides whom He wills. And He knows best those who are the guided." Furthermore, the foundation of the Islamic state in Madinah was based on brotherhood.

The Ansar (Helpers) and Muhajirun (Emigrants) were interwoven into one brotherhood in Islam. The Islamic state/one nation Islam/ Muslims communities is not an end in itself, but a means to an end, the end being the development of a community of people who stand up for equity and justice, for right against wrong. Leaders and followers who are spiritually and morally strong and adhere to the teachings of Islam as decree by Allah/God. Again, Prophet Muhammad (PBUH) is the model to follow. Moreover, at the same time, leaders and followers of the Muslims Ummah should be aware that the biggest enemy of Islam is the ignorant Muslim, whose ignorance leads him to intolerance, whose actions destroy the actual image of Islam, and when the people look at him, they think that Islam as argued strongly by Sheikh Ahmed Deedat (May Allah have mercy on him) and is strong reminded us all.

Finally, the last even in Palestine give us hope that the Ummah is still strong even though there are some division here and there. The world have shown that injustice cannot prevail even with the might of gun and bomb powers and that who hold powers are the followers not the leaders. The apartheid regime in South Africa did not succeed despite their might and support from the west and the case in Palestine is not that different.

The fear of coexistence is just a pretext for perpetuating crime against humanity. The leaders and followers of the Muslims Ummah should not forget their history. For example the case of Sumaya (RA) and Yasir (RA), the first martyrs of Islam, the Crusades in Jerusalem where the streets ran red with blood, until now, the Ummah has faced oppression and is still the target of oppression, slander, killing, persecution, as the case going on in the Middle East today, but they should not follow the food step of those who oppress them, but rather should follow the Islamic teaching for Allah/God have decree them victory. We all know that any person with an ounce of sympathy in their heart would pray for them. The whole world is crying and praying for them as we can see in our television screen, especially in western capitals were their leaders have become indifferent.

The Messenger of Allah, Muhammad (PBUH) says: "The parable of the believers in their affection, mercy, and compassion for each other is that of a body. When any limb aches, the whole body reacts with sleeplessness and fever." (Bukhari, Muslim). Muslims and non-Muslims should be keeper of one another and fight injustice and pray for effective leadership in their rank to serve mankind as Khalifah/Vicegerent of Allah/God on earth. See Surah 61 Al-Saff (61:8-9) 8, They intended to put out the light of Allah (i.e. the religion of Islam, this Quran, and the prophet Muhammad (PBUH) with their mouths, But Allah will bring His light to perfection even though the disbelievers hate it. 9, He it is who Sent His Messenger(Muhammad (PBUH) with guidance and the religion of truth (Islamic monotheism) to make it victories over all (other) religions even though the Mushrikun (polytheists, pagans, idolaters, and the disbelievers in the Oneness of Allah and in His Messenger (PBUH) hate it. Muslims leaders and followers and also non-Muslims should be keeper of one another and should not fear the pressures from the big powers to form alliances that are against the Ummah interest and fear

Allah/God only alone for leadership is trust (Amanah) and is selfless servitude purely for the pleasure of Allah/God.

Allah/God in Surah 22 Al-Hajj (22-41) has decree Muslim leaders as 42, Those (Muslim rulers) who, if we give them power in the land, (they) enjoin iqamatul-Salat (i.e. to perform the five compulsory congregational Salat(prayers) the male in mosques)] to pay the Zakat and they enjoin Al-Maruf (i.e. Islamic Monotheism and all that Islam order one to do), and forbid Al-Munkar (i.e. disbelief, polytheism and all that Islam has forbidden), [i.e. they make the Quran as the law of the their country in all the spheres of life]. And with Allah rests the end of (all) matters (of creatures).

This is my reflection on hearing of the normalisation of the relationship between Israel and some Muslims countries. Those countries should remember their responsibility with regards to the Issue of Majid Aqsa the third Holy Majid after Haramin Sherifine in both Makkah and Madinah. Those who are making these decision should be aware that Masjid Aqsa is the heart beat of the Muslim Ummah in general, the right to two state solution and the freedom for Muslims to visit Majid Aqsa if they do desire to do so freely. Remember that Islamic Jerusalem is the

Holy Land and it was liberated to bring it under the fold of Islam. The significant of the place requires great thinking before making a final decision with regards normalisation of relationship, so that our brothers and sister should leave in peace as was the case before the 1948 crises.

There is a need for coexistence so that both parties can have the right for self-determination and the process of democracy and peace for all. See Surah 5 Al-Maidah (5:8) as translated into English by Khan and Al Hilali (1996, p.146), O you who believe! Stand out firmly for Allah as just witnesses; and let not the enemy and hatred of others make you avoid justice. Be just: that is nearer to piety; and fear Allah. Verily, Allah is well-Acquainted with what you do. Also see Surah 8 (Al-Anfal (8:56-

61) as translated into English by Khan and Al Hilali (1996, p.235), 56, They are those with whom you make a covenant, but they break their covenant every time and they do not fear Allah. 57, So if they you gain the mastery over them in war, punish them severely in order to disperse those who are behind them, so that they may learn a lesson. 58, If you Muhammad (PBUH) fear treachery from any people throw back (their covenant) to them).

Certainly Allah likes not the treacherous. 59, And let not those who disbelieve think that they can outstrip (escape from the punishment). Verily, they will never be able to save themselves (from Allah's punishment). 60, And make ready against them all you can of power, including steeds of war (tanks, planes, missiles ,artillery) to threaten the enemy of Allah and your enemy, and others beside whom, you may not know but whom Allah does know. And whatever you shall spend in the cause of Allah shall be repaid unto you, and you shall not be treated unjust. 61, But if they incline to peace, you also incline to it, and (put your) trust in Allah. Verily, He is the All-Hearer, the All-Knower. Thus, the Islamic Ummah and non-Islamic need an effective leadership to steady the ship of humanity as was the case of Prophet Muhammad (PBUH) who was send by Allah/God as a mercy for mankind.

Muslims leaders and followers should remember their history and learn from past mistakes, especially from those people who disobey Allah/ God and their prophets, and subsequently what happened to them, we have to remember that the collapse of the Ottoman Empire lead to the colonisation of the Muslim Ummah and the change in the education systems in the Muslims Ummah and we are still suffering from the secularisation of the education systems in the Muslims Ummah today. We have to remember the Hadith of the prophet Muhammad (PBUH) the Messenger of Allah/God as narrated by Thawban:

The Prophet (PBUH) said: The people will soon summon one another to attack you as people when eating invite others to share their dish. Someone asked: Will that be because of our small numbers at that time? He replied: No, you will be numerous at that time: but you will be scum and rubbish like that carried down by a torrent, and Allah will take fear of you from the breasts of your enemy and last enervation into your hearts. Someone asked: What is wahn (enervation). Messenger of Allah (PBUH): He replied: Love of the world and dislike of death". Sunnan Abu Dawud 4297, Sahiha Al-Albani Hadith 4284.

This hadith explains the first form of weakness, which has befallen the 'Ummah in all corners of the world, as being a result of inclination to this world, love of it, and being preoccupied with it, whilst turning away from the Hereafter, being distant from it and hatred of death. Hatred of death is a sign of loving this world, since the one who loves this world, hates death. Since, with death, comes the meeting with Allah/God, the Most Perfect. How could the Muslim Ummah not speak with one voice with these atrocities engulfing the Muslim Ummah today, this can only be explain by the Hadith of the Prophet Muhammad (PBUH) who was send as mercy to mankind as was narrated by Thawban in Sahih (Al-Albani) refence in Abu Dawud (no. 4297). The above Hadith remind us as Muslims leaders and followers how some European powers carved at will during the Berlin Conference of 1884 Africa for their own interest and colonized Africa. For example King Leopold of Belgium very famously referred to his colonial ambitions as "this magnificent African cake."

Finally, we in the Muslim Ummah should remember the declaration of Prophet Muhammad (PBUH) that, "There will never cease to be a group from my nation victorious upon the truth, unharmed by those who will oppose them, until Allah/God decree comes to pass." So many religions have come and gone, and yet the prophet (PBUH) boldly expressed that despite all the corruption and moral degradation, true believers in Islam will endure. Even when the adversity involved in preserving Islam will be tantamount to "grasping onto a burning coal," Muslims will always exist who value their faith over their lives, and hence the Prophet (PBUH) further described them in another hadith by saying, "The Hour will not commence until a man passes by the grave of his brother and says, 'I wish I were in his place.'" Ibn Baṭṭāl (d. 1057) explains that this will not be due to any suicidal ideation, but rather an anxiety that the prevalent evils and the strength of their adversaries may cost them their religion. The youth of the Muslim Ummah are resolute and united in their belief in the unity of the Ummah. However, there are certain leaders who are undermining this unity and causing division. These leaders are serving the interests of the enemies of the Muslim Ummah in order to maintain their own power and political positions. It is important for these leaders, as well as the followers of the Muslim Ummah, to be reminded of their responsibility to work for Islam and the unity of the Ummah, wherever Muslim communities may be. Within the Muslim Ummah, we are in need of effective leadership that emulates the example set by our beloved Prophet Muhammad (PBUH), who serves as a role model for all, regardless of religious affiliation or political ideology. We should also look to the four Rightly Guided Khalifas and other great leaders throughout history for inspiration.

Glossary

'Abd: Slave

Abu Bakr: A close and trusted friend of Muhammad; one of the first converts to Islam; the father of 'A'isha, the beloved wife of the Prophet

Abdullah ibn 'Abd al-Muttalib: The father of Muhammad, who died before he was born

Abu Jahl: "Father of Insolence," the nickname given by the Muslims to Abul-Hakam; the most virulent of Muhammad's early opponents

Abu Sufyan ibn Harb: Chief of the Qurayshan clan of 'Abd Shams; a leading opponent of Islam.

Abu Talib ibn 'Abd al-Muttalib: Muhammad's uncle, guardian, and protector. 'A'isha bint Abi Bakr Daughter of Abu Bakr; Muhammad's beloved young wife

Ali ibn Abi Talib Abu Talib's: son; the ward of Muhammad and Khadijah. He married Fatimah, the Prophet's daughter.

Ahl al-beit: People of the household. Muhammad's immediate family.

Ahl al-kitab: People of the Book. Usually Jews and Christians.

Allahu akhbar: "God is greater." A phrase that reminds Muslims of the transcendence and supremacy of God.

Al-Rahim: The Merciful. One of the names of God.

Al-Rahman: The Compassionate. One of the names of God.

Ansar: The Helpers. The Medinese Muslims.

Asibiyyah: Tribal solidarity.

ayah: (Plural: ayat): Sign, parable, symbol, a verse of the Qur'an

Allah: God

Al-Amanah: The trust or the moral responsibility or honesty, and all the duties which Allah has ordained

Arafat: A famous place of pilgrimage in the southeast of Makkah.

Arafat: A mountain sixteen miles east of Mecca; one of the stations of the hajj, where pilgrims made an all-night vigil.

Ameen: O Allah, accept our invocation

Ayaat: Proof, évidences, lessons, signs, revelations etc.

Badr: A place about 150 Km to the south of Al-Madina where the first great battle in Islamic history took place between the early Muslims and the infidels of Quraish

Badr: A watering hole on the Red Sea coast, where the Muslims achieved their first victory over the Meccan army.

Bait-ul-Maal: (the house of money) was the department that dealt with the revenues and all other economic matters of the state

Bilal: An Abyssinian slave who converted to Islam; he became the first muezzin to call the Muslims to prayer.

Dhikr: Reminder, remembrance.

Din: Religion, way of life, moral law, reckoning

Gabriel: The angel or spirit of the divine revelation.

Hadith: A saying of the Prophet Muhammad (PBUH), the Prophet (PBUH) act on see also Sunnah

Hadith: (plural: ahadith) Report, a maxim or saying attributed to the Prophet

Hajj: Pilgrimage to Makkah /The pilgrimage to Mecca.

Hajji: pilgrim.

Hijrah:: Literally it means migration. It is used for (a) the migration of Muslims from an enemy land to a secure place for religious causes (b) the first Muslim migration from Makkah to Abyssinia and later to Al-Madina (c) the migrations from Makkah to Abyssinnia and later to Al-Madinah d) The Prophet's migratory journey from Makkah to Al-Madinah e) The Islamic calendar year which started from the Prophet's migratory journey from Makkah to Al-Madinah

Hijrah: Migration, especially the Muslims' migrations to Medina.

Hijab: Curtain, veil, a covering for something precious or sacred.

Hira: A well-known cave in a mountain near Makkah

Hudaybiyyah: A well within the confines of the Meccan sanctuary, where Muhammad(PBUH) made a peace treaty with the Quraysh in 628

Islam: Surrender, submission, the name eventually applied to the religion of the Qur'an

Isra: A night journey, especially that of Muhammad to Jerusalem.

InshaAllah: God willing. i.e. I will meet you tomorrow, Insha'Allah

Jahannam: Hellfire

jahiliyyah: Traditionally translated "Time of Ignorance," and used to apply to the pre-Islamic period in Arabia, but in the Muslim sources its primary meaning is violent and explosive irascibility, arrogance, tribal chauvinism

Jihad: Striving, applies to any sort of effort or activity made by any person arriving out of love for Allah; Struggle, effort, endeavour.

Jinn: A creature or spirit of fire

jinni: (plural: jinn) "Unseen being," usually one of the sprites who haunted the Arabian desert, inspired poets, and led people astray; also stranger, a person hitherto "unseen.

Ka'bah: The cubic stone structure or House of God at the centre of the Haram Mosque in Mecca, the foundations of which were built by Abraham (PBUH) and his son

Kabah: Literally, cube. The granite shrine in the Haram, dedicated to Allah. It is a place all Muslims face when they are in their prayer all over the four corners of the world. When Muslims circle the Kaaba they walk in the footsteps of their prophet Muhammad (PBUH) in devotion to Allah/God. What unite the Muslims from all over the world is during their circulation of the Kaaba is a desire to emulate the life the prophet (PBUH).

Kafir: (Plural: kafirun) traditionally translated "unbeliever." More accurately it refers to somebody who ungratefully and aggressively rejects Allah and refuses to acknowledge his dependence on the Creator.

Kalifa: The successor of Muhammad, the caliph.

Caliphate or khilāfah/Caliph: a person considered a political-religious successor to the Islamic prophet Muhammad and a leader of the entire Muslim world (ummah).

Khadijah bint al-Khuwaylid: Muhammad's first wife.

Kufr: Disbelief in any of the articles of Islamic Faith

Layla al-qadr: Night of destiny; the night when Muhammad received the first revelation from God.

Marwah: A hill to the east of the Kabah; during the hajj, pilgrims would run seven times between Marwah and Safe.

Masjid: A place for prostration; later, mosque

Mecca: The commercial city ruled by the Quraysh; the birthplace of Muhammad.

Medina: The name given by the Muslims to the settlement of Yathrib; the city of the Prophet.

Mina: A valley about five miles east of Mecca; one of the stations of the hajj.

Mu'min: Those who faithfully live up to the Muslim ideal

Munafiq: A hypocrite

Munafiq: (Plural: munafiqun) Waverer; hypocrite; the term applied to an uncommitted Muslim who followed Ibn Ubbay.

Mushrikun: Polytheists, pagans, idolaters and disbelievers in the Oneness of Allah and His Messenger Muhammad (PBUH)

Muslim: A person who has surrendered his or her entire being to God; who has made the act of Islam.

Muttaqun: Pious believers of Islamic Monotheism who fear Allah and love Allah.

Nadhir: A messenger who brings a warning to his people.

P B U H: Peace Be upon Him Whenever the name of the Prophet Muhammad (PBUH) is mentioned, Muslims are required to follow the name by pronouncing '"Sallallahu alaihi wa sallam" and 'is the Arabic equivalent of Peace Be upon Him

Qiblah: The direction of prayer.

Qur'an: "Recitation." The scripture that was revealed to Muhammad by God.

Quraysh: Muhammad (PBUH) tribe, rulers of Mecca; Adj. Qurayshan; Qurayshi; a member of the tribe.

Ramadan: The Holy month of the Islamic calendar during which Muslim fast; the Holy Qur'an is believed to have been revealed in this month

Rashidun: The "rightly guided" ones; the first four caliphs.

Riba: Usury, of two major kinds: a) interest on lent money b) taking a superior thing of the same kind of goods by giving more of the same kind of goods of inferior quality. Islam strictly forbids all kinds of usury

Safa: A hill to the east of the Kabah; during the hajj, pilgrims would run between Safa and Marwah.

Salat: The ritual worship performed five times a day by Muslims.

Shahadah: The Muslim declaration of faith: "I bear witness that there is no god but Allah and that Muhammad is his prophet."

Shari'ah: The code of behaviour for the Islamic way of life, the law that determines the rightness (halal) or wrongness (haram) of any particular action

Shari'ah: Originally, the path to the watering hole. The lifeline of a nomadic tribe; later applied to the body of Muslim law.

Shaytan: A "Satan." A tempter who could be a human being or one of the jinn, who leads people astray and inspires facile, empty desires.

Shirk Idolatry: associating other beings with God, putting other deities' or purely human values on the same level as Allah. The cardinal Muslim sin.

Sunnah: Ways of the Prophet Muhammad (PBUH). For

example: Growing of his beard for a male Muslim is Sunnah

Surah: Surah, chapter surah/ a chapter of the Qur'an.

Taqwa: God consciousness/ Mindfulness; an attitude of sensitivity to and consciousness of God

Tawheed: Monotheism. Believing in one God, unity principle/ the unity of God, realized in the integration of the human person.

Umar ibn al-Khattab: The nephew of Abu Jahl; at first passionately opposed to Muhammad, but later became one of his closest companions.

Uthman ibn 'Affan: One of the earliest converts, with family connections to some of the most powerful clans in Mecca; he became Muhammad's son-in-law.

Waraqah Ibn Nawfal: Cousin of Khadijah; a hanif who had converted to Christianity.

Umrah: A visit to Makkah during which one performs Tawaf around the Ka'bah and the Sa'y between As-Safa and Al- Marwah. It is also called the Lesser Hajj'/the Lesser Pilgrimage. The rites of the hajj that were performed within the city of Mecca.

Uhud: A mountain to the north of Medina; the Meccans inflicted a severe defeat over the Muslim army on the adjoining plain.

Wahy: The Revelation or Inspiration of Allah to His Prophets.

Yathrib: The first name of the city of Madinah i.e. Madinah was earlier called Yathrib, so named after the man who founded it

Yawm ad-din: Day of reckoning; moment of truth.

Zakat: To purify. Muslims 'cleanse' their material possessions and money by donating a percentage of it (2.5% of surplus income) as a compulsory payment to help the poor, needy and the sick.

Zakat: Literally "purification" Alms; a charitable donation to the needy. One of the essential practices of Islam.

Zalzala: An Earth quake

Zamzam: The sacred well inside the (the grand mosque) Haram at Makkah

References

Abu Dawud, S. (2008). Sunan Abu Dawud. Riyadh: Darussalam Publishers.

Abū Dāwūd, Sunan Abī Dāwūd, 4:111, no. 4297; authenticated by al-Albāni in the comments.

Abu-Munshar, M. Y. (2013). Islamic Jerusalem and its Christians: A History of Tolerance and Tensions. London & New York: I.B. Tauris Publishers.

Abu-Rabi, I. (1997). Facing modernity: Ideological origins of Islamic Revivalism. Harvard International Review, 19 (2), 12-13. Retrieved from https://www.jstor.org/stable/42764024

Abu-Saud, M. (1983). Concept of Islam. Riyadh: International Islamic Publishing House.

Al-Bukhari, M. I. I. (1997). The Translation of the Meanings of Sahih Al-Bukhari. Riyadh: Darussalam Publishers

Adair, J. (2010). The Leadership of Muhammad. On a journey the leader of people is their servant.London: Konganpage.

AlKhuli, M.A. (1981). The Light of Islam. Riyadh: International Islamic Publishing House.

Al-Jibouri (2016) Inviting Rulers of Neighboring States to Islam (628 A.D.) http://www.imamreza.net/eng/imamreza.php?id=8952[assesed on 7/01/2016]

Al Omar, A. (1975) Islam the True Religion of Truth. Riyadh: Al Farazdak press.

Al-Salabi, M.R. (2001a). Al-Khulafaa Al-Rashedeen: Abo-Bakr. http://saaid.net/book/open.php?cat=7&book=2146, downloaded on December 30, 2008.

Ali, S. A. (2020) A short history of the Saracens. Alpha Edition.

Al-Salabi, M.R. (2001b). Al-Khulafaa Al-Rashedeen: Omar ibn Al-Khattab.. http://saaid.net/book/open.php?cat=7&book=2924, downloaded on December 30, 2008.

Al-Sallabi, A. M. (2007). The Biography of Abu Bakr As-Siddeeq. Riyadh: Darussalam Publishers.

Al-Suyuti, A. (1995). The History of the Khalifahs (3rd Revise). London: Ta-Ha Publisher Ltd. Al-Tabari, I. J. (1990). The History of al-Tabari Vol.9: The Last Years of The Prophet. New York: State University of New York Press

Al-Wāqidi, A. I. (2011). Kitāb al-Maghāzī (R. Faizer, Ed.). New York: Routledge.

Al-Wāqidi, A.-I. (2005). The Islamic Conquest of Syria. London: Ta-Ha Publisher Ltd

Alvesson, M. (1995), Management of Knowledge Intensive Companies,Walter de Gruyter, New York, NY.

Amstrong, K (1992) Muhammad: A Biography of the Prophet.

Amstrong, K (2006). Muhammad A Prophet for Our Time. HarperCollins Publishers Inc.

An Interview with Egypt's Mufti," *Asharq al-Awsat Daily*, 25 Nov. 1998. https://kennedy.byu.edu/alumni/bridges/features/islam-and-western-culture

Avolio, B.J., Soik, J.J., Jung, D., I., & Berson, Y.(2003) Leadership model, method, and applications. In W.C. Borman, D.R. Ilgen. &R,J. Klimoski (Eds.), Handbook of psychology (vol.12,pp.277-307).

Hoboken. NJ: Wiley.

Avolio, B. J., (2005), Leadership development in balance: Made/born. Mahwah, N.J.: Lawrence Erlbaum Associates.

Avolio, B. J., & Gardner, W. L., (2005), Authentic Leadership Development: Getting to the root of positive forms of leadership. Leadership Quarterly, 16, pp. 315-338.

Bamyeh, Social Origins of Islam, 32. Bamyeh, Social Origins of Islam, 22–24 Bamyeh, Social Origins of Islam, 25–27

Bass, B. (1997). Does the transactional-transformational leadership paradigm transcend national boundaries? American Psychologist, 52(2), 130.

Barker, R. A., (2002). On the nature of leadership. Lanham: University Press of America.

Bass, B.M. (1985). Leadership and performance beyond expectations. New York: Macmillan.

Bennis, W.G., & Nanus, B. (1985). Leaders; The strategies for taking change. New York: Happer & Row.

Bhasin, Hitesh, (2021) What is Ethical Leadership? https://www.marketing91.com/ethical-leadership/

Bilal Philip, A. (No: 1040). The True Religion of God. Jubail:Jubail Dawah & Guidence Center.

Bilal Philip, A. (1979). The Purpose of Creation. Dar Al Fatah. Riyadh.

Blacke, R.R., and Mouton, N. (1986) Executive Achievement: Making it at the Top. New York: McGraw-Hill Book.

Blacke, R.R., and Mouton, J.S. (1985) The managerial Grid, Huston, TX: Gulf.

Boal, K.B., and Bryson, J.M. (1987) "Charismatic Leadership: A

Phenomenological and Structural Approach." In Hunt, J.G., et al. (Eds.). Emerging Leadership Vistas (pp. 11-28). Lexington, MA: Lexington Books.

Bradford, D.L., and Cohen, A.R. (1984) Managing for excellence: The guide to developing high performance organisations. New York: John Wiley

Brown, M. E., L. K. Treviño, and D. A. Harrison. "Ethical Leadership: A Social Learning Perspective for Construct Development and Testing." Organizational Behaviour and Human Decision Processes 97.2 (July 2005): 117–134.

Bryman, A. (1992). Charisma and Leadership in Organization. London: Sage Publication, Inc.

Bryman, A. (1993). Charismatic leadership in organisations: Some neglected issues. Leadership Quarterly 4, pp289-304

Britannica (2023) Biography of Abu-Bakr. https://www.britannica.com/biography/Abu-Bakr Bukhari, Hadith 1.3, in Lings, Muhammad, 44–45

Burns, J. M (1978). Leadership. New York: Harper & Row. Burns, J. (1978). Leadership. New York: HarperCollins.

Bush, T. (1995) Theories of Educational Management. London: Harper and Row.

Bycio, P.; Hackett, R.D.; & Allen, J.S. (1995). Further Assessment of Bass's (1985) Conceptualisation of Transactional and Transformational Leadership, Journal of Applied Psychology, 1995, Vol.80, No.4, 468-478.

Bass, B. (1990). Bass & Stogdill' s handbook of leadership: Theory, research, and managerial applications. New York: Free Press.

Casimir, G. (2001). Combinative aspects of Leadership style The ordering and temporal spacing of leadership behaviours. Pergamum. The Leadership Quarterly 12 (2001) 245-27.

Chamber, S. (2021). Islamophobia in western media is based on false premises https://theconversation.com/islamophobia-in-western-media- is-based-on-false-premises-151443

Chapter1591 (2023): Nations Summoning One Another To Attack Muslims https://sunnah.com/abudawud:4297

Cheng, B. S., Chou, L. F., Wu, T. Y., Huang, M. P., and Farh, J. L. (2004). Paternalistic leadership and subordinate responses: establishing a leadership model in Chinese organizations. Asian J. Soc. Psychol. 7, 89–117. doi: 10.1111/j.1467-839x.2004. 00137.x

Ciulla, J.B. (1995). Leadership ethics: Mapping the territory. Business Ethics Quarterly, 5 (1), 5-28.

Cook, B. J. (1999). Islamic versus Western conceptions of education: reflections on Egypt. International Review of Education, 45(3/4), 339-357

Conger, J.A. and Kanungo, R.N. (1988) "Behavioral Dimensions of Charismatic Leadership." In J.A. Conger, R.N. Kanungo, and Associates (Eds.). Charismatic Leadership: The Elusive Factor in

Organizational Effectiveness (pp. 323-336). San Fransico, CA: Jossey Bass.

Conger, J.A. and Kanungo, R. (1998) Charismatic leadership in organisations, Sage Publication

Covey, S.R.(1990). Principle-Centered Leadership. New York (NY: Simon& Schuster.

Covey, S.R.(1989). Seven habits of highly effective people: Restoring the character ethic. NewYork: Simon &Schuster.

Cumbo, L. J. (2009). Ethical leadership: The quest for character, civility, and community. Current Reviews for Academic Libraries, 47(4), 726-726.

Daft, R.L. (2018). The Leadership Experience (7th ed.). Cengage Learning.

Darcy, K. T. (2010). Ethical Leadership: The past, present and future. International Journal of Disclosure & Governance, 7(3), 198-212.

Daun, H., Arjmand, R. & Walford, G. (2004). Muslims and education in a global context. In Daun, H. and Walford, G. (Eds), Educational strategies among Muslims in the context of globalisation: Some national case studies (pp. 5-36). Leiden: Brill

De Vaus, D. (2002) Survey in Social Research. Taylor and Francis Group: Routledge.

Den Hartog, D.N. (1997) Inspirational leadership. Doctoral, University of Amsterdam.

De Hoogh, A. H. B., & Den Hartog, D. N. (2008). Ethical and despotic leadership, relationships with leader's social responsibility, top management team effectiveness and subordinates' optimism: A multi-method study. The Leadership Quarterly, 19(3), 297- 311.

Den Hartog, D.N, & Koopman, P.L. (2001). Leadership in Organizations. Handbook of Industrial, Work & Organizational Psychology, 2, 166-187. https://doi.org/10.4135/9781848608368.n10.

De Pree, M. (1990). Leadership is an Art.

DePree, M. (1989). Leadership is an Art. New York: Dell Publishing. Dov Seidman (2021), Moral Leadership: Meaning, Characteristics and

Examples https://harappa.education/harappa-diaries/moral-leadership/

Durbrin, A.J. (2007). Leadership. (5th Ed.). New York: Houghton Mifflin.

Dvir, T. (1998). The impact of transformational leadership training on follower development and performance: A field experiment. Doctoral dissertation, Tel Aviv, Israel.

Edgan,p. (2019). Educational Renaissance: Promoting a Rebirth of Ancient Wisdom for the Modern Era https://educationalrenaissance. com/2019/04/05/why-study-western-civilization/

Elmessiri, A. (2002). Secularism, immanence and deconstruction. In

J.L. Esposito & A. Tamimi (Eds.), Islam and secularism in the Middle East (pp. 52-80). London: Hurst & Co.

Eicher-Catt, Deborah (2005). The myth of servant-leadership. Women and language, 28 (1), 17-25.

Esposito, J. L. (2002). Introduction: Islam and secularism in the twenty-first century. In J.L. Esposito & A. Tamimi (Eds.), Islam and secularism in the Middle East (pp. 1-12). London: Hurst & Co.

Fazaile-Amal, The Stories of Companions, Raisul Muhadditsin Allama Mohammad Zakariya R.A, Sheikhul Hadits, Mazahir Ulum, Saharanpur,p: 14.

Freeman, E., & Stewart, L. (2006). Developing ethical leadership. Institute for Corporate Ethics. www.corporate-ethics.org. Retrieved on 26/11/2014

Fiedler, F. E. (1967). A Theory of Leadership Effectiveness. New York: McGraw- Hill.

Gandhi. M. (1924). The Young India. https://islamigems.com/blog/ https://islamigems.com/huge-respect-for-great-caliph-of-islam-hazrat-umar-mahatma-gandhi/

Gardner, J.W. (1990). On Leadership. New York: Free Press.

Graham, J.W. (1987) Transformational Leadership: Fostering Follower Autonomy, Not Automatic Followership. In Hunt, J.G., et al. (Eds.).

Emerging Leadership Vitas. Lexington, MA: Lexington Books.

Graham, J.W. (1998). Servant leadership and enterprise strategy. In

L.C. Spears (Ed.). Insights on leadership (pp. 145-156). New York: John Wiley & Sons.

Geewax, M. (2002). Enron scandal expected to touch every American. Bnet.com. Retrieved June 11, 2011, from www.bnet.com

Gianluca Paolo Parolin, Citizenship in the Arab World: Kin, Religion and Nation-state (Amsterdam University Press, 2009),

Gill,R., (2006). Theory and Practice of Leadership. CA: Sage Publications.

Gini, A. (1998). Ethics: The heart of leadership. Westport, CT: Greenwood.

Green, M.T., & Odom, L. (2003). Law and the ethics of transformational leadership. Leadership and Organization Development Journal, 24(1/2), pp. 62-69.

Greenleaf, R.M. (1977) Servant Leadership: A journey into the nature of legitimate power and greatness. New York: Paulist Press.

Greenleaf, R.K. (1991). The Servant as a Leader. Indianapolis, IN: The Robert K. Greenleaf Center. [Originally published in 1970, by Robert K. Greenleaf].

Greenleaf, R. K. (1977/2002). Essentials of servant leadership. In L. C. Spears & M. Lawrence, M. (Eds). Focus on leadership: Servant-leadership for the 21st century (3rd ed.) (pp. 19-25). Hoboken, NJ: Wiley.

Hain, M.(2023). The Ten Commandments. https://www.ewtn.com/catholicism/library/ten-commandments-10336

Hart, M.H. (1978) The 100: A Ranking of the Must Influential Person in History.

Harter, N., and Evansky, D. (2002) Fairness in leader-member exchange theory: Do we all belong on the inside?Leadership Review, 2(2)1-7.

Heifetz, R. A. (1994). Leadership without easy answers, Cambridge, MA: Harvard University Press.

Heifetz, R. A. (2006). Anchoring leadership in the work of adaptive progress. In F. Hesselbein & M. Goldsmith (Eds). The leader of the future: Visions, strategies, and the new era, pp. 78-80. San Francisco, CA: Leader to Leader Institute, Josey Bass

Heller, T., and Van Til, J. (1983). Leadership and followership: Some summary propositions. Journal of Applied Behavioural Science, 18, 405-414.

Herbert, T.T. (1976). Dimensions of Organizational Behaviour. Macmillan Press Co., Inc.

Hickman, G. R. (1998). Transactional and transforming leadership leading organizations perspectives for a new era (First ed.). Thousand Oaks: Sage.

Hollander, E.P. (1992) Leadership, followership, self and others. Leadership Quarterly, 3(1), 43-54.

Hollander, E.P. (1978). Leadership Dynamic. A practical guide to effective relationships. New York: The Free Press.

Hooper, R., and Potter, A. (2000) Intelligent Leadership. London: Random House Business Books.

House, R. J. (1971). Path-goal theory of leadership effectiveness. Administrative Science Quarterly, 16, 321-338

House, R. J., Woycke, J. & Foder, E. M. (1988). Charismatic and noncharismatic leader: Difference in behaviour and effectiveness. In Conger & R. N. Kanungo (Eds), Charismatic Leadership: The Elusive Factor in Organisational Effectiveness. San Francisco, CA: Jossey- Bass.

House, R.J., and Howell, J.M. (1992) Personality and charismatic leadership. Leadership Quarterly 3 pp. 81-98.

Howell, J.M., & Avolio, B.J. (1993). Transformational Leadership, transactional leadership, locus of control and support for innovation: Key predictors of consolidated-business-unit performance. Journal of Applied Psychology, 78, 891-902.

Historie de le Turquie, Paris 1854, Vol.11.Pages 276-77

Hunt, J.G. (1991). Leadership A new synthesis, Newbury Park, CA: Sage

Ibn Kathir, I. (2004). Al Bidayah Wan Nihayah. Jakarta: Darul Haq. Ibn Ishaq, Sirat Rasul Allah, 143, in Guillaume, Life of Muhammad

Ibn Ishaq, Sirat Rasul Allah, 151, in Guillaume, Life of Muhammad, 105.

Ibn Majah, M. I. Y. (2007). English Translation of Sunan Ibn Majah. Riyadh: Darussalam Publishers.

Islamiaonline. The Prophet's Life in Brief. https://islamonline.net/en/the-prophets-life-in-brief/

Islamic Finder.https://www.islamicfinder.org/knowledge/biography/story-of-ali-ibn-talib-ra/

Islamic Finder.

Jago, A.G. (1982). Leadership: Perspective in theory and research. Management Science, 28, 315-336

Janin, H. (2005). The pursuit of learning in the Islamic world, 610-2003. Jefferson, North Carolina: McFarland & Company, Inc.

Johnson, C. (2001). Meeting the ethics challenges of Leadership. Thousand Oaks, CA: Sage.

Keane, K. (2002). The limits of secularism. In J.L. Esposito & A. Tamimi (Eds.), Islam and secularism in the Middle East (pp. 29-37). London: Hurst & Co.

Khan, M.M., & Al-Hilali. M.T. (1996). Interpretation of the Meaning of The Noble Quran in The English Language. Maktab Dar-Us-Salam: Riyadh.

Knights, D and O'Leary, M. (2018) Reflecting on corporate scandals: the failure of ethical leadership. Business Ethics: A European Review.

Kotter, J.P. (1990). A force for change: How leadership differs from management. New York: Free Press.

Kotter, J.P. (1999). What Leaders Really Do. Harvard Business Review Book.

Kotter, J. P. (1989). What leaders really. Harvard Business Review, 67(3), 103-11.

Kirkpatrick, S.A., and Locke, E.A. (1991). Leadership: Do traits really matter. Academy of Management Executive: 48-60.

Kanugo, R.N. (2001). Ethical values of transactional and transformational leaders. Canadian Journal of Administrative Sciences, 18,257-265.

Kanungo, R.N. & Mendonca, M. (1998). Ethics of leadership. Encyclopedia of Applied Ethics, 1, 49-58.

Karcic, F. (2001). Applying the Shari'ah in modern societies: Main developments and issues. Islamic Studies, 40(2), 207-226. Retrieved from https://www.jstor.org/stable/20837095

Kellerman, B. (2004) "Leadership: Warts and All", Harvard Business Review, January 2004, 40-45.

Kennedy, I. (2022). Ethical Leadership Principles & Examples | What is Ethical Leadership? https://study.com/learn/lesson/ethical-leadership-principles-examples. html

Khatami, M. (1997). The Islamic World and modern challenges. Retrieved from https://www.al-islam.org/islam-dialogue-and-civil-society-khatami/islamic-world-and-modern-challenges

Khan, S. M. (2020, May 21). Uthman. *World History Encyclopaedia.*

Retrieved from https://www.worldhistory.org/Uthman/

Kidwai, A.R. (2012). Daily Wisdom Saying of the Prophet Muhammad. Leicestershire: KUBE Publishing.

Kincheloe, J., and McLaren, P. (1998) 'Rerthinking critical theory and qualitative research 'in Denzen, N. and Lincoln, Y. (eds.), the landscape of Qualitative Research, Thousand Oaks, California:Sage.

King, M.L., Jr. (1957). Stride Toward Freedom: The Montgomery story. New York: Haper &Raw

Kirkpatrik, S.A., And Locke, E.A.(1991) Leadership: Dotrait matter? The Excutive, 5, 48-60

Kohlberg, L. (1976). Moral Stages and Moralization: The Cognitive Developmental Approach. In T. Lincona (Ed.), Moral Development and Behavior. New York: Holt, Rinehart & Winston.

Kotter, J. P. (1990). A Force For Change: How Leadership Differs From Management. New York: The Free Press.

Kotter, J. P. (1990). What Leaders Really Do, Harvard Business Review No. 90309

Kotter, J.P. (1999). What Leaders Really Do. Boston, MA: Harvard Business School Press.

Kotter, J.P. (1995) "Why Transformational Efforts Fail." Harvard Business Review, Mar-Apr, 59-67.

Kouzes, J.M., and Posner, B.Z. (1987) The leadership challenge. San Francisco: Jossey-Bass.

Leadership Themes. A Paper Presented to the BEMAS Annual Conference, September 1999.

LaMartaine, A (1857)..*Histoire de la Turquie* Paris, 1854, vol. II, pp. 277-276

https://ballandalus.wordpress.com/10/08/2012/alphone-de-lamartine-regarding-the-prophet-muhammad/

https://www.islamicity.org/6435/a-view-of-prophet-muhammad-from-france-1854/

Leo Tolstoy quotes on Prophet Muhammad (PBUH).

https://www.quora.com/What-had-Leo-Tolstoy-said-about-the-Prophet-Muhammad-PBUH

Likert, R. (1967) The Human organisation: Its Management and Value. New York: McGraw-Hill Book Company.

Marriner-Tomey, A. (1993). Transformational Leadership in Nursing. St. Louis: Mosby-Year Book, Inc.

Mawdudi, A.A. (1993). Towards Understanding Islam. Leicster: Islamic Foundation.

McClelland, D.C. (1975) Power: the inner experience. New York: Ivington.

Meindl, J.R. (1990) On Leadership: An alternative to the conventional wisdom. In: Staw, B.M. and Cummings, L.L. Research in organisational behaviour, vol.12 JAI Press, Greenwich, CT, pp159- 203.

Moaddel, M. (2002). Discursive pluralism and Islamic Modernism

in Egypt. Arab Studies Quarterly, 24(1), 1-29. Retrieved from https://www.jstor.org/stable/41858401

Mohammad A. Bamyeh, The Social Origins of Islam: Mind, Economy, Discourse (Minneapolis, 1999), 17–20.

Muhammad ibn Ishaq, Sirat Rasul Allah, 120, in A. Guillaume, Trans The Life of Muhammad: Translation of Ishaq's Sirat Rasul

Allah (London, 1955); cf. Leila Ahmed, Women and Gender in Islam (NewHaven and London, 1992), 42.

Mhd Omar, M.H (2022). Humane Leadership in Islamic Approaches https://www.intechopen.com/chapters/81164

Mullins, L.J. (1987). Management and Organisational Behaviour. London: Pitman Publishing.

Muthi, A.D and El-Awaisi, K. (2022). THE CONTRIBUTIONS OF CALIPH ABU BAKR TO THE FIRST MUSLIM LIBERATION OF ISLAMICJERUSALEM. Journal of Islamic Jerusalem Studies, 2022, 22 (2): 133-152 DOI: 10.31456/beytulmakdis.1208278 https:// dergipark. org.tr/en/download/article-file/2787115

Nair, K. (1994). A higher standard of leadership: Lessons from the life of Gandhi. San Francisco: Berrett-Koehler.

Nanus, B. (1992) Vissionary Leadership. San Francisco, CA: Jossey-Bass press.

Newstrom, J.W. (2011). Organisational Behavior: Human Behavior at Work. London: McGraw Hill. Ng, T. W. H., and D. C. Feldman.

"Ethical Leadership: Meta-analytic Evidence of Criterion-Related and Incremental Validity." Journal of Applied Psychology 100.3 (2015): 948–965.

Northouse, P.G. (1997). Leadership: Theory and Practice. London: SAGE Publications.

Northouse, P.G. (2010). Leadership Theory and Practice Fifth Edition. London: Sage Publication,Inc.

Northouse, P.G. (2001). Leadership: Theory and Practice. London: SAGE Publications

Northouse, P.G. (2010). Leadership: Theory and Practice. London: SAGE Publications

Northouse, P.G (2013) Leadership: Theory and Practice. London: SAGE Publications Sixth Edition.

Omar, A. (2006). Towards the Conquest of Islamicjerusalem: The Three Main Practical Steps taken by Prophet Muhammad. Journal of Islamicjerusalem Studies, vol.7, 55–100.

Omar, A. (2008). The Preparation and Strategic Plan of the Prophet Muhammad for Islamicjerusalem. Unpublished PhD thesis, University of Aberdeen

Panjwani, F. (2004). The Islamic in Islamic education. Assessing the discourse. Current Issue in Comparative Education 7 (1), 9-29.

Peters, F.E (1994). The Hajj: The Muslim Pilgrimage to Mecca and the Holy Places (Princeton, 1994), 24–27.

Phillips, D.T. (1999). Martin Luther King on Leadership: Inspiration & Wisdom for challenging times. New York: Warner Books, Inc.

Plinio, A. J. (2009). Ethics and leadership. International Journal of Disclosure & Governance, pp.277-283.

Plinio, A. J., Young, Judith, M., & Lavery, L. M. (2010). The state of ethics in our society: A clear call for action. International Journal of Disclosure & Governance, 7(3), 172-197.

Podsakoff, P.M., Mackenzie, S.B. and Bommer, W.H. (1996) Transformational leader behaviours and substitutes for leadership as determinants of employee satisfaction, commitment, trust and organisational citizenship behaviours. Journal of management 22, 259-298.

Podsakoff, P. M., MacKenzie, S. B., Moorman, R. H., & Fetter, R. (1990). Transformational Leader Behaviors and their Effects on Followers' Trust in Leader, Satisfaction, and Organizational Citizenship Behaviors. Leadership Quarterly, 1, 107-142.

Prentice, W.C.H. (1961) Understanding leadership. Harvard Business

Review (2004).

Prophet Muhammad's Hijira (2016).The state information services https://www.sis.gov.eg/Story/106146/Prophet-Muhammad's-Hijra?lang=en-us#:~:text=According%20to%20Muslims%20 tradition%2C%20when,kill%20him%20in%20the%20morning.

Ridah (1922). Al-Khilafa aw al-Imama al-'Uzma (The Caliphate and the Greater Imamate)

https://en.wikipedia.org/wiki/The_Caliphate_or_the_Supreme_ Imamate_ (book)

Robbins, S.T., & Judge,T.A.(2012). Essentials of Organisational Behavior. London:

Rost, J.C. (1991) Leadership for the Twenty-first Century. New York: Prager.

Rost, J.C. (1995). Leadership: A Discussion about Ethics. Business Ethics Quarterly, 5 (1), 129-142.

Sahih Muslim 1652c. In-book reference: Book 33, Hadith 15. USC-MSA web (English) reference: Book 20, Hadith 4487.

Saunder, J. J. (1978) A History of Medieval Islam. Routledge

Sheikh Ahmed Dededat. The Daily Reminder Network.

www.reddit.com/r/islam/comments/3haz13/the_greatest_enemy_of_ islam_is_the_ignorant/

Sergiovanni, T. (1984) 'Leadership and Excellence in Schooling', Educational Leadership, 41(5):4-13.

Seleny, A. (2006). Tradition, Modernity, and Democracy: The Many Promises of Islam. Perspectives on Politics, 4(3), 481-494. Retrieved from https://www.jstor.org/stable/20446203

Shaw, G, B. (1936) 'The Genuine Islam',. Singapore. Vol. 1, No. 8, 1936 http://www.ahmadiyya.org/islam/bernard-shaw.pdf#is-rev

Sharma, G.D.,Aryan, R., Singh, S., and Kaur, T., (2019). A Systematic Review of Literature about Leadership and Organization. *Research Journal of Business Management, 13: 1-14.*

Scott, K.T. (1994). Leadership and spirituality: A quest for reconciliation. In J.A. Conger & Associates (Eds.), Spirrit at work (pp.63-99). San Francisco: Jossey-Bass.

Smith, J.A., and Foti, R, J. (1998). A Pattern Approach to the Study of Leader Emergence. Leadership Quarterly, 9(2), 147-160.

Spears, L. (1996). Reflections on Robert K. Greenleaf and Servant-Leadership. Leadership & Organisational Development Journal, 17(7), 33-35.

Stogdill, R. M., and Coons, A. E. (1957). Leader Behavior: Its Description and Measurement. Ohio: The Bureau of Business Research College of Commerce and Administration, The Ohio State University Columbus.

Stogdill, R.M. (1974). Handbook of Leadership: A Survey of Theory and Research. New York: Free Press.

Stogdill,R.M. (1948). Personal factors associated with Leadership: A Survey of the Literature. Journal of Psychology, 25, 35-71.

Stogdill, R.M., 1974. Handbook of Leadership: A Survey of the Literature. Free Press, New York, USA

Stone, A.G., Russell, R.F., & Patterson, K. (2003). Transformational Versus Servant Leadership a difference in leader focus. Leadership & Organisational Development Journal, 25(4), 349-361.

Tan, C. (2017). Colonialism, Postcolonialism, Islam, and Education.

In: Daun, H., Arjmand, R. (eds) Handbook of Islamic Education. International Handbooks of Religion and Education, vol 7. Springer,

Cham. https://doi.org/10.1007/978-3-319-53620-0_22-1

Tan, C. & Abbas, D.B. (2012). Madrasahs and the State: Which Worldview?. In Tan, J. (Ed.), Education in Singapore at the beginning of the 2010s (pp. 89-99). Singapore: Prentice Hall.

The University of Villanova (2021) What is ethical leadership. https://www.villanovau.com/resources/leadership/what-is-ethical-leadership/

Tichy, N. M., & Devanna, M. A. (1986). The Transformational Leader. New York: John Wiley Inc.

Treviño, L. K., & Brown, M. E. (2005). The Role of Leaders in Influencing Unethical Behavior in the Workplace. In Kidwell, R., & Martin, C. (Eds.) Managing Organizational Deviance. Thousand Oaks, CA: Sage.

Watson, I. B. (1997). Islam and its challenges in the modern world. Retrieved from http://www.ifew.com/insight/v12i01/ibw.html

Werpehowski, W. (2007). Practical Wisdom and the Integrity of Christian Life. Journal of the Society of Christian Ethics, 27(2), 55-72.

West, M. and Ainscow, M. (1991) Managing School Development A Practical Guide. London: David Fulton Publishers.

Whetstone, J.T. (2002). Personalism and Moral Leadership: The Servant leader with a Transforming Vision. Business ethic: A European Review, 11(4), 385-390.

World Civilisation Chapter 77 The Rise and Spread of Islam. https://courses.lumenlearning.com/suny-hccc-worldcivilization/ chapter/ early-life-of-muhammad/

White, B. W. (1996). Talk about school: Education and the colonial project in French and British Africa (1860-1960). Comparative Education, 32(1), 9-26.

Wright, P. (1996). Managerial Leadership. London and New York:

Routledge.

Wright, P., & Taylor, D.V. (1994). Improving Leadership Performance: Interpersonal Skills for Effective Leadership. (Place): Prentice Hall.

Wilferd, M. (1997). The Succession to Muhammad: A Study of the Early Caliphate. Cambridge, England: Cambridge University Press.

Wirba, A.V. (2012). Leadership Styles. LAP LAMBERT Academic Publishing.

Yaqeen Istitute(2023). The immortality of his nation

https://yaqeeninstitute.org/read/paper/the-prophecies-of-prophet-

muhammad

Yukl, G. A. (1994). Leadership in Organizations. Englewood Cliffs, NJ: Prentice-Hall.

Yukl,G.A. (2006). Leadership in Organizations (6th ed.). Upper Saddle River, NJ: Pearson-Prentice Hall.

Yukl, G. A. (1981) Leadership in Organizations. Englewood Cliffs, New Jersey: Prentice-Hall, Inc.

Yukl, G. A. (1989) Leadership in Organization (2nd ed.) Englewood Cliffs, New Jersey: Prentice-Hall.

Yukl, G. A. (1998) Leadership in organisation (4th ed ed.), New Jersey: Prentice-Hall.

Yukl, G. A. (2006). Leadership in Organizations (6th ed.). Upper Saddle River, NJ: Pearson/Prentice Hall.

Yukl, G. (2012). Leadership in Organizations (8th ed.). Upper Saddle River, NJ: Pearson/Prentice Hall.

Yukl, G. (1994). Leadership in organizations, 3rd ed. Englewood Cliffs, NJ: Prentice-Hall.

Yukl, G.A. (2002). Leadership in organizations (5th ed). Upper Saddle Rivers, NJ: Prenice Hall.

Yukl, G., (2006). Leadership in Organization (8th Ed.). Pretice Hall: Pearson Education, Inc

Yusuf Ali,A. (1989). The Holy Qur'an: Text, Translation & Commentary. Brentwood, Marylan: Amana Corporation.

Yusuf Ali, A. (1992). The Holy Qur'an: Text, Translation and Commentary. Brentwood, MD: Amana Corporation, 1989, 68:4. All references to this translation of the Qur'an by Abdullah Yusuf Ali will be referred to as Qur'an.

Zaleznik, A. (1977) Managers and Leaders: Are They Different? Harvard Business Review, 55(5), 67-80.

Zalelznik, A. (1977), "Managers and Leader: Are they Different?" Harvard Business Review, May-June.

Zaleznik, A., & Ket de Vries, M.F.R. (1975). Power and the Corporate Mind. Boston: Houghton.

Internet sources:

www.radianceweekly.com/ISLAMIC_HISTORY http://atheism.about.com/library/glossary/Islam/bldef_umar.htm Smith, Huston the World's Religions http://www.al-islam.org/muhammad-yasin-jibouri/prophet-madina- 622-ad http://www.al-islam.org/muhammad-yasin-jibouri/prophet-madina 622-ad https://sunnah.com/abudawud:4297

NOTE: Please keep this book in a clean place because it contain verses of the Quran.

Thanks.